I'm currently planning on studying Environmental Engineering at Yale next year, and it is my sincere hope that one day I'll build, do, or be a part of something that will secure a sustainable future for our planet.

—Daniel Monteagudo

I was born in a small, rural village in Nepal. Currently, I live in the capital of Nepal. I want to explore how things work and use that knowledge for the betterment of humanity, so I want to study mechanical engineering and help disabled people with prosthetic limbs and autonomous robots.

—Diwas Gautam

I am studying in an international school in Shanghai, China. I dream to be a journalist; I have faith in the truth.

—Nanfan Yi

I'm a student, artist, sculptor, singer, debater, and "whatever-er" living in the Seattle metropolitan area. I got into Stanford through early action despite having little or no idea of what I'll major in—but that's just fine. I have two years of exploration to do.

I took a lot of long walks while applying to colleges, scrawling down essay ideas as they came to me while sitting on curbs or park benches. This particular essay's source material came directly from my browsing habits. The webpages open on my computer are wildly diverse, and in a sudden moment of inspiration, I realized that they would be perfect for showcasing my diverse range of interests.

—Michelle Bae

College essays are hard to write. There is an expectation to capture your essence in 650 words. I tried this and came to a blank page—until I decided to do something different. I wrote about what I'm not. I wrote about the "what ifs," diving deep into my hypothetical past.

—Mina Khan

The basis of this essay was a conversation I had with my grandfather several years ago. It is a story that reminds me both of who I am and where I came from. I had wanted to use this story in an essay, but it was only when I started thinking about my idiosyncrasies did I realize the small ways that who I am is linked to my family history.

—Conor McGlynn

A member of a large family, I live in a colorful but impoverished town on the Mississippi coast where my father pastors a historic Methodist church. I hope my college education will allow me to join the intense, creative collaboration of a think tank dedicated to alleviating poverty and educational inequity.

In today's racially charged world, I found it difficult to describe the Deep South's deeply ingrained division between black and white, penury and prosperity, without resorting to either blame and victimization, or callousness and complacency. Nevertheless, the circumstances I have grown up in have so permanently shaped my outlook on life and goals for an education that I found myself compelled to take on the subject, despite taboos and complexities.

—Natalie Newton

I live in Kanpur, a small city in India, and come from a humble background. I'm a striving visual artist and a science enthusiast. For me, engineering is not limited to quenching my intellectual curiosity, but a medium to spread awareness and provide aid to people. I am motivated to explore new sustainable energy sources to power the remote regions of Asia and Africa and work toward empowering underprivileged people.

—Harshit Ranjan

Growing up in Beijing, I've witnessed firsthand its slow but steady degradation from a relatively pristine city to the smog-covered metropolis that it is today, and this transformation accompanied my own flourishing goal to become the next international leader in environmental science and policy.

—Angela Zhou

It was a cold Friday night in October. I was seated at the desk (the one I am typing this on), and I started writing whatever came into my head. I originally planned on writing about identity, because I wanted to highlight the love I have for my religion and my culture. Eventually, I realized that the most beautiful lesson I learned was because of my name, and I learned that lesson from the experience I recall in my essay (I won't reveal any details because everyone loves a little suspense!)

—Tarek Meah

To brainstorm ideas, I went to a quiet place and put on soft, inspirational music and just started writing. Just by putting words down on paper, I got a better idea of what I wanted to say.

—Elizabeth Gibbs

I was born in Sri Lanka but I reside in New York City. I spend most of my time on trains, where I read too much and I don't write enough and I'm trying to do more of both. Ironically, I was told by many trusted adults that my essay was too bold. I am willing to compromise, but not when it comes to my writing. I left the tone of my essay in its original state because I am confident the message is clear.

—Tehani Gunaratna

I'm a senior at Columbus School for Girls in Columbus, Ohio. I will be attending Columbia University next year and aspire to be an editor and live in New York City for the rest of my life. Writing this essay, I underwent agonizing pain and stress (just kidding…it was actually pretty fun). I reminisced about my family and my burgeoning career as a fashion designer.

—Madeline Woda

I live in a small town in Washington. My goals are to break out of this small town and really make something of my life. I found an old photo of myself water skiing and it sparked the memory that became my essay.

—Erika Groudle

This is written by an awkward turtle who thrives on writing personal essays. I'm currently dwelling in the murky winter season of Troy, Michigan, but hope one day to work in the medical field with an awesome college degree earned by becoming one with the mightiest weapon: the pen.

—Sarah Chung

I live in New York City, but I'm originally from Brazil. I plan on majoring in neuroscience, or biology, while doing a premed track. The University of Chicago is known for its provocative prompts. In order to tackle the prompt, I had to think, think, and think, and read a lot of fiction to find inspiration.

—Pedro Del Cioppo Vasques

I live in New Jersey. I'm a high school senior dedicated to unflinchingly defending human rights and empowering people to reclaim them via a major in international business.

To write this essay? I just sat down and wrote. I always find that my best writing—for school or for art—comes most natively and expressively when I don't try to outline or force my words into something they're not. I built my essay from the ground up, then went back and edited out unnecessary parts, added in more relevant concepts, and finally, when I was all done, went to friends, parents, and my guidance counselor to see what their feelings were about it.

—Daniella Tang

Born and raised within a stone's throw of downtown Houston, I will always be rooted in the southern lifestyle, but certainly not defined by it. Growing up, I had an unconventional answer to the hackneyed question: "What do you want to be when you grow up?" The answer always has been, and always will be, simply: "Proud of myself."

—Tyler Pugh

I live in New York City. This is my fifth country of residence; my dad is a diplomat. I want to see the potential that Bangladesh, my home country, is absolutely brimming with, become actualized, and I want to use my worldly experiences and education to play an active role in making this happen.

—Rayat Rahman

The Handmaiden's Tale was my inspiration for my essay. I wanted to mimic Margaret Atwood's ability to trick the reader as well as make the reader an active part of the essay. I wanted the reader to be able to see the continuous reconstruction of memory work and take part in it while they read. My process included digging through a lot of photo albums. As I looked through the albums, I would write my immediate memories from the images. It was actually a wonderful experience. I am proud of what I was able to create and I enjoyed the process!

—Lauren Robinson

I live in Evansville, Indiana, and my greatest passion in life is exploring religions. Although I myself do not belong to an organized religion and I do not worship according to the practices of any one religious code, I consider myself to be a very spiritual person who is constantly searching for answers that only lead to more questions.

—Cam Cook

This essay was written at the beginning of my senior year and was one of the most difficult essays I have ever written because of the pain I went through as I had to visualize the thoughts that had been cultivating in my mind throughout my entire childhood. To actually say I started writing this essay at the beginning of my senior year would be a false statement because I had been thinking about how I wanted to convey these emotions for a long time. It wasn't until my senior year that I wrote my thoughts down.

I live in Benton Harbor, Michigan, and I plan on earning my PhD in Classics and becoming a professor and archaeologist. For this essay, I took a poem I had written and expanded upon it, turning it into a college admissions essay.

—Julia Spiegel

I have attended the Churchill School since I was seven years old, and with anxiety-tinged excitement, I am looking forward to attending Kenyon College next fall. I have no clue what I want to do, but I hope to stumble upon it.

It took me a while to figure out a direction for my paper, but once I settled on an idea, I spent two weeks writing, re-writing and editing several drafts until it resembled an essay. I had to kill many "darlings," sentences that I grew attached to and inevitably had to delete. My final draft arose from this carnage.

—Lydia White

It took me a couple years pondering exactly what would happen when college applications rolled around, and what would be the hit story that would change lives and drive admissions officers to tears. But in the end, I decided to tap into what really created the person I am today: my past mistakes. After sitting in a car in the middle of the night watching the rain pour down, I found a certain peace with myself, and an acceptance of how all my past mistakes have most greatly created me.

—Reine Defranco

Best College
Essays 2016

Edited and with an
Introduction by
Gabrielle Glancy

ONEIRIC
PRESS

Oneiric Press
www.oneiricpress.org

Book Layout ©2016 Tracy R. Atkins
Book Cover by Kit Foster

Best College Essays 2016 / Gabrielle Glancy. —1st ed.
ISBN 978-0-9973529-5-5 (Paperback)

Contents

Introduction.. 1

The Best Hat I'll Never Wear (Second Prize Winner)........................ 5

To Catch a Crab 8

Growing from Not Growing (Second Prize Winner) 11

The End of the World.. 14

Unnoticeably Noticed 18

A Villager's Self-Account 21

Are You a Science Person or a Humanities Person?.......................... 24

The "Bumps" in My Road.. 27

My Canvas 30

There Is No Fault in Our Stars.. 33

Eerily Beautiful 35

Alternate Lives... 38

I Hate Socks 41

To Name Oneself.. 43

I Choose Not To (First Prize Winner).. 46

The Troubles I've Seen.. 49

50,000 Pennies.. 52

The World Through My Eyes 55

"Smog Log".. 58

Bittersweet 61

The Blank College Form 64

Gertrude Vanderbilt Whitney Houston...................................... 67

My Mother Never Had to Worry.. 71

Tarek, طارق, তারেক.. 74

The Kingdom of Elizabeth 77

A Girl with No Country... 80

A Story Untold 83

Alive 86

Craniosynotozilian Lais 89

Ever Since 92

Butterflies 96

My Home Team 99

The Grayish Area 101

Run-On Sentences 104

Loose Strings Theory 107

Revise 110

Blue Skies 113

Confidence Is Key 115

Tree Rings 118

Hidden Lake 121

Sharks in the Lake 124

Creating My Path 126

Becoming a Spokesperson 129

Undercover Tweety 132

Redemption Song 135

The Countdown 138

Grandpa Stephen 141

Finding My Sea Legs 144

Montuno: Learning Music in Cuba 147

Am I a Vampire? 150

Traveling Is a Part of Me 153

Behind the Bars 156

Crop Top Rebellion: The Day I Was Asked to Change at a Feminist

Camp 159

It Comes, It Goes 162

If Curiosity Killed the Cat, My Dad Was an Accomplice 165

On Being the Oldest Sibling 168

Thank You, Shu-Li 171

Going Against Tradition 174

The Dock 177

Blood 180

Embrace the Rain 183

Touch 186

Penny-Colored Oasis 189

Candles 192

A One-Inch, Plastic Story 195

The Leftover 198

Elephant Theory 201

My Experience With Satanic Social Networking 204

Hearthrob(bing) 207

As Easy as Riding A Bike 210

Helen Keller 213

Mudville 215

The Coliseum 218

A Whole New Balance 221

There Are Cows in the Story 224

Why Carleton 226

There's No Place like Camp Tuolumne 228

Invisible 231

Engineering My Future 234

Finding the Woman Inside 237

To My Fellow Emmas 240

Jesus's Vacation House 243

The Show Must Go On 246

The Girl with the Paper 249

Not as Easy as It Looks 252

Mighty Minnow 255

World of Words 258

Mind, Hands, and Values 262

The View from Behind 265

The Princess Party 268

Rain and Rust: My Soggy Childhood 271

The Good Life...274

Gravel, Cacti, Rain 277

A Memory of My Father...280

Feminine Feminism...283

I'm a Teacher..286

Where Olympians Rule 289

N/A 291

Running Free..294

The Weight Room...297

An Unbroken Embrace..300

Counting Elephants..303

Mud People 306

Disaster in Thirty Minutes or Less.................................309

Yellow...312

Food for Thought...314

Moments That Shape a Life...316

Lost in Paradise..318

To Infinity and Beyond 321

Bust a Move 324

The Crimson Tablecloth 327

I Said Something 330

Immeasurable Growth 333

Las Tres Sofias 336

About the Editor Gabrielle Glancy 340

In the process of writing what is surely the most important essay of their lives, students are called upon to reach deep inside themselves for what moves them, while reaching toward the world they will soon enter. In these essays, you will feel this yearning, as students unfold their stories, first to themselves and then to those who will take part in deciding their future.

The process of writing a college essay is a beautiful journey—and one that merits recognition and respect.

May this book be an inspiration and a guide to those who enter its pages. May it honor those who came before and forge new paths for those to follow.

My thinking spot is atop my horse, because horses are my thing and the barn is my place. On my horse, Khedar, my mind wanders; I let it float around, branch out, pursue different avenues, and perhaps most important, I allow it to backtrack. During this stage, I dictate the piece in my head: I match the cadence of my sentences to the rhythm of his canter, punctuate them with his transitions, and become fully consumed by ideas, language, and the gentle movement beneath me. And then I write.

—Charlotte Knopp

INTRODUCTION

To write an amazing essay, students must take an amazing journey—a journey within—to locate what has moved and formed them, and find a way to put what they discover into words.

This is no easy task, especially because students are asked to write in a form they may never have heard of, let alone mastered—the narrative, personal statement.

The college essay is not like the five-paragraph essay students have been taught to write in school. Nor is it a simple reflection. The fundamental building block of a narrative personal essay is the anecdote. What is an anecdote? A short piece of writing that tells a story. But an anecdote alone does not a great narrative essay make. You also need reflection on the story you are telling—and dialogue and description to bring it to life. You must, as they say, show *and* tell in your college essay.

While other factors such as grades, test scores, and extracurricular activities certainly play an important role in deciding a student's fate, the essay—especially an honest, interesting, beautifully written (though not necessarily perfect) essay—can indeed tip the scales in the student's favor.

I know. I worked in college admissions.

The job of an admissions officer is daunting. To be tasked with the awesome job of deciding who will get in and who will not—now that is a lot of responsibility.

The job of an admissions officer is also (often) boring. She stretches, sighs, takes another sip of coffee, and waits for the inevitable—a big, fat yawn.

I don't mean to be insulting. I mean to make clear that the essays that get students into the colleges of their dreams—or, as I said, at the very least, tip the scales in their favor—must grab the admissions officers by the collar and not let go.

1

I know that when I read an essay from start to finish, with real interest, compassion, delight, or fascination—if everything else was in order—it was hard to say no.

The essay needs to be gripping (not gimmicky), honest, and unique. The job of the essay is to embody in two dimensions what exists in three—to bring you to life in front of the admissions committee so that they have a real sense of who you are and what you're made of. They want to know how you think, what's important to you, how you handle adversity, where you see yourself headed, and how you deal with the hand you've been dealt, so they can decide whether you would be a good fit for their school. But you can't tell them directly. You must somehow *show* them by writing an essay that embodies your essence.

I can't tell you how many times I've read essays that began, "Last summer I volunteered for organization A, B, or C..." and went on to describe in chronological order all the events of the summer, the student touting his or her accomplishments every step of the way.

What makes a great essay great is not a list of accomplishments but a flavor of uniqueness, a glimpse into the life and heart of the writer, an embodiment of a student's *je ne sais quoi.*

And yet, although it is probably the single most important essay a student will ever write in his or her life, the college essay gets sent to admissions offices never to be seen again. Students pour their hearts out in these essays. They spend more time on this particular part of the college application than they do on all the other parts put together. The college essay is the expression and culmination of seventeen years of living on this planet. But when the admissions committee is done reading it, where does it go? What happens to those essays?

We know the answer to that question. They are shredded, tossed into recycling, virtually erased from existence!

The mission of *Best College Essays* is to exhume these diamonds in the rough, destined to be discarded as soon as the process is over, and expose them to the light of day in an effort to mark, showcase, and honor this often overlooked rite of passage.

A byproduct of this worthy goal is that this book provides a plethora of high-quality examples of what a college essay can be or do.

Writing from models is a great way to learn.

I am always amazed at how students respond when I show them sample essays. "You can write about that?" they often say.

They have no idea what a wide (read: infinite) range of topics is available to them. And, as I already mentioned, many have never even seen a narrative essay before.

Best College Essays 2016 offers more than a hundred examples—all very different from one another—of essays students have written that got them into the schools of their dreams.

It's not a book to be read from start to finish necessarily—although you are welcome to do so, if you so desire—but to be tapped into, read randomly, even. We did not group the essays in any particular order. We did not put the winning essays or finalists first, though, of course, we have recognized them. Rather, we have organized the essays randomly. All of them are equally worthy—although you may prefer one to another.

We have also chosen not to revise the essays in this book. Proofread, yes. Revise, no. What this means is that some of the essays are a little rough around the edges. But remember, we wanted authentic voices telling a real story. We did not want essays written by college counselors, creative writing teachers, and parents. We wanted student voices to be represented as nakedly as possible and to be valued for what they are.

Best College Essays represents submissions from students all over the world applying to American universities. Are these really the *best* essays anywhere out there? They are the best from those we received.

Our judges read hundreds of submissions. We are hoping that in the coming year—once this book comes out—the next generation of students will be inspired to write essays they may never have thought possible and submit them to the competition so that they, too (the students and the essays), may stand up and be counted. I am certain that, for every essay we have published, there are hundreds of other worthy essays out there. May this book forge the way to stronger, more risk-taking, more open and powerfully written essays to come.

Rather than analyze what worked in each essay, we have let students speak for themselves about the process they went through in writing these essays. Where we could—it was not always possible—we included the prompt and the college that the student plans to attend. Often, when the prompt was not indicated, the essay was a response to Common Application Question #1: *Some students have a background or story that is so central to their identity that they believe their application would be incomplete without it. If this sounds like you, then please share your story.*

You will see in the essays that were chosen moments of brilliance, vulnerability, and self-reflection. You will see heartache and triumph. You will hear voices of students struggling to make sense of the world and to be heard. These essays are artifacts of human consciousness (true for all writing, really). The essays in this anthology, however, give us a glimpse into the dreams, lives, and stories of young adults at the moment they are reaching toward, and about to step into, the world.

The record of these journeys would be lost, like the island of Atlantis, without books such as this one.

I am honored to be part of such an expedition.

—Gabrielle Glancy

THE BEST HAT I'LL NEVER WEAR
(SECOND PRIZE WINNER)

Daniel Monteagudo

I have a hat that I will never wear but will forever treasure. It's a ranger hat from Yellowstone National Park, and it's too dorky to ever be put on my head. What it is good for, however, is holding pins. Each time we visit a national park, I buy a pin and stick it on the hat. Now, nine years later, the band of pins reaches halfway around the brim, from Yellowstone, Acadia, Glacier, Grand Teton, Grand Canyon, Bryce Canyon, Kenai Fjords, Denali, and more. Sometimes I like to look at the hat and think about the parks I've visited, because it's more than just pins that I've been collecting.

I've been collecting memories. Experiences. Moments of realization. From each place, I've learned more about the natural world and about myself. From hiking to Grinnell Glacier, for example, and comparing it to photos from a hundred years ago, I learned that mistakes can accumulate, and that I don't want to hand my kids a dying world. From unzipping our tent for a glimpse of snowcapped Denali, I learned that the wilderness is precious, and that living in harmony to preserve nature's awe-inspiring beauty is worth a lifetime of effort.

I've hiked the hoodoos at Bryce and watched the sun set over the north rim of the Grand Canyon, and yet my favorite park, if I had to choose, would be the lesser-known Acadia, in Maine. It's probably one of the least impressive ones I've visited, but I love it because of its place in my life. Acadia was my first national park, and also the only one I've been to over and over again. Acadia doesn't have the power of the Grand

Canyon, the scale of Denali, or the uniqueness of Yellowstone, but it's where I learned to love things like glacial erratics, intertidal zones, and birds of prey, and it's where I first became concerned about the environment.

I'm a city kid from Queens, having grown up riding the gritty subways and buses of NYC, so when I go to a national park, I start thinking differently. I wonder about life and living things, and how we fit into the world. I ponder Earth's history, all the way back to when the solar system was just stardust. But sometimes, national parks can even get me to stop thinking altogether. The first time I remember that happening was when I found a perfect little rock chair sculpted by the waves in Acadia. I sat in it, looked out at the sea and felt utterly at peace. I find myself thinking all the time, sometimes too much and without really getting anywhere, so these moments when I can simply be, without thinking, are as precious as my hat.

I don't want to just go through life collecting these experiences like pins, however. I want to ensure that future generations can revel in the biodiversity and beauty of a healthy planet. I will do whatever it takes.

About the Author: My name is Daniel Monteagudo. I'm a senior at the Bronx High School of Science in New York City who loves being outside—biking, hiking, reading a book, or playing ultimate Frisbee. I'm currently planning on studying environmental engineering at Yale next year, and it is my sincere hope that one day I'll build, do, or be a part of something that will secure a sustainable future for our planet.

High School Attended: Bronx High School of Science, New York, NY

The Process: I started with a couple free-writing sessions on the topic (my interest in the environment) to get some of my ideas into words. I then took what I liked best and figured out how to make all the ideas fit together and flow with a logical progression. Then I revised it a few more times, making tweaks here and there and moving sentences around, usually getting someone else to read it and give comments in between edits.

Acknowledgments: My mom, and my college coach, Ian Fisher.

To Catch a Crab

Katherine McLaughlan

I hear the crisp crunch as my teeth sever another fingernail. "Here's your test, Katie." I glance up and take the paper. As I do so I look into the eyes of a classmate, the eyes of someone who has seen my grade before I have. I feel incredibly exposed.

I keep the test facedown as it exchanges hands to hide my likely less-than-satisfactory grade from the math whiz sitting to my right, a move which I have mastered after many months of disappointing myself in this calculus class. I take a deep breath and prepare myself for the worst. Like a game of Russian roulette—where the risk is my GPA—I secretly fold over the upper right hand corner of the page to view my grade: 73%, a C.

I don't understand. I felt so confident in my understanding of the material. My mind begins to race. This was the last test of the quarter, making my grade unsalvageable and my GPA a few points under my already-lowered expectation. I once strove for A's and now I'm striving for B's. Will this render my chances of college acceptance impossible? How will I get into medical school? What if I end up at community college? Maybe I'll suffer from depression as a result of my inability to achieve my goals. I will live in my parent's basement and participate in activities at the expense of my liver. I'll get married just for a sense of achievement. I won't encourage my children's dreams because the process didn't seem to work for me.

What came to mind was a rowing term called "catching a crab." It's when a rower loses control of their oar and it gets swept under the boat, disrupting the swing and rhythm of the rest of the crew. Crabs can be lethal in the moment. I once witnessed a girl get flung out of her seat into the frigid January waters and another get a concussion when the oar smacked her head. Crabs are devastating; they embarrass the victim and cost seconds in a race. I realized this test was my crab. The point of crabs is that they don't have to ruin a practice, a race, and especially not a life. You catch one, you twist your oar back around, and the boat moves on, recovering quickly from this sudden lapse in control.

Crabs have run rampant in my life: test grades, judgment calls, failing to make the top boat, clothing choices, and, yes, actual Maryland blue crabs. In a school full of high performers and overachievers, it is easy to get caught up in the swell of doing well. It's easy to believe a life is based on test grades, and it is even easier to let yourself be pulled under by one bad score.

On that day, I realized one test in 11th grade calculus doesn't have the power to alter the trajectory of my life. This test presented a chance to change my mindset, to be resilient, and to work harder the next time. I had to bounce back and regain control of my oar.

One month later, I was back in that calculus class, waiting to receive my grade on another test. I see a classmate approaching with the stack of papers. My mind begins to race. My GPA will drop. . . . Wait. I take a deep breath and flip over the paper: 91%, an A-. Later that day, I check my email. I open the most recent one and find I have been offered an incredible internship at the biotech lab I applied to. Relief spreads over me. Life is so much easier when I forget the crabs.

About the Author: My name is Katherine McLaughlan. I live in South Riding, Virginia and would like to work in the field of medicine or biotechnology in the future.

High School Attended: Thomas Jefferson High School for Science and Technology, Alexandria, VA

The Process: I began the process by writing about the two of activities that occupy most of my time, school and rowing, and the essay flowed from there.

Acknowledgments: I would like to thank my parents, Ted and Kelly McLaughlan, for supporting me through the challenges described in this essay.

GROWING FROM NOT GROWING
(SECOND PRIZE WINNER)

Jacob Brawer

Suddenly I was a baritone. Almost overnight, my voice changed just in time for my seventeenth birthday. In seventh grade, I was diagnosed with Constitutional Growth Delay (CGD), an endocrine condition that placed me four years behind my peers in puberty and skeletal development. As a ninety-pound twerp with twig-like limbs, I stood no chance with the freshman girls when compared to the sideburned studs in my class with their tree-trunk legs. Sophomore year, I was mortified to still be shopping for boxers and school clothes in the "big boys" section at clothing stores. The first time I entered this department at age eight, I thought I'd arrived—goodbye Incredible Hulk briefs and hello Quiksilver boxers. Seven years later, this annual trip had become a painful reminder that, while my peers were celebrating their growth, my body had stalled out.

Trapped inside a body that was growing too damned slow, I focused on "growing" the only part of my body I could control—my brain. I'd always been a straight-A student, but my slow growth drove me to even greater levels of studiousness. Having CGD meant that my bones fractured easily. Within three years, I'd broken a radius, an ulna, another radius, and my fifth metatarsal. Immediately following fracture four, I started searching online for solutions that might quicken my healing process. All I found was lactoferrin, a glycoprotein in mammalian milk that strengthens the bones of rats. Desperate for help, I decided to experiment, taking lactoferrin orally, to see if it could also assist with bone *regrowth*. My healing was so accelerated that I invited a friend with

11

a recently broken tibia to participate in my pilot study. He took lactoferrin too, and his bone mended at an equally rapid rate. When my orthopedist saw our X-rays, he was so enthusiastic that he volunteered to recruit subjects at his UCLA clinic for an ongoing study.

Because of my slight build and susceptibility to injury, I've had to work harder than most to keep up with my basketball teammates. Every week, determined to be the best three-point shooter on the team, I shot thousands of baskets. What I lacked in size, I made up for in accuracy and grit. At the end of my sophomore year on JV, I was voted MVP and moved up to varsity. Being a strong shooter made me feel temporarily "big and tall," in spite of my seventh-percentile weight and twentieth-percentile height. When the physical disparity between my peers and me was at its greatest, I would have been amazed to know that as a rising senior, I'd be playing in college recruitment showcases alongside the top D3 level academic players in the country.

I'm now 6'2" and still growing, thanks to inheriting "tall" genes that kicked in just in time for my senior year. Even though my CGD has a finite end, "developmental delays" have enabled me to cultivate compassion for people who suffer with no end in sight. Seeing a line of mentally challenged adults, holding hands while walking down the street, reminds me of the true meaning of developmental delays. I've also learned to be more sensitive to those who suffer in less obvious ways. Because I was so good at masking my struggle, hiding behind my superficial strengths, I can look beyond a person's external presentation and wonder if they, too, are struggling internally.

CGD also provided me with an opportunity to look inward in search of emotional strength. Although there was no escaping my slow-growth reality, being conscious of my feelings and articulating my pain to family and close friends helped me endure the humiliation of being physically out-of-sync with my peers. Ultimately, it was this ability to connect with others regarding my struggle that enabled me to get comfortable being uncomfortable. And while I had no choice in the matter, I ended up growing from not growing.

About the Author: My name is Jacob Brawer. In the fall, I will be studying premedicine at Pomona College, and I plan to pursue a career in the medical field someday.

High School Attended: Flintridge Preparatory School, La Canada, CA

The Process: The idea for my essay came to me during the summer before my senior year. After multiple edits and revisions, my school essay mentor felt that my essay was ready to be submitted. Just to be sure I was on the right track, I decided to consult with Gabrielle Glancy before submitting. She assisted me in removing the "tell" and improving the "show" in my essay. We worked together for a week, and then I submitted my essay with my early decision application in the fall.

Acknowledgments: I would like to thank the following people for reading my essay at least once: Ms. Cooper (essay mentor), Ms. Ventura (college counseling director), Rhona Blaker (essay specialist), Leanne Watt (my mom), and Gabrielle Glancy.

THE END OF THE WORLD

Diwas Gautam

September 9, 2013. Kathmandu, Nepal.

10:01 a.m.—The whole world suddenly falls into a complete silence. I can see the dark clouds hovering around my head, and I swear I would've heard the scattering noise made by my heart hadn't the tears made it through. I feel like this is the end of the world. All because I couldn't secure my name in the only public engineering college in Nepal.

1:00 p.m.—I reach home. I don't know how, though. I can only remember telling myself I can't afford to join expensive private colleges. I don't have the strength to call my parents and inform them that their son's journey of getting scholarships—from a small village in eastern Nepal to a district headquarter and finally to the capital— had come to an end, and their loans won't be paid in their lifetime. Still, I decide to call; nothing worse can happen, right?

3:38 p.m.—My mom cries. The conversation doesn't go well. I lock myself in my room. I keep on seeing the "talented" tag hovering around my head and faces of people laughing at me. This is it. I am going to rot here.

A week later—Still low on self-esteem, I decide to take some time off my studies and volunteer to help children like me who can't afford an education. My conscience yells, GUILTY, but it actually feels good.

A month later—I'm tutoring basic math to orphans, collecting funds for needy students of Jumla, and hanging out with HIV-positive students on Saturdays. My relationship with my parents is still on the rocks. I live with orphans and with the happiness they find when they understand simple algebraic problems. Here, I am a teenager who recently failed his entrance exam, drowning in his own misery, thinking this is the end of the world, and there I see HIV-positive kids, with their sparkling little eyes asking if I can go there again the next week to play with them. This is the beginning of new hope as the beginning of a journey where I will forget about my failures and learn to move forward in life.

A year later—my mom sees my community service efforts in Jumla in a newspaper and calls me to say, "We are proud of you!" I am glad I faced my failure, wore it as my armor and experienced an eye-opening journey that textbooks wouldn't be able to teach me in a lifetime.

During my volunteering days, I saw people living on piles of garbage. I saw kids satisfying their appetite by sniffing dendrite. I saw the courage the cold, hard ground gives you when you have nowhere to go. I saw the walls showing the slogans of children's rights, but seldom practicing them. I saw millions of dreams being shattered because of the country's poverty and illiteracy levels.

Yet, among these imperfections, I found inspiration. I found inspiration in the optimism of a kid in Jumla, Dhurba, who walks miles every day without shoes just to attend school. I found inspiration in the eyes of children I helped. They taught me to stay strong no matter how cruel the experiences life has to offer. They taught me about survival, renewal, and reinvention of myself and taught me that small moments do matter and that life is what you make of it.

As I leave Nepal for my education, I will forever carry these memories and inspirations. With the education and experience I will receive, I will come back to the same streets of Kathmandu, the same villages in Jumla, and serve my dying nation, whether it's in engineering, public service, or any other way. And I look forward to my engineering career like I did my gap year: facing difficult challenges, discovering truths, gaining perspectives and moving toward the dream for which I left my village five years earlier.

After all, it wasn't the end of the world.

About the Author: My name is Diwas Gautam. I was born in a small, rural village in Nepal. Currently, I live in the capital of Nepal. I want to explore how things work and use that knowledge for the betterment of humanity, so I want to study mechanical engineering and help disabled people with prosthetic limbs and autonomous robots.

High School Currently Attended: Ambition Academy Higher Secondary School, Kathmandu, Nepal

The Process: At first, I made a list of all the things I wanted to tell colleges through my personal essays. And using those clues, I composed a biographical sketch of me, which was my first draft. It was about 1,000 words, so I worked for several weeks to cut redundant parts and organize my essay. After several drafts, I came up with something that was okay to read and that was within the 650 words limit. Having come from a Nepali medium school with little experience of English literature and writing, it was hard for me to express my feelings and passion. So I was going through several websites for tips to write personal essays and this one website called www.collegeessayguy.com had really good step-by-step procedures. After taking suggestions from this website, I composed a new draft and sent it to Ethan Sawyer, the owner of the site. He introduced me to Susana A. de Urruela, one of the best advisers I have found in my life. I sent Susana my draft and she made remarks and suggestions about it. Keeping in mind her words, I edited my draft and sent her the updated draft. This process of sending her drafts, receiving feedback, and improving my essay went on for several months. And finally I was able to come up with this essay.

Acknowledgments: I would like to thank Susana A. de Urruela for her valuable suggestions and feedback. I would also like to thank Ethan Swayer, and my friend Bani Karki, who helped me with my writing skills.

UNNOTICEABLY NOTICED

Elena Howes

I fought with this prompt for a very long time. It stumped me. So I made a list of all the qualities that made me me. After finishing the list, I realized most of the words fit into the same category: loud, unfiltered, headstrong, confident. I started to ask myself, why am I only fitting into one category?

I came to the conclusion that, as with almost everything, there are a multitude of factors—but only one of them is unnoticed. This factor, however, is only an effect of one of the most noticed thing about me: my breasts. They came in earlier, faster, and larger than normal, and I have been receiving unwanted male attention on the streets of New York City ever since. Men on the street stared and hollered at me, unconcerned with my age or how uncomfortable it made me feel. They sexualized me when I barely understood sex itself.

I realized very early on when this started happening, I was maybe ten or eleven, that because of how I was built and who I was, I couldn't afford to be quiet. I realized that this attention was coming from not only disgusting perverts on the street but from my friends and my peers as well. I convinced myself that I had to always be strong and fearless so that I could stay in control. I hated the way those men made me feel. I hated that they had control over my emotions or my perceived safety. I figured that if I was always strong and independent, they would stop making me feel that way, and I could have my control back.

People don't talk about how catcalling affects people. It's completely unnoticed, but it changed who I was. Now, many years later, I am proud of the person I am. I love that I am loud and that I will say things that others are afraid to. I am proud that I am bold and always confident. But it came about partly because a vulnerable, scared, ten-year-old girl got sick of walking home with her keys in between her fingers.

Ironically, the most noticed thing about me—my physique and loud personality—is a result of a deeply unnoticed problem: the effects of the hypersexualization and objectification of women. Many girls allow their personalities to be shaped by the way that people see them—the way men see them. This isn't only about seeking approval, it's also about learning to deal with undesired attention.

It's extremely important to me that people take more action to combat this problem—and not just the surface problem of catcalling. I think the issue goes much deeper. I think that many men have been taught in multiple ways, the media being one of the most powerful, that women are sexual objects. Because certain men are taught to think this way, they believe it gives them license to catcall or even take advantage of women. I know that not all men are sexist and misogynistic, but I think far too many of them are. *Don't blame media— we control it too, even though men have it better*

I know many girls who are not as tough as I have trained myself to be. They still quiver when they see a man, much older than they, look at them and wink. I have realized how important strength is, and it's important to me that other girls do, too.

OK but what was the prompt?! It's the books fault for not telling us

About the Author: My name is Elena Howes. I am from New York City. I have always been interested in writing and someday hope to be a journalist.

High School Attended: The Calhoun School, New York, NY

The Process: I kept the prompt in the back of my head while I went about my daily life. I wrestled with it. One summer afternoon, a man whistled at me. Following my disgust, I remembered the prompt and quickly sat down to write.

Acknowledgments: Mrs. Goldbaum.

A VILLAGER'S SELF-ACCOUNT

Nanfan Yi

Just like a plasma membrane, I am a "selectively permeable" person.

One part of me is activated. I need to run. I need to learn. I need to absorb. I need to "be" internationally minded. I need to think critically. I need to catch up with the trend. I need to internalize the "nutrition" the world has given to me. I need to hit my highest potential. I need to adapt to the dynamic environment. Do all of these things, I keep reminding myself. Who should I be? I keep asking myself. This part of me is *not real*, not alive, customized to reach society's expectation of a great person, and does not know how to live a *life*.

The other part of me is quiet, is *real*, is living perpetually inside of me and denies changing. It is called *family*. My whole family was born in a village in central China, a distance away from the cosmopolitan cities of China. I am proud to call myself a villager. As a villager, I sometimes speak in a strange accent; as a villager, I am bound with Mother Nature; as a villager, I am *dumb* in a sense to the outside world, because I do not know what the outside world looks like. I inherited all these lovely traits from my family; I am fortunate. The world is changing rapidly. People do get lost along the way. I, as well, do get confused and frustrated. However, I have a family as my backup. Time does not steal away my memories. I am still the little girl who is settled in the light-green field, eating a handful of nameless grass in the spring; I am still the little girl who grabs a wooden chair out in the yard, enjoying the chilling air of a summer night and counting the twinkling stars; I am still the little girl who pushes the jujube tree in front of the house and waits for the jujube rain to hit the ground in the advent of autumn; I am still the little girl who could not wait to pick up the soft pure white snow and turn it into the shape of a family of three people despite the coldness of winter. Those memories are more precious and more valuable than any awards that I could possibly get. My family is always the fountain of my happiness, my security, and my direction. It is the phospholipid bilayer that protects me from the distraction, the depression, the sadness, and the darkness in the outside world. Whichever road I choose to walk, or whoever I choose to be in the future, will not affect the fact that I am from my family, my village. I know that. Nothing will ever change my *roots* and I will always defend this part of me and the tranquility it brings to me.

This is it. This is me. My individuality comes from the unity of my family. I am malleable, yet deep inside my heart I am the snowman, "undissolvable." The stronger the backbone is, the less possible that one would break down; the stronger the connection between my family and me is, the more probable that I would strive to seek for a way to live and propel.

About the Author: My name is Nanfan Yi. I am studying in an international school in Shanghai, China. I dream of being a journalist; I have faith in the truth.

High School Attended: Kang Chiao International School

The Process: I really care about my identity. When I first saw the essay prompts, I outlined things I wanted to address. Then the phrase "selectively permeable" came through my mind; I learned it in my biology class. I began to think how I am related to this phrase, and I began to elaborate my thoughts. Finishing the first draft, I requested Ms. Ackerman give me some suggestions. I revised it after that, adding more emotions and sensory details into it. At last, the final draft came out.

Acknowledgments: I want to thank Ms. Ackerman (my extended essay coordinator) for telling me about this contest and giving me suggestions.

ARE YOU A SCIENCE PERSON OR A HUMANITIES PERSON?

Emma Clark

Are you a science person or a humanities person? When I was younger, this was one of the hardest questions for me to answer. If I was reading a novel that I couldn't put down, I'd answer: *humanities.* If I was learning about a particularly interesting topic in biology, like genetics, I'd answer: *science.* It wasn't until I became a writer for curiousSCIENCEwriters, a blog that focuses on communicating science to the world through storytelling, that I learned you don't have to be a science person *or* a humanities person. You can be both.

My pencil flew across my notepad as I listened to Melissa Marshall speak about science writing at my first curiousSCIENCEwriters (cSw) conference: "Scientists are the ones tackling our grandest challenges . . . if the public doesn't know about their work or understand it, then the work isn't done." I stopped writing and looked to the front of the room as these words sunk in. The point of the conference was to teach cSw writers the importance of our roles, but I understood the importance after hearing that single sentence. My mind started racing as I sat in the auditorium chair. I realized that scientists are changing the world every day, yet many people are unaware. There is a barrier between scientists and the general public because of the specialized language that is used to describe scientific research, but this gap needed to be bridged. Explaining research using engaging language brings people the knowledge that they are entitled to and connects nonscientists to the scientific community, which creates advancements in society.

I left the conference that day with a newfound perspective on my passions for both science and humanities. I realized that my interest in understanding the human body could be combined with my love of writing to provide something important and beneficial to the world. I threw myself into my CSW role as a science blog writer, first beginning with the science. I studied articles, websites, and journals. I spoke with specialists. I learned about incredible scientific breakthroughs ranging from the studying of grizzly bear hearts, to developing a cure for heart disease, to the creation of PolyAspirin, a polymer synthesized for localized drug delivery. After understanding the science, I moved to the writing. For each topic, I wrote a story to explain the science in an interesting, informative way. The feeling of writing a story that makes an amazing scientific breakthrough relatable to nonscientists is unforgettable. Maybe people who think that science is boring will read a story I wrote and change their minds. Maybe people who want to understand more about the development of a cure for a disease affecting their loved ones will read a story I wrote and have hope. Maybe it is okay to be a science person *and* a humanities person.

Cornell's College of Arts and Sciences is the perfect place to be a science and humanities person because it promotes curiosity and diversity of interests. Here, I would be able to successfully pursue my passions for both biology and writing because of the interdisciplinary nature of the school. For example, I would be able to take classes related to my interest in biology such as comparative physiology, but I would also be able to take classes related to both my interest in biology and in writing, such as the writing seminar Lives on Trial: Histories of Biomedicine. The academic diversity and rich intellectual atmosphere of the College of Arts and Sciences would provide the opportunity to create my own path to success through the combination of two fields that aren't traditionally combined. I belong in the College of Arts and Sciences because, there, it is a good thing to answer my longstanding question with: *I am both a science person and a humanities person.*

About the Author: My name is Emma Clarke. I live in Spring Lake, NJ, and attend High Technology High School, a pre-engineering high school. I will be attending Cornell University in the fall of 2016 to pursue my love of both science and the humanities. My goal in life is to work in biomedical research or as a science writer.

High School Attended: High Technology High School in Lincroft, NJ

The Process: In order to write this essay, I thought about my high school career and the times that I was most excited about whatever I was working on or involved in. My experience as a science writer immediately came to mind. I thought about all the times I excitedly explained how incredible curiousSCIENCEwriters was to my mother, and I tried to embody that excitement and passion in my essay.

Acknowledgments: Mrs. Gross.

THE "BUMPS" IN MY ROAD

Nicole Kruss

[handwritten: intriguing mysterious first line ✓]

Most people have one mother, but I have five. Technically, only one is truly my mother, but I don't have a better way to refer to my dad's revolving door of girlfriends. When my skin began to break out in middle school and I became insecure about my complexion, I turned to whomever I could for guidance and support. As a product of divorce, constantly split between two households, I had to reconcile my mom's lessons about beauty with what my dad was inadvertently modeling through his relationships. My mom and his girlfriends took turns teaching me about the true value of internal and external beauty, about the person I strive to be and the one I will never be. *[handwritten: love the all caps]*

SKIN OFTEN SHOWS THE FIRST SIGNS OF DISEASE. Patricia was my dad's first girlfriend post-Mom. She had severely blemished skin and resembled the villains in children's stories. True to form, she became my evil stepmother, and I, her Cinderella. Dad was smitten blind by her and always took her side. In my naiveté, I thought that her pimples and blackheads were signs of wickedness. She classically conditioned me to fear bad skin, which would make my "Acne Years" particularly problematic. Mom had taught me not to judge books by their covers, but Patricia taught me that some books are rotten inside and out. *[handwritten: lesson]*

SUNBURNS AT A YOUNG AGE CAN CAUSE LIFELONG DAMAGE. My dad's next girlfriend was also named Patricia, but we called her Patricia II out of respect. I looked up to her not only because she was kind, but also because she had beautiful, golden skin. She took

[handwritten annotations in margins: "cool phrase", "into to essay", "big idea", "en cliché"]

27

me to the beach once to get a "base tan" and promised that tanning oil was better than waterproof sunscreen. That was my first memory of sunburn . . . and betrayal. When my mom saw me, she burst into tears, muttering curses that ended in a rendition of "Isn't it bad enough *he's* ruining our lives?!" I learned that exposure to bad role models increases the likelihood of emotional scarring.

SKIN HAS A LONG MEMORY. Lauren was the first girlfriend significantly younger than my dad, but her pockmarked skin suggested otherwise. She was remarkably negative, finding flaws in everyone. Karma was apparently working itself out on her face through her constant picking. I wondered what crimes I had previously committed to now face a lifetime of Proactiv and cover-up. Lauren was the Ghost-of-Nicky-Future, showing me what I might become if I didn't learn to be content with my complexion. My mom's cryptic advice: You can pick your nose, and you can pick your skin, but you can't pick your dad's girlfriends. Lauren taught me to pick wisely because some picking leaves nasty scars.

BEAUTY IS ONLY SKIN DEEP. His latest girlfriend, Martha, is gorgeous and has perfect skin, but there isn't much going on upstairs. She's 37 but acts 20, and although she's not the type of woman I want for my dad, I don't dislike her. She's obviously with him because he caters to her expensive tastes. She buys me stuff with his credit card, hoping that gifts will bring us closer. Martha proves that beauty can't buy love any more than money can. I now know that if I want to attract someone intelligent and deep, I have to nurture those qualities in myself first.

Skin is the page on which our lives are written, recording every sunburn, every scar, every vice. Skin is not only our largest organ, but it can also be our greatest teacher. When I reflect on my skin and the "bumps in my road," I realize how each imperfection has helped to define and shape me. Likewise, my dad's relationships have taught me about the kind of woman I want to be. Thankfully, my mom has been my mirror throughout it all, showing me that true beauty is a product of love, wisdom, and compassion.

About the Author: My name is Nicole Kruss, and I live in Hollywood, Florida. I have many aspirations that I'm determined to accomplish, but my main goal is to earn a degree for athletic training in order to strengthen people physically and mentally.

High School Attended: American Heritage, Plantation, FL

The Process: I went through weeks of brainstorming and rough drafts in order to portray this essay exactly how I wanted. The story I tell is personal, but I attempt to bring forth some comic relief. I had to find the perfect balance of sincerity and comedy.

Acknowledgments: My seventh grade English teacher, Mr. Daniel Swerdlow.

My Canvas

Shangyi Fu

My great-grandfather always told me to paint my own canvas.

As an artist, he used painting to lift his family out of poverty with expressions of love and happiness. As his strokes expertly glided across pages of bamboo paper, my strokes attempted to follow with blobs of paint, matching his example with sweat and tears, tripping along while gaining priceless life lessons. From then on, I always had complete control over my canvas. My rough strokes danced across the paper until my essence brilliantly shone in myriads of vibrant hues of precious awards and achievements spanning from fine arts to academics. Even though my family members expressed their impassioned disapproval of my talent, pressuring me to find better opportunities, I held my head above their negativity, remembering the words of my great-grandfather and, clinging to my canvas, determined to paint my own life and aspirations, all displayed in the art studio of my heart where my parents could not reach.

Unfortunately, at age fifteen, my thousands of paintings, precious oils and vibrant acrylics, life and aspirations shattered. Within the cracked bits of charcoal and limp shreds of paper, my mother's osteoporosis finally conquered her when she fractured her ankle. She braced herself to face the pain and agony of surgery and rehabilitation; the image of my mother's face contorted in suffering remains a permanent sketch in my memory, a memory that sparked flames of determination to help those who have been sick and injured to find comfort and happiness again. From then on, my paintbrush forged the images of Leonardo Da Vinci and began sketches of Louis Pasteur, the inventor of vaccines, and Hippocrates, the father of medicine.

Before I could start anew, financial difficulties pried my paintbrush out of my hands. Our lack of medical insurance made it difficult for us to sustain the injury's overwhelming costs. As my father attempted to make ends meet with a promotion in a different city, I became the "man" of the house, the baby-sitter, the maid, the launderer, the cook, and, hardest of all, the student. With advanced classes piling up with my chores and extracurricular activities, I found that my responsibilities drowned me in a sea of dirty dishes and textbooks. Exhausted, I quickly realized I was wasting away.

Without control over my canvas, I discovered the extensive psychological and physical trauma that can result from stress. My grades were dropping and my health was waning. I was terrified to face the gaunt stranger in the mirror. As I sunk deeper and deeper in my responsibilities, my pencils and charcoal fell farther and farther out of reach. In the darkness, I suddenly realized I couldn't let an injury and its effects control my life.

Awakened by a new sense of purpose, I began to swim toward my art supplies. It was crucial for me to take ahold of my canvas again in order to balance the mass amounts of responsibilities in my life. I began to grab things that would propel me toward my canvas. I took hold of a planner, organizing every minute, squeezing in homework and chores. As a person who rarely showed vulnerability, I slowly struggled to open up to my friends and ask for help. Hardest of all, I prioritized my family by temporarily letting go of my own desires, such as club activities and competitions. Little by little, these small acts of hope pushed me closer and closer until my fingers grazed over the smooth handle of my paintbrush. As I reached the surface, I finally filled my lungs with sweet relief and renewed dedication.

I know that my life all comes down to my delicate control of hues and textures on my canvas. Although years have passed since I have seen my great-grandfather, his words ring in my ears every day, cementing my grip on my paintbrush: It's interminable and unbreakable.

About the Author: My name is Shangyi (Shelly) Fu and I live in Houston, Texas. I aspire to be a physician who has a knack for both art and medicine.

High School Attended: DeBakey High School for Health Professions, Houston

The Process: This essay focuses more on the basis of who I am as a person, including where I come from and my journey to become who I am today. By speaking with friends and family while doing some simple introspection, I was able to find the basic entities that define me as me: art, my heritage, and a certain incident that showed me everything is possible.

Acknowledgments: I would like to thank Ms. Bull, my Emerge Coordinator, who has spent hours helping me construct my thoughts. I would also like to recognize my family, who has supported me through it all.

THERE IS NO FAULT IN OUR STARS

Rylen Sigman

One of my earliest, most distinct memories is that of sitting on the docks in New Hampshire, gazing at the stars with my parents. It is late summer and the lake laps softly against the rugged sand. We sit in old beach chairs as we do every night, the three of us, and my mother hands me a book of constellations. Although I am only six, I have already developed a love of reading and am enthralled by the myths and legends presented on each page. I run my hand over the illustrations, white bumps that bulge with phosphorescent paint, and try to match the patterns beneath my fingers with those reflected over the lake. I break into a grin as I spot Cygnus, the grieving swan, soaring through the sky as if his wings are more than a collection of dots. My mother points out Ursa Major and my father searches for Leo. *family connected*

I have always felt a personal connection to the constellations. To me, they represent the intersection of science and art, a blend of logic and creativity stemming from astronomy and myth. Likewise, I am very much a melting pot of left brain and right brain, with interests in earth science and creative writing alike. I remember thinking that Orion was designed specifically for me because our names sounded so similar. Even now, I still recognize that shape, the roughly hewn hourglass cinched by three bright stars that make up the hunter's belt—Alnitak, Alnilam, and Mintaka. Orion was, supposedly, the greatest hunter in the world of ancient Greece and the doomed lover of Artemis. By extending the hourglass shape above Orion's head, one can make out his choice of weapon: a large, silver bow.

What makes the constellations so wondrous is that they may not be a pattern at all, but rather an archetype of the human tendency to look for meaning in the meaningless. As a species, we have centered our religions, customs, and beliefs on the habits of the natural world. And we always look up. Since Cygnus first took flight, to the discovery of Pluto, we have always looked up, whether our reasons are spiritual, technological, or merely based on curiosity. My love of constellations is closely bound to my love of Greek mythology and the idea that the behavior of every leaf, every bug, every star, is tied to a fantastical source. The ancients looked up and saw stories of their creation and ways of life. It would be interesting to know whether they based their myths off of the patterns they saw, or if they found the constellations with specific meanings in mind—a classic "chicken or the egg" dilemma. Either way, the constellations have, in part, defined our existence and our relationship with the universe. The night sky is a pattern found in the natural world, yes, but it is also a pattern deeply rooted in human essence. Our ability to look into a litter of Pollock-esque cosmos and derive purpose is the reason I smile every time I stargaze.

About the Author: My name is Rylen Sigman. I was born in Manhattan and have lived in Harlem for the past seven years. I have always aspired to be a novelist and am currently working on my first book.

High School Attended: Bronx High School of Science, Bronx, NY

The Process: After reading the prompt, which asked for a wondrous pattern in the natural world, my mind immediately jumped to the constellations. It was an easy topic for me to write about because I love the constellations so much. After that, the words flowed and I finished the essay in less than an hour.

Acknowledgments: My parents.

EERILY BEAUTIFUL

Eve Alterman

Hundreds of tiny specks of light danced in the night sky. The lights from the stars and the city of Jerusalem dimmed for the show, and the echo of the explosion overhead was deafening. As it thundered, I froze, and my eyes followed the sparks as they fell and dissolved into black. It was unnervingly beautiful. But that beauty could not conceal the ugly truth: I was watching a Hamas missile and an Israeli Iron Dome counter-missile afire above me. As the lights faded and sirens blared, I rushed to meet my friends inside the bomb shelter. At that moment, my summer in Israel stopped being just a trip with my camp and started to become something more.

I had just witnessed what felt like two worlds colliding directly over my head. Somewhere between my awe, fear, and confusion, I almost didn't hear my peers' whispers. "Muslims are monsters," one said. "Palestinians are murderers," said another. "Palestinians are people," I thought.

At Bronx Science, a significant portion of the student body is Muslim. As I heard the hateful words spoken in the shelter, I thought about Asanul, who tutored me in trigonometry. I remembered Shabab and Ishrat helping me with my chemistry homework and laughing over coffee in Starbucks. I knew what my peers were saying was false, and it was painful to hear it. I began to feel more and more isolated as I refused to join them. As a Jew who has spent every summer in Jewish camp and years in Hebrew school, I was surely tempted to join in the bonding over the common enemy. But when I watched those missiles, I didn't see two missiles colliding—I saw two cultures colliding.

Culture clash is not a concept with which I am unfamiliar. Bronx Science has a highly segregated student body, divided by both race and class. Often, cafeteria lunch tables eerily resemble borders of our respective countries of origin. Throughout my time here, I have tried to push past these borders. My breakthrough occurred, however, when I joined the debate team.

Our team was both open to everyone and financially subsidized, which made it possible for any student to join, regardless of background. As novice director and later co-captain of the Congress squad, I was forced to figure out how to work with people who were different than me. I learned early on that the key to a successful team was collaboration. I relied on my new teammates for research, critique, and support throughout practices, tournaments, and late-night prep time in less than clean hotel rooms. I developed a love and a dependence on these new friends who had not grown up on the upper west side of Manhattan.

Before I arrived in Israel, I was unaware of how deeply these experiences had influenced my view of the world. As the trip progressed, however, I began to hear echoes of the hostility I had heard in the bomb shelter. My friends did not appear to think twice about voicing openly racist sentiments about Palestinians, Muslims, or anyone else who did not share their worldview. And maybe if I had not gone to a school like Bronx Science or even devoted myself to debate, I might have felt the same way. But my school had changed me. The complexity of the conflict and my own confused feelings made it impossible for me to share their simplistic view of what was going on around us. And after all, Israel/Palestine is nothing if not complicated.

That summer made me realize not only how much I didn't know yet, but also how important it is, even under the most difficult circumstances, to see the gray behind the black and white. And as I get older, I want to continue to explore the gray, no matter how challenging, or at times uncomfortable, it may turn out to be.

About the Author: My name is Eve Alterman. I am from New York City. I am extremely politically minded. When I am an adult, I am hoping to be a campaign manager.

High School Attended: Bronx High School of Science, NY

The Process: All of my opinions I hold very strongly. I know that I arrived at all of them through experience and personal thought. Whenever I struggle with an idea, I am not content until I have worked it out in my head. This prompt forced me to reflect on that experience.

Acknowledgments: Ms. Robinson.

ALTERNATE LIVES

Mina Khan

There's not much to do on a subway but think. This morning on the way to school, my mind wandered around the turns, the paths I could have taken, or rather, the ones that could have been taken for me. For reasons beyond my control, I could be on three starkly different paths: with my mother, with my father, or here.

When my mother was eight months pregnant, she made the fourteen-hour journey from New York City to Seoul, Korea. Her arms clenched a passport, a bloated stomach, and a one-way ticket. But after her C-section, she changed her mind; she returned to America, her husband, and her two children. If she hadn't, my life would be drastically different.

I would have grown up in Korea. I have noticed that the Korean side of my family is more inclined toward those of their own ethnic background. I am half Korean, half Pakistani. Although this is invisible to the American eye, it's blaring to the Koreans. There's something different about me; perhaps I'm the victim of some botched plastic surgery. But when the truth is revealed, I am no longer a victim; I am simply no longer pure, not really Korean. I have not yet been fully accepted into Korean society. If I lived there, I would have to lie about my ethnicity to avoid judgment. I would feel shame for what is most important to me today: my diversity and individuality.

My next timeline begins when I was seven, when my mother was diagnosed with hematoma. Blood clots littered her brain and spilled onto her spinal cord, washing over her nerve endings. It didn't look like she was going to make it. Luckily, she's a fighter. But arrangements were still made. I heard my father's family discuss it when my mother went to bed. His family is traditional. The girls are kept at home and are found suitable husbands as soon as they menstruate. Only my mother insisted on my education. If she had passed, I would be different. I would have been taken out of school in the third grade. My uncle, Abrar, would have found me a husband by thirteen. By now, at seventeen, I would be the reluctant mother of three. Family photos would feature young skin worn by suffering, tired hands clasped by my forty-something husband and three vibrant little boys. *paints a scene*

Although there might be perks to all of these timelines, I must say, I'm happy with mine. These other timelines take from me my key identifiers: my ethnic background and my educational opportunities. My Korean timeline would have stripped me of the duality of my cultures and the racial identity that I'm now able to explore.

Here, in America, I have been gifted an education; I am able to read for pleasure, whereas many of my Pakistani cousins remain illiterate. This very well could have been me, but my education has changed my trajectory. My circumstances have made me liberal, informed, and outspoken. I am not afraid of confrontation; rather, I bask in it, as it leads to discussion. I have learned to confront, explore, and eventually take pride in every facet of myself.

It's absolutely bizarre to think that if things went differently, if my mother had not lived to leave my father at the specific time she did, I would not be the person I've become. While I was probably born with certain attributes, different attributes have been made stronger through my experiences. Pakistani Mina or Korean Mina, although the same person, would be almost unrecognizable to American Mina. Lives are a series of coincidences that compile into experiences and those experiences compile into people. I am made not only by my experiences but by others' too. I am made out of anonymous mistakes and successes that bounced off one another and settled into one solid space: here.

About the Author: My name is Mina Khan and I live in New York City. I have dreams of making my passions for art, writing, anthropology, and social justice into a career.

High School Attended: Hewitt School, New York, NY

The Process: College essays are hard to write. There is an expectation to capture your essence in 650 words. I tried this and came to a blank page—until I decided to do something different. I wrote about what I'm not. I wrote about the "what ifs," diving deep into my hypothetical past. I realized that I am who I am due to external choices. I discussed these circumstances and, finally, I found my personality typed in 648 words.

Acknowledgments: Ms. Stevens, my English teacher, for looking it over.

I HATE SOCKS

Conor McGlynn

good first line [handwritten annotation]

I hate wearing socks.

It turns out that this is a family trait. My mother, growing up in the frozen Canadian tundra, was noted as a child for not wearing socks, even under winter boots in deep snow. However, this idiosyncrasy goes back much further. My grandfather grew up in the olive orchards of Palestine, in a small village near Jerusalem. He and the other kids in the village would not only eschew socks but shoes, too, as they played in the village square. The village is now long gone, destroyed in war, the olive trees uprooted, and the villagers never to return to their fields. But sometimes, when I look down at my bare toes, I think of him.

I remember the first time my grandfather showed me his most precious possession. He reached into a drawer and pulled out a single key. It was a large iron key, clearly old, with a simple design. At first, I was confused, thinking that his most precious possession would have been a valuable family heirloom. He explained to me that this was the key to his house in Palestine and that, on being forced to evacuate, the last thing my great-grandmother did was to use this key to lock the door to her house. As she did this, she was thinking that she would be away a matter of days, unaware that just hours later, her house, her orchards, and her village would be permanently erased from Earth and that she would never again set foot in her homeland. This single key is all that ties my family to the past.

It should not be surprising that those in boots destroyed the lives of the barefoot. Even today we see too many examples of the strong oppressing the weak. My distaste of socks may seem silly, but it sometimes helps me to remember where I come from and that there are still many barefoot people in our world who need our protection.

About the Author: My name is Conor McGlynn and I live in Walnut Creek, California. After college, I would like to start my own business that uses creativity and innovation to solve current and future environmental problems.

High School Attended: Acalanes High School, Lafayette, CA

The Process: The basis of this essay was a conversation I had with my grandfather several years ago. It is a story that reminds me both of who I am and where I came from. I had wanted to use this story in an essay, but it was only when I started thinking about my idiosyncrasies that I realized the small ways that who I am is linked to my family history.

Acknowledgments: Gabrielle Glancy, Pat McGlynn, my grandpa.

TO NAME ONESELF

Jacob Levitt

I seldom considered names important. On paper—my birth certificate, my math test—I am Jacob, but everyone calls me Jake. Because my parents had no particular inspiration in mind when I was born, to me names were purely aesthetic, labels even, that said nothing about who a person was or what they were like.

But during an English class discussion on their meanings, my classmates held sharply different opinions. Take one student, named after a mountain in India known for its beauty during sunsets, or the girl whose mother named her after an African country—her mom didn't care which one—as a testament to the importance of her Afro-Caribbean identity. As more origin stories filled the room, with incredible details of foreign nations and ancient histories, I began to see my peers in a different light. There was much more to them than I knew from my classes and clubs; they possessed a wealth of knowledge not found in any textbook.

That got me thinking. Names were a cultural window to the many worlds contained within the walls of my school. In this newfound forum, I was learning about the wealth gap in Bangladesh before chemistry, the role of women in Islam at lunch, and the relaxed style of Moroccan Arabic after speech practice. Conversations with my friends about the linguistic roots of their names brought distant societies into clearer focus. Yet these stories and histories were not only educational; my hunger to learn was not satiated by facts and figures alone. Within a name was a friend's culture, with telling details of her value system, her beliefs, and her family life. I found a more complete picture of my peers than I had expected at a large and fast-paced school, and delving deeper into someone's character was as easy as asking about their most basic identifier.

Maybe it was time to reconsider my own name.

I had little to start with. "Jacob" is derived from the name of the Jewish prophet, Ya'akov, which contains the Hebrew verb "to supplant." However, my parents didn't factor etymology into their decision; they gave me a formal option, a casual nickname, and a choice between them. At first, I saw no struggle between "Jacob" and "Jake," because neither seemed to hold more weight nor reveal more of me than my personality alone. But names had been such a reliable gateway to forming deeper connections with others in my high school, so perhaps constructing the cultural significance of my own name would make a large part of my identity more accessible.

Jacob, as the biblical story goes (and as suits the verb), journeyed from his native land to Egypt with God's word that his descendants would build the Israelite nation. My family's tale, though mortal, contains many parallels. A century ago, my great-grandparents uprooted their lives in Eastern Europe to escape persecution for practicing the same faith that Jacob worked to pass on. I have the ability to learn from Jewish principles and partake in Jewish traditions, from community service to family dinners, because of the sacrifices made by those before me.

My parents didn't name me after Jacob the prophet, but who's to say that I can't look to him and his story for significance?

The next time I participate in an exchange about names, I hope I reciprocate the wisdom I've gained from my school community with a lesson or two from my own heritage. I hope I will come to form deeper connections with others as they get to know me beyond the basics.

But maybe I can still carry out these goals as Jake. Because that's how my brother, best friends, and teachers know me. While I've gained a new appreciation for my birth name, I have yet to discover which option I prefer. These realizations have shown me that I can embody—and that I am—both.

About the Author: My name is Jacob Levitt. I live in New York City and go to the Bronx High School of Science, where I find interest in both my studies and the diversity of people around me. I will be studying biochemistry at Yale University starting this fall and hope to do humanitarian work with the pharmaceutical industry as a career.

High School Attended: Bronx High School of Science, NY

The Process: I began writing over the summer on a variety of different topics to get a feel for what makes me tick. For Yale University, my other supplements essays were going to focus on my academic and extracurricular interests, but for this essay I wanted to focus on the personal—the way I interact and bond with others, my interest in world cultures, and my connection to my own religious and cultural heritage. After about ten drafts over a period of two months, I was finally satisfied with my work.

Acknowledgments: I would like to thank Hana Albertz, Lauren Casey, and my parents for their support and guidance throughout this process.

I Choose Not To

(First Prize Winner)

Michelle Bae

A quick trigger finger is all it takes. *Click.* Tips on the proper handling of ball pythons, various articles on MSM blood donation controversies, and recipes for avocado cheesecake—all gone, thanks to the death sentence in the upper right hand corner: the x.

The x, though unassumingly located in the corner of your computer screen, is surprisingly divisive. Whether you use Google Chrome, Internet Explorer, Firefox, or Safari, all netizens can be split into two parties. Some, utterly without mercy, compulsively close tabs after they are done with them, while others—like myself—can't bear to cut short the life of any browser tab, because each is part of an aggregation of knowledge and inspiration. My YouTube searches for Stacey Kent's jazz recordings nestle between Bandcamp explorations of new music and my Spotify. In a new window, articles on the best ways to survive a zombie apocalypse accompany exposés on racial imbalances in our justice system. And without shame, I can admit that at least ten of my tabs are reserved for web comics, text-adventure games, and art blogs.

I respect those who can keep their browsers limited to under ten tabs—because their organization and focus is admirable. I also respect those who, embodying their browser habits, have managed to prune their interests in the same way they prune their tabs: learning to play the violin exclusively for ten years, or focusing all of their efforts on JSA alone. But I can't bring myself to close my tabs, nor can I bring myself to stop accumulating interests until my schedule overflows.

Perhaps, like my computer's desktop, I lead a cluttered lifestyle. It's rare that I don't have anything to do—no club meetings, no ASB duties or art projects—during lunch or after school. I'm the only one in my school who managed to bypass our limited electives to take both art and choir. It's fair to say that I've tried my hand at nearly everything my school has to offer. There, though, lies the greatest disadvantage of my tab-embracing, club-hopping way of life: I have so many interests that I can't bear to choose just one. Despite years of soul-searching and analysis of my activities for the sake of putting something down under "Intended major," I'm hard-pressed to decide on anything other than "Undecided."

It may seem unfocused. It may seem less noteworthy than the other applicant who wanted to be a doctor since she was four or the student who talks, lives, and breathes computer science. But I embrace it— dancing, singing, delegating, writing, sculpting, coding, debating, etc.— because even though I can find x, I choose not to.

About the Author: My name is Michelle Bae. I'm a student, artist, sculptor, singer, debater, and "whatever-er" living in the Seattle metropolitan area. I got into Stanford through early action despite having little to no idea of what I'll major in—but that's just fine. I have two years of exploration to do.

High School Attended: International School, Bellevue, WA

The Process: I took a lot of long walks while applying to colleges, scrawling down essay ideas as they came to me while sitting on curbs or park benches. This particular essay's source material came directly from my browsing habits. The webpages open on my computer are wildly diverse, and in a sudden moment of inspiration I realized that they would be perfect for showcasing my diverse range of interests.

Acknowledgments: Mercer Education was a good, casual place to fine-tune essays with my peers.

THE TROUBLES I'VE SEEN

Natalie Newton

Welcome to my Mississippi hometown, a time capsule from the '60s. One side has shaded sidewalks lined with well-kept homes. The other side is more youthful, but the residences are old, dirty, dilapidated, and the commercial strip consists of pawn shops and liquor stores, title loan and payday advance enterprises, gun and ammo stores. Unsupervised children, roaming the streets, suffer the pernicious effects of boredom and make sport of vandalizing property. Many older youth graduate to more serious crime—drugs, theft, assault. Our tiny public school system has its own police force to break up fights and escort expelled children home. The school administrative building has bullet holes in the windows. The squad car parked outside had its windows replaced after teenagers smashed them. Last year, middle-school students killed a classmate on the playground, and a teacher was hospitalized after intervening in a fight. A high percentage of students drop out before graduation. Would things improve if the state took over this recently F-rated system? As things stand, middle-class citizens enroll their children in expensive private schools. And my siblings and I homeschool.

Two months ago, my two sisters and I were awakened in the middle of the night by red lights pulsating on our bedroom's walls. We gathered at the window to watch firefighters responding to an arson attempt at the high school directly across the street from our home.

Mississippi is not burning, but economic and racial rifts are real. The median income for African-Americans is half that of whites. Homogeneity of low-income neighborhoods (the product of shockingly recent government-sanctioned discrimination) contributes to poverty being defined along racial lines. If education is "the gatekeeper," black children in the South are denied access to opportunities to escape generational poverty: "In 24 of the 40 Mississippi districts to receive a D or F grade from the state, African-Americans make up at least 95 percent of the student body" *(Washington Post)*. Lacking examples of success, expectations of success, and enrichment for success, as bestowed in middle-class neighborhoods, poor African-American youth are disenfranchised and frustrated.

"Separation has never produced mutual understanding and respect. It has produced ignorance, suspicion, impersonal stereotyping, demeaning innuendo . . ." (*Bloodlines*, John Piper). Restricted daily contact between blacks and whites gives credence to the notion that the "other" is of a different essence. America chuckled at a 1980s *Saturday Night Live* skit called "White Like Me," in which a black person, with the help of makeup, went undercover to infiltrate white society. The comedy hinged on the assumption that blacks see the white world as alien. Less amusing, while pushing neighborhood children on playground swings, I overheard an African-American child insult her dark-skinned friend, "You can't push me down that slide, you little white girl!" "Oh yeah?" the other indignantly retorted, "You're blond, blond at the roots!" I was sickened when my Caucasian roommate at Mississippi Girls State matter-of-factly announced, "I'm racist." Telling me about her background, she had just contrasted her homogeneous white school with a nearby poorly funded and troubled minority school.

I straddle dualities: rich and poor, black and white. I live in a low-income household and appreciate financial struggles and hindrances, but I received a rich education in academics and arts due to my parents' own educational background. Seven years ago, my family adopted two African-American half-siblings who had grown up in the streets and projects where poverty was virtually insurmountable. My new siblings' self-application to the challenges of school and life is still stymied by self-doubt springing from disturbing surrounding demographic disparity. I believe it is naive to expect poverty and racism will be fully and forever eradicated: Human psychology and sociology are complex; moral consciousness ebbs and flows throughout history. Yet there is no excuse for complacency when inequitable and injurious conditions can be ameliorated. I am burning to do something. I have been a witness to injustice in my Mississippi microcosm, and I cannot walk away.

About the Author: My name is Natalie Newton. A member of a large family, I live in a colorful but impoverished town on the Mississippi coast where my father pastors a historic Methodist church. I hope my college education will allow me to join the intense, creative collaboration of a think tank dedicated to alleviating poverty and educational inequity.

High School Attended: Home School, Moss Point, MS

The Process: In today's racially charged world, I found it difficult to describe the Deep South's deeply ingrained division between black and white, penury and prosperity without resorting to either blame and victimization or callousness and complacency. Nevertheless, the circumstances I have grown up in have so permanently shaped my outlook on life and goals for an education that I found myself compelled to take on the subject, despite taboos and complexities.

Acknowledgments: Parent.

50,000 PENNIES

Atticus Wakefield

Fifty thousand pennies, each with a broken matchstick on top. Those were the only elements in Chris Burden's "The Reason for the Neutron Bomb." I loved it. The piece was the perfect mix of my father's conceptual outlook and my mother's sense of design, and it was about war, which I loved because I was 12. It was ideationally brilliant and aesthetically beautiful. "Each penny represents one tank in the Russian Armada," my dad told me as I tried to count them. I couldn't imagine how long it must have taken to set it up, let alone to think of it. I turned to my brother, who didn't seem to share my enthusiasm.

I think I was predestined to fall in love with art. Although I didn't admire the creative careers of my parents and extended family when I was little, I am now grateful for my genetic makeup and the influence of those people I love most in the world. I realize that my best childhood memories are inherently intertwined with my mother's aesthetic sensibility and the warmth of her home. My dad, on the other hand, is a writer and curator and taught me that the thought behind any creation is more important than its manifestation: He is conceptually driven. I'd like to think that I am my parents' synergism: I admire Chris Burden's pennies for its aesthetic beauty and for its conceptual foundation; I would not feel the same if either was lacking. My parents, through the union of their autonomous strengths, gave me an incredible gift: They gave me the love of making art, a practice that requires both integrity and tenacity, two traits that I know must guide my life.

Although I loved going to museums and galleries from a young age, I didn't seriously begin making art until I was 15. Initially my drawings and paintings were only for me, but in time I realized that I wanted to participate in the visual conversations I had visited in exhibition spaces all my life. I decided that in order to do this I must first improve my rendering. I began to draw anything that was in front of me: my brother, a candle, a bug. My drawings were disappointing. I lacked the technical skill I desired and doubted having the necessary ingenuity to make work like Chris Burden's. I lost faith and had trouble sustaining my drive. Until I saw one of Robert Longo's mammoth drawings.

Longo's charcoal drawing measured roughly 20' x 5' and depicted a crashing wave. I had never seen anything like it: the perfect integration of Old Master skill and punk rock violence. I discovered, for the first time, what it felt like to be jealous of another artist. I became determined to achieve this level of technical prowess and, in that moment, I realized that I was willing to fight for it, that I was willing to work for it. And I was excited. I took every available art class. I watched countless drawing tutorials online. I assisted any artist who would let me. And I committed myself to drawing for at least an hour every day. At first the act of forcing myself to draw for a complete hour was arduous. It seemed similar to how people describe beginning to meditate: It was a journey of my own making, one I chose, and yet I often fought against it. With time, however, I transcended the fidgeting and the frustration and soon that committed hour of drawing became time I coveted. I wasn't concerned with whether the drawings I produced were good; the point was to keep the commitment to myself and to the work: one hour, no interruptions. No matter what, I wouldn't stop before the hour was up. I continue this practice every day. And I know that I won't stop until I have made my own fifty thousand pennies.

About the Author: My name is Atticus Wakefield. I've grown up in New York City and hope to become a professional artist.

High School Attended: Friends Seminary, New York, NY

The Process: I knew I wanted to incorporate dialogue and specific anecdotes in the essay because I always find that's the best way for me to convey who I am and to describe the relationships I have. I also knew I wanted the essay to focus on the role that art plays in my life: how, growing up, going to galleries was a family activity, what making work now means to me, and how my relationship with art in many ways defines who I am.

Acknowledgments: Ellen Ross, my college adviser.

THE WORLD THROUGH MY EYES

Harshit Ranjan

I am seventeen, Indian, born in Kanpur. I went to school there, private, co-educational, on the plains to the south of Kanpur. I am the only Hindu in my class. Well, I like to draw, invent, dance, and be in peace. I like to dream, read, play, and understand complexities.

However, there is more to me than these few introductory lines can convey. I live in a world of my own, they say. I often prefer it that way. The concepts that seem too idealistic for everyone are real and tangible in my world. A world where no race, no religion, no class or boundary divides us. A world that remains untainted by the imperfections of this world. That is the world where I truly belong and it's the purpose of everything I do. I am not just an idealist who conceives of a world without problems, but an activist who wants to make things happen. Like Langston Hughes, a 22-year-old black man who faced the oppressive racial climate of America, I see various segregations in India, too, that have divided not only us but also our ideologies.

Thinking about the evident issues around me motivates me to cast a stone in the water to create many ripples and inspire a difference.

As I grew up, my mind opened up to racial and religious dynamics in India. I started to see how these ideologies governed people's actions, even if some people were not aware of the causes or consequences. From advocating false stereotypes of female inferiority to the distinctions made on the basis of caste, creed, and religion, every manmade division ignores the existence of one universal classification—humanity—or rather, I prefer, "*Homo sapiens*." In fact, I was one of those victims who had undergone the consequences of religious segregation throughout my schooling years. "We cannot be friends, we are different, our religion is different," one of my peers explained, gladly following his father's footsteps. All this never consumed me; instead, it encouraged me to bring a change in their ingrained beliefs. I believe in a world without religious segregation, and just one religion, of being human and altruistic.

As a result, my passion for equality motivated me to discuss my viewpoints at every opportunity—while volunteering for community service programs to teaching visual arts to underprivileged students to even portraying the message though my artwork.

Religious discrimination is just one amongst the several forms of imperfections I have observed around me—education that limits our imagination, gender-based violence, and corrupt governments—to name a few. The journey to make this world akin to the one in my imagination is going to be a long and arduous one. I aspire to begin with one issue and keep turning new leaves along the way. Idealists like me are often disregarded as impractical. But it is only because of idealists that the world progresses from one century to the next. I do live in a world of my own. But someday, I hope I shouldn't have to.

About the Author: My name is Harshit Ranjan. I live in Kanpur, a small city in India, and come from a humble background. I'm a striving visual artist and a science enthusiast. For me, engineering is not limited to quenching my intellectual curiosity, but a medium to spread awareness and provide aid to people. I am motivated to explore new sustainable energy sources to power the remote regions of Asia and Africa and work toward empowering underprivileged people.

High School Attended: Dr. Virendra Swarup Education Center, Kidwai Nagar, Kanpur, Uttar Pradesh

The Process: The essay portrays my actions, opinions, and motivations for creating an ideal world. It was a spontaneous (as the title demanded) catharsis of my views, based on all that I have seen happening around me. I juxtaposed the issues I feel strongly about with the little steps I have taken to work toward their solutions.

Acknowledgments: I want to thank my teachers for reviewing my essays and my parents for encouraging me to explore my talents.

"Smog Log"

Angela Zhou

The onyx orbs of a yak shine at me with curiosity. I'm five hours from the nearest town, on the Tibetan plateau, twelve thousand feet above sea level. As a bewildered city girl lost amongst meandering yaks and a soft blue mist, I feel like an intruder. Yet there is something magical, even sacred, in this image, as if I've accidentally stumbled into nature's last haven. A memory surfaces.

It's years before, and I'm staring forlornly out of the car window as I travel with my family. Outside, a smoky haze imprisons our vehicle, suffocating us the same way it extinguished the sun that morning.

My father turns abruptly from the driver's seat, "You know, this isn't fog. It's smog."

I didn't know it then, but that marked the beginning of a personal mission and a life-long relationship with pollution.

It's amazing how in my daily life I forget I live within a dangerous experiment. Ever since its introduction in middle school, my awareness of air pollution has been pushed steadily toward the back of my mind. I'd gaze at flying plastic bags as if watching clouds, joke about my decreasing lung capacity, and shrug carelessly when particulate concentration goes off the charts, yet again. I had forgotten what Earth should actually feel, smell and even taste like.

But the Tibetan plateau is a wake-up call. The velvety clouds serve as a powerful reminder of the beauties I've lost, and they urge me to cherish the beauties I can still savor. In this moment, my feeling of intrusion falls away and is replaced by hope: hope abandoned months prior; hope that once glistened in a coat of pungent water.

It had been less than two months since I nearly fell into Duck Lake, trying to gather samples for my experiment. It was pouring that day, acid rain spattering from murky clouds and down my bangs like a mini waterfall. Twelve miles from Beijing city center and right in the middle of my school campus, this duckless lake was turbulent with untreated residential and commercial effluent. The lake's surface reflected the gathering storm overhead: a whirlpool of harsh charcoal, shimmering silver, and glossy wax. As I collected my water sample, I felt myself sinking into the muddy ground. Creatures of unknown origins nibbled my vulnerable fingers, and I realized I was drenched in poisonous waters. I asked myself: Why am I here?

Only now, amid surreal yaks and clouds, do I fully understand my dormant motivations. Like streams converging to become a continuous current, my emerging ambitions come from discolored visions conceived on a fateful gray day, ideas that nudged me toward Duck Lake, and a sense of purpose revived by crisp, clean air and innocent jet-black eyes. Inside me burns an innate scientific inquisitiveness, one that needs to be set free to blossom. I was once just an urbanite, too accustomed to air pollution and toxic water, but now, my polluted city urges me daily to protect others from suffering the same fate.

I shivered under that acid rain because I yearned to break apart the components of Duck Lake water, to identify the criteria pollutants in classroom air, and to explore my community as fertile ground for environmental research. And I can put that moment into greater context here on the Tibetan plateau. Even without its startling vistas, this plateau is a place of refuge for my urban-battered self. It revitalizes my dreams and aspirations for the future. It breathes meaning into my gray-colored past. And, most of all, it drives my present, unbroken resolve to recapture this stunning scenery for others.

About the Author: My name is Angela Zhou. Growing up in Beijing, I've witnessed firsthand its slow but steady degradation from a relatively pristine city to the smog-covered metropolis that it is today, and this transformation accompanied my own flourishing goal to become the next international leader in environmental science and policy.

High School Attended: Western Academy of Beijing, Beijing, China

The Process: For months, I lived in constant fear of the task that was my personal statement. I knew I wanted to write about my intended major, environmental science, but I didn't have the right words to do so. It wasn't until weeks later, with the due date looming above me, that I experimented with the idea of juxtaposition. I remembered vividly my trip to Tibet just months before, but in my mind, it was simply a vacation destination. However, when I managed to contrast my place of residence to this pristine landscape, I found that the result suited my personality as comfortably as my favorite pair of pajamas. Dozens of drafts, countless cups of coffee, and couple of screaming matches between me and my peer-editors later, I proudly clicked the submit button with tired eyes.

Acknowledgments: I would like to thank Ms. Michelle, my high school counselor, for making my dream come true.

BITTERSWEET

Elif Kurkcu

From first to fourth grade, I grew up without a mother. The reason was not because my mother had died or my parents were divorced; my mother, who is now a forensics scientist specialist, had to complete her specialization away from me. For four years, I lived with my father and my grandparents. I was always loved, never neglected, but I still remember the pity in other adults' eyes when they saw my father alone at parent meetings or when he was the one organizing my birthday parties. They pretended she was dead. My friends were careful to not to speak about their mothers; they were probably warned by their parents. I always became angry when I realized the change in people's actions, though it often was seen as sadness to others. It was my father who knew that it was not sadness but anger that grew in me, and it was him who always took me out to eat *ashure*, a traditional Turkish dessert, and told me how things were going to be different.

I never liked ashure really, it tasted sweet but bitter at the same time. It refreshed you but also made you wish you were eating something else. My father one day told me that I was like ashure. I didn't want to be ashure. It was not as sweet as other desserts, and it did not taste as good as them. Still, he insisted I was like it. My father explained that, as ashure, I had a mixture of every emotion, every personality trait in me. The sour taste and the sweet taste combined. I had my good sides along with the bad, but that's what made me myself. I was angry with myself for being angry toward people who wanted the best for me, but I didn't want anyone to pity me. My father showed me that the reason I was mad at myself and others was because I wanted to slice out half of myself. I wanted to cut out my sad emotions, my bad parts, and became a child that everyone could love because I felt lonely and forgotten.

After my talk with my father that day in fourth grade, I understood why I was the way I was. I was punctual because I hated to be late, I didn't trust anyone other than me because I was strong enough to do what they would help me with. I never cried after that about being lonely. I laughed when they looked at me with pity in their eyes to show I was okay. I worked hard to achieve the best and show I could do what others could without any help. I did my own hair in the mornings, prepared my own breakfast, and left the house by myself without waking anyone up because I was capable of taking care of myself. I was not a motherless child who should have been pitied or seen as vulnerable; I was a grown-up now, who was capable of caring for herself.

Independence has come to define who I am. I am strong, hardworking, and punctual. I learned in difficult ways to take care of myself and decide things that would determine my future, but I am thankful for that. I see people around me, dependent on their friends, family, or teachers, and I realize how lucky I was to be able to become who I really am this young. With both my good sides and bad sides, I am me, and I stand with full control over my own life, without depending on any other.

About the Author: My name is Elif Basak Kurkcu and I live in Turkey, Adana. I go to Tarsus American College, one of the only American schools in Turkey, and going abroad to study was always my aim since I started high school. I want to major in marketing in college and work in the field of digital marketing in the film industry. I wish to be able to experience entertainment and the film industry while I do my major.

High School Attended: Tarsus American College, Mersin/Tarsus

The Process: I wrote a couple of drafts for the same prompt. It took me a long time to decide what to write in order to explain my characteristics in the best way. While choosing what to write, I looked into my past. I asked the question to myself, "What made me the person that I am today?" I also wanted to represent my country and where I came from. The answers to these two topics were the bases of my essay. I decided to base my essay on one of my childhood memories and how that memory reflected on my life.

Acknowledgments: I would like to thank my college counselor since she was the one who edited my essay and led me to the topic.

THE BLANK COLLEGE FORM

Jessica Chen

In the end, what really made me start writing on the blank college form was my mother.

Originally, I was staring at the blank form in front of me, waiting for my hand to automatically write something. I wanted to study finance, since it seemed to suit my personal level of mathematical interest, but that resulted in a frantic search of several colleges that had finance majors and connections that could potentially lead me on the right path. Still, that search only limited the numbers of colleges that sufficed my needs and wants—it didn't help me decide.

While gazing blankly at the blank form, I saw my mom entering the warm room after being outside, wrinkling her forehead as she picked up her reading glasses and notebook and sat on the couch. I thought of the endless days she spent caring for both myself and my brother alone. To make a living, she spent countless weeks, months, and even years working a variety of jobs—taking care of several kids while also taking care of her own, working long-hour shifts at a tiresome bakery, all while studying to earn a permit to help the elderly. Even though my mom didn't like working at places like the bakery because she disliked the tedious jobs of hauling out packages and making sandwiches, she still agreed to work extra hours to earn the extra money. With all of that going on in her life, she still made time in her schedule to pay attention to my brother and me; she helped me through my college process and my brother through his SAT and ACT preparation.

Throughout my junior year, I always found myself asking: "Hey, Mom. *Ni jue de na yi ge da xue bi jiao hao*? (Which college do you think is good?)" Like clockwork, my mom would always answer the same thing: "*Sui bian ni. Ni xiang qu na li dou ke yi.* (Wherever you want. You can go anywhere.)"

Her words struck me—the college process was bigger than me. I have this opportunity because of Mom, but what I do with it is my own.

Empowered, I wanted to do something in return. I wanted to stop being distraught and figure out what college would suit me. I invested myself in research but this time with improvement. I focused on colleges that were closer to home, so that I could visit more regularly without burdening my mother. Afterward, I looked at the courses colleges had listed on their websites, taking notes of differences that would influence my decision whether or not I would be satisfied at those colleges. I wanted to find something that set my mind alight.

Feeling accomplished, I set down my pen and looked at what used to be scrap college mail turn into a bunch of notes with occasional scribbles. I turned to my mother, who still had her eyes glued to the notebook, and said, "I'm done."

She looked at me with a content smile and in a Chinglish accent replied, "Good job."

Pleased, I looked back at the blank form and started to write.

About the Author: My name is Jessica Chen and I'm from New York City, with a pursuit in the field of finance and a goal to one day give back to society.

High School Attended: Bronx High School of Science, Bronx, NY

The Process: When I originally saw the prompt, I immediately decided that I would incorporate my college process experience, despite the fact that it would be a "dangerous" topic to write about. I wanted to show how the college process itself affected me. With that idea in mind, I made a first draft, with inspiration from my hard-working mother and followed a classic procedure afterwards—revise, draft, revise, draft—until I completed the final draft.

Acknowledgments: I applaud, with gratitude, my mother, my guidance counselor, Mr. Elia, and my creative writing teacher, Ms. Brooks, for guiding me along the way when I was writing this essay.

GERTRUDE VANDERBILT
WHITNEY HOUSTON

Manuela Ortiz

"Darling, don't forget to tend to Whitney Houston today!" Her husband kissed her cheeks as he bade her farewell. It was very much like him to remind her of such simple things she already took care of on a daily basis. Letting her legs take her down to the lobby of her Fifth Avenue home, she made an exit, thanking the doorman that opened the same door every 7 a.m. At the curb waited her Porsche, chauffeur inside, destination known far ahead of time. Elegant as ever, she entered the car, sinking into the fine black leather. Luckily, the weather was neither hot nor humid, and for this she was thankful. In her purse, her compact calendar accompanied her. Pulling out the notebook with rather worn corners and notes jotted everywhere, she took a look at the day's plans. "Whitney Museum of Art: 103, Whitney Houston Art Gallery: 49." Gnawing on her lip, she added "Minton's: 9." She was always preoccupied with work. And yes, art was her thing, but maybe it was performing arts that called for her rather than the fine variety. Arriving at the Whitney Museum, she was greeted with much enthusiasm. *Duty calls, of course*, she thought before returning a tight smile, lips pressed together and barely visible.

It was 8:55 at night and she breathed heavily through the mask that pressed snugly against her face. She knew behind the curtain was the stage, and behind that was the crowd, an anticipating one at that. Here, she was no longer the artist, the curator, the sculptor. Here, she was Vanney. Vanney, the masked soul artist. Vanney, the unknown woman who sang her heart out. As the emcee introduced her, she gave a small smile and the curtains parted, revealing her and the band. Her double life was hers and hers alone.

Gertrude Vanderbilt Whitney, named precisely after her great-grandmother. Born in New York City in the early '60s, she was one with much character. However, her own father did not particularly favor such a unique personality. He adored his grandmother and wanted his own daughter to be identical, or as identical he could possibly make her. She was given private tutors and sent to the Brearley School for women, the same in which her dear great-grandmother attended. She found it boring. Gertrude Vanderbilt Whitney existed already; why was it necessary for there to be another one? Her father did not see it the same way.

It was at the age of twenty when Gertrude was introduced to soul music for the first time. Coming from her grandfather's residence in Old Westbury, homebound, going through Harlem, clubs were booming with the compassionate African American beats, voices, and lyrics. She was never exposed to such culture in her life, considering her father had much control over her life. It was then when she invested in a Walkman. When asked what she was listening to in her study, she would confidently state the notorious "Chopin Nocturne Opera 9, Number 2" and continue to feel the smooth, liquid gold sound, later singing it herself.

At twenty-three, Gertrude Vanderbilt Whitney Houston was married and busy as ever. With her own recently opened gallery, named after both her father and her husband, she found that keeping her secret had become more and more difficult. The pressure of having to fulfill duties as a wife while consistently working at two locations had her stressed. She needed a break. She needed relief. That was when she started to attend clubs in Harlem. Yes, it was dangerous. And, yes, she was desperate.

The audience, the stage, the lights. Every aspect of the scene made her heart melt with joy. The performances astonished her and left her with a satisfied and fulfilled feeling. On many occasions, she simply closed her eyes and swayed in her seat. Quite frankly, she couldn't help it. It was that moment where she tried. She spoke to the owner, offering an extraordinary price to allow her to perform one night. And there she was, every Friday night at Minton's and no one even knew, which added to the thrill of it. She was no longer Gertrude Vanderbilt Whitney Houston. She was Vanderbilt Whitney. Vanney.

After one particularly exhausting night, running from place to place, she returned home to her husband, arms and legs crossed, face unamused. "Where have you been? It's half past midnight. Where have you been, Gertrude?" There was an obvious sense of anger in his tone. He had let it go the week prior and the week prior to that and the week prior to that, but this time he was not going to let it fly past him. She knew if she did not confess the truth, conflicts would arise. "I'll show you next week."

About the Author: My name is Manuela Ortiz. I am from Brooklyn, NY and have lived here all my life. I am half German and half Dominican with four sisters, who are the main factors that have influenced who I am as a person. I hope to major in biochemistry in college.

High School Attended: Bronx High School of Science, Bronx, NY

The Process: As a kid, I was always taken to museums and shows by my parents. Now, in my teenage years I go to museums at least once a month on my own or with friends. My favorite museum is the Whitney Museum of American Art in lower Manhattan and it is the museum this piece is based on. Also, as a family, I used to go on countless road trips, and my parents often played music not necessarily from the 2000s, including the Beatles, the Rolling Stones, and, of course, Whitney Houston. Therefore it only seemed right to mash these two aspects of my life into this writing piece.

Acknowledgments: I'd like to thank my guidance counselor, Mr. Ralph Elia, for always quoting me on how, "I'm more likely to be at a museum than the movies." Thank you for guiding me throughout this process!

My Mother Never Had to Worry

Emily Harvey

"Now, listen up . . ."

Even at twelve, I knew what those words meant. Standing in the hangar of the airport, I took a long look at my mother, my father, and my three siblings. With my father in the military, I can only remember him coming and going. We were a family living in states of interruption.

"I love you." I began reciting the speech along with him, echoing those departing words I knew all too well.

"Be strong." *Be strong.*

"I'll call you as soon as I can." *I'll call you as soon as I can.*

"Take care of your mother." *Take care. Of your mother?*

Adulthood took shape in twelve letters.

For as many deployments as I can remember, the speech always ended with "take care." It was deceptively meaningful; our interpretations allowed us to hide behind the vague phrase. The specificity brought on by twelve letters shined a light on what used to be shadows. I could still hear it.

"Take care of your mother." *She needs it more than you do.*

Without much consultation from me, it was decided I was past being my own priority.

Over the next five years, I learned to be more independent and responsible for my own actions. I am thankful my dad added those three words, whether he intended to or not; they guided my first steps into adulthood. It took me longer than it should have to realize how I could take care of my mother. However, I found that sometimes the best way we can care for others is by caring for ourselves. With over 900 wives in the battalion to supervise and her own job to keep up with, my mother had enough to worry about. She did not need to worry about me as well.

I made the first real changes in school. I relied less on my mother's help and took my education into my own hands. While I knew my mother was always willing to help, seventh grade science fair projects were definitely one thing she could do without. After a while, I found myself wanting to excel in school not for my mother's sake, but for my own. I lost myself in school. I fell in love with my English and history courses. Creating and destroying ideas, I built my own opinions like Lego towers. Going into high school, I possessed a strong work ethic and focus unlike those of my peers. I pursued my passions at every chance, joining the school's literary magazine staff and drama program. I took pride in the work I did. My mother never had to worry.

I also began taking more initiative at home. I did not have to be assigned chores, I just saw what needed to be done and did it. At times it seemed thankless, but I knew my efforts were helping my mother. In some ways, they helped me, too. In and out of the classroom, if something needed to be done, I was the first to do it. I learned how service works hand in hand with leadership. By high school, volunteering lost its role as a graduation requirement and settled itself into a special place in my heart. There is no number of hours I could give back to the military community for all they have given me. My involvement with the Hugh O'Brian Youth Leadership program had an incredible influence on my philosophies as a volunteer and as a leader. I became a better soccer captain. I became a better class officer. I became a better person. My mother never had to worry.

As I head to college, I take comfort in knowing I am prepared for the adult world. I am not worried, and my parents should not be worried either.

Mom and Dad,

Now, listen up, I love you. Be strong. I'll call you as soon as I can. Take care.

Emily

About the Author: My name is Emily Harvey and I am a senior at Columbus High School in Columbus, Georgia. In college, I plan on working toward becoming a journalist.

High School Attended: Columbus High School, Columbus, GA

The Process: Once I selected the prompt, I spent a few days thinking of ideas on how to make it creative and personal. I knew that this essay would be my best chance to represent myself to colleges. After deciding what I would write about, I spent roughly a week writing and editing the rough draft. Thankfully, I started the whole process early enough to give myself some time to finalize before submitting.

Acknowledgments: I would definitively like to thank my parents, Ken and Janice Harvey, for reading every draft and helping through the entire process.

TAREK, طارق, তারেক

Tarek Meah

"Enan?" I turn around. "Enan, where are you?"

My screams are being muffled by the sounds of the city. No one understands me. Cars zip past me and people shove me in different directions; lightning strikes the hapless skyscrapers until the sky is a maelstrom of light and thunder. I'm soaked in sweat and rain and tears, the latter a result of my failure to protect Enan.

The adhan for maghrib, which coincides with the sky's transition from scarlet to a tender indigo, blares from the minarets. I would normally find the imam's nasally call to prayer comforting; at this moment, however, it signals that darkness will soon blanket the city. The fairy lights that dangle from the stores in the Centre Bazaar will soon flicker on, and the congested street replete with motorcycles, Toyota and Honda sedans, the occasional bus, three-wheeled motorized CNGs, and rickshaws will be lighted by these meager Eid decorations and the dim lights of the vehicles themselves. I have never been in a situation like this in a city like this. I'm not in Fair Lawn, New Jersey, I'm in Chittagong, Bangladesh. Street lights are scarce, traffic lights are nonexistent, there are no lanes, and people almost carelessly weave through the speeding vehicles.

Just moments before we were separated amidst the chaos of other shoppers, Enan, my thirteen-year-old cousin, agreed to walk with me to Aarong, the city's largest antiquities store. While our mothers were trying on gold necklaces, "It'll take a while," my mother told us, eyeing rows upon rows of the flashy metal, Enan and I crossed the shopping plaza.

And now I have no idea where he is.

As I'm looking for Enan, there's a buzzing in my ears. The hum comes and goes at unexpected intervals; I'd prefer a constant stream of noise.

In Chittagong, there is never silence. White noise surrounds you, drowns you, becomes you so that you become the white noise. But I can't be the white noise. I must be the beacon of sound that cuts through it.

The buzzing escalates, as if all the shrieks and screams and cries of the beggars and youth and burqa-clad women emanate from a spirit, the metaphysical manifestation of the sounds of the city that stalks me as I'm searching for my cousin. The thrumming eventually quells as I continue making my rounds of the boutiques. Defeated, I walk back to the jewelry store, preparing myself for my mother's lengthy diatribe; "He's your younger brother!" she'll start. I'm thinking about when she'll begin the waterworks, either before, after, or during the tirade, when I see Enan standing behind her in front of the boutique; her arms are crossed.

"Crud."

She tells me how worried she was, how I didn't need to look for him for so long because he was smart enough to return to the store. But my aunt tells me she's proud of me: My relentlessness is demonstrative of my sense of responsibility.

My name means "night visitant." The responsibilities of AtTariq are dictated in chapter 86 of the Quran: Each human has a celestial protector who is forever watching over its person. AtTariq also means "The Piercing Star." I am to serve as the beacon of light, of hope, of eternal safety. When it's dark, I'm supposed to be bright. Juliet Capulet called names meaningless, but she didn't realize that Juliet means youthful and it was her childishness which ultimately led to her untimely demise.

It's these two syllables "tˤa" and "ˈrɪq" that determine my course of action; it's these two syllables that determine the course of all of my actions. I am outspoken, I am vigilant, I am accepting. I refuse to be drowned by the deafening sounds of everythingness or nothingness because, even in the most chaotic of situations, a star still stains the purple of the surrounding sky.

About the Author: My name is Tarek Meah. I currently reside in Fair Lawn, New Jersey, although I plan on enrolling in a six-year program at Johns Hopkins University in Baltimore to receive a BA and a MA in International Studies. My dream job is to anchor a news show focused on international affairs, like *GPS with Fareed Zakaria.*

High School Attended: Bergen County Technical High School, Teterboro, NJ

The Process: It was a cold Friday night in October. I was seated at the desktop (the one I am typing this on), and I started writing whatever came to my head. I originally planned on writing about identity because I wanted to highlight the love I have for my religion and my culture. Eventually, I realized that the most beautiful lesson I learned was because of my name, and I learned that lesson from the experience I recall in my essay (I won't reveal any details because everyone loves a little suspense!). The essay was originally flawed, and as I kept rereading it, I became more upset about it. Then, one day, while I was in New York City en route to an overnight program at Johns Hopkins, I sat down at Hudson Yards Park close to Penn Station. There was something about the park—I don't know if it was the cold air blowing in from the Hudson, or the water fountain in front of me, or even the sounds of the city—that inspired me to write what I've submitted. I wrote it with my black G2 gel pen on my favorite Docket Gold pad of yellow paper, and finished it on a computer at the Milton S. Eisenhower Library at Johns Hopkins University. I wrote my college essay at my dream college.

Acknowledgments: My sister, Mumtahana Meah.

THE KINGDOM OF ELIZABETH

Elizabeth Gibbs

I'm going to let you in on a little secret: It really stinks being an only child. I'm actually not an only child, but my brother and sister are so much older than I am that I barely saw them growing up. I don't blame them. When you're a teenager, your five-year-old sister is not supposed to be your best friend.

As I grew up without my siblings, I rapidly jumped to the conclusion that I owned the place. Welcome to the Kingdom of Elizabeth. I had servants, their names were Mom and Dad. My kingdom was stocked with Flamin' Hot Cheetos and Pop-Tarts. It also came with 24/7 cable coverage. There was no one to threaten my kingdom, and so I became the queen of selfishness.

My egotistical mindset was only encouraged by a new Nikon Coolpix camera. The perfect instrument to develop my creativity and make memories, right? Well, looking back at my photo library from six years ago, I only see selfies. If you were to look in the dictionary for the definition of narcissism, you would find one of my selfies. It was a new source of self-glorification and I reveled in it.

The kingdom I had built was soon uprooted and transplanted to a new place. My family made a move, but not to the next street or next state. More like, a move across the Atlantic Ocean. Finding myself in a new culture that didn't swallow new selfies and statuses by the minute, this self-absorbed girl was forced to transform. The amount of selfies in my photo library began to decrease.

Fast forward a few years, and I'm moving again. It wasn't until I moved six hours away from my parents that the selfie obsession finally ceased. I was given the opportunity to live with family friends to attend a school in a city instead of being homeschooled in a remote town. The kingdom had been obliterated. I now had a "sister."

When you live with someone else, your flaws are easily exposed. One of my biggest flaws was believing the lie that I could get whatever I wanted in life. Now that I had to share with someone, I was forced to look around at others instead of at myself. Living with my "sister," Madeleine, taught me the hardest lesson of all: I was not the center of the universe. People will not flock to serve your desires, like they did when you were a child. After wiping the self-absorbed fog off my glasses, I derived so much joy from the new eyes I had. I began to see the marvel of others that had been placed in my life. My photo library started filling up with photos of memories with friends that I will cherish for years to come.

My favorite picture from that year I spent with my second family was of Madeleine and me. We were sprawled out on a bed in the middle of a West African hot season. The power was cut, and we couldn't find a way to make ourselves any cooler. Sure, we were miserable, but we were content because we had each other to laugh the sweat away. Instead of looking back on my photos from that year and seeing a self-absorbed girl, I see a young woman "living deep and sucking the marrow out of life" (Thoreau).

The child-like concept of the sun, moon, and stars revolving around me was directly correlated to the amount of selfies in my photo library. Thank goodness my kingdom was destroyed, because building it with others is a million times more rewarding than a compliment on a selfie on social media.

About the Author: My name is Elizabeth Gibbs. I am an expat living in Burkina Faso, a country in West Africa. I aspire to be a teacher that works in difficult places like inner city schools or in a developing country.

High School Attended: International School of Ouagadougou, Burkina Faso

The Process: To brainstorm ideas, I went to a quiet place and put on soft, inspirational music and just started writing. Just by putting words down on paper, I got a better idea of what I wanted to say. After coming up with a rough draft, I went through and polished it with my counselor and my mom.

Acknowledgments: My high school guidance counselor and my mom, who taught me to love writing.

A Girl with No Country

Elizabeth Nsabimana

There is no place where I feel content. I am a girl with no country.

When I was six years old, visiting my paternal grandparents, kids my age yelled at me, "Muzungu, muzungu," a derogatory word in Rwanda used to describe white people. One of the kids even rubbed my face with her dirty hands and afterwards rubbed her face. She asked the others, "Did I change?" They replied, "No." I yelled at them, "I am not white!" But I was filled with self-doubt, thinking—"Am I a white? Why is she rubbing dirt on me?"

Six months later, we went back to Russia to visit my maternal grandparents. I always ran in front when I went out with my family. Kids shouted, "Черный уходить," which means "Black, go away." My mother told me to ignore them, but that was too much to ask a six-year-old. I refused to go out anymore. I hid in my room wondering—"Who am I exactly?"

I am a mixed Rwandan-Russian, as my father is Rwandan and my mother is Russian. I was born in Russia and lived there for two years until we moved to Rwanda in 1998. I love both my countries, but they don't love me back. If I am not accepted where I am, am I truly of that country? Am I truly a girl with no country?

I fell prey to self-pity—"Why me?"

I did my best to fit in. In primary school, my classmates used to pull my long hair when the teacher was out. It hurt and I cried. When the teacher came back and saw my red eyes, she was shocked and asked me what happened. I responded "Nothing. It's just that I am sick and my eyes are hurting." My classmates were surprised that I didn't tell the truth. The next day, they pulled my hair again; again I didn't tattle on them. They asked me, "Why are you being nice to us while we are so mean to you? Why don't you tell the teacher?" I replied, "I don't want to get you in trouble because of my hair." They apologized, and we soon became good friends.

I have both white and black friends, but I often feel uncomfortable around them. When I am with my white friends and they start saying bad things about black people, it hurts me deeply. I can't stop myself from opposing them, telling them how things actually are. When I am with my black friends, they also criticize white people, and I can't stop myself from defending whites because it also hurts me.

So my burden has become a mission. I know who I am, and I am used to the names people call me. I learned not to care about what people say about me as long as it is not true. I learned to not only deal with being a misfit, but to thrive in such a setting. With feet in both worlds, I am always defending everyone, never content to allow the stereotypes to perpetuate.

A few months ago, a Russian representative of East European universities came to school, and my "plotting" headmaster assigned me to be his tour guide. I began the tour talking to him in English, but when we reached the math class, I asked him a question in Russian, and he replied quickly without thinking. He was so taken aback, thinking he was back in Russia again, but seeing the words coming from my café au lait face. I knew that he would never look at Rwandans the same way again.

I have never found a place where I am content, but I have found a purpose; I am an ambassador of both blacks and whites, trying to promote peace and understanding. Though I am never content, I have found my place. I am mixed, but not mixed up.

About the Author: My name is Elizabeth Ituze Nsabimana and I'm from Rwanda. I'm now studying material sciences at Yonsei University in South Korea. In the future, I want to be an engineer who does more than engineering; I will use my skills to inspire others through our collaborative work to improve Rwanda's infrastructure.

High School Attended: Gashora Girls Academy of Science and Technology

The Process: I first wrote an essay about playing volleyball and the role of teamwork and sportsmanship. But my headmaster, who knows me well, challenged me to write a more personal essay that would distinguish me from so many other applicants. I resisted at first because the memories I would write about were still painful, but with his support, I began to express those feelings I had bottled up for so long. Even if this essay is not accepted for the book, it was a therapeutic experience for me, and I am very proud of what I wrote.

Acknowledgments: My headmaster at GGAST.

A STORY UNTOLD

Tehani Gunaratna

I have lived between the lines of a story; a story of struggle, of sacrifice, of the labor of love—a story that I have been told not to share.

My story begins in Sri Lanka, an island nation with a modern history of civil war and poverty; I was born to this land, and spoke the language with my family and stray dogs. My parents tell me it was as if the war paused and I was born, the first child of two people who bore their hopes and dreams in a swaddled infant who had no interest but to suckle, sleep, and stir. Changing countries at six is no easy task—it is a strange age to assimilate; being young enough to learn the new culture, but too old to forget your own. Language drew an obvious boundary, but there were subtle challenges. My father was away at night and rubbed his eyes in the day, visits from child services analyzing our family in our one bedroom apartment with two beds shoved against an eggshell wall were regular, and the house-beating noise of the railroad above our complex hummed while I devoured mountains of books.

I began my academic career mastering a language that struck fear in my mother, becoming proficient at navigating tax forms, Medicaid forms, and job applications. Now, my 65-year-old family friend Terry encourages me to not grow up too fast; she tells me that I owe it to myself to create an amazing future, to move on from the childhood that I was unintentionally denied. These particular statements are well-intentioned, but lack reflection about what it means to move on from my absent childhood, one filled with erasure—I have grown up not knowing many like myself, not seeing myself in my books, on TV shows, so it is disheartening to hear people respond to my reality by telling me to leave this burden behind. This reality is my own and is expounded on by many other kids in this country. Is it fair to say this is not an adequate childhood, that it is a cliché and overwrought to write about it—like so many of my reviewers have said? Do I only weave an ever-so-common tale of immigrant resilience?

I, like many others, cannot move on from my struggles because my family is still struggling: my father with his income, my mother with her English, and me with my calculus. However, these circumstances did not destroy my childhood; instead they made me resilient. Yet I have been told too many times that my story is too much of a burden for others to read, that my experiences are a cliché and overused, that admissions officers are sick of reading them. In turn, I, too, am tired, but from how many times I have been told my story is too stale.

Truly it would have been incredible if I did not have to confront issues of poverty and discrimination, but I am no longer that first grader struggling to string my discombobulated syllables into words in English. I now use my words wisely. I have an understanding of a language that does not comfort my parents, but it is one that I consciously utilize to create a story, a story that may be echoed by ten thousand other students, but still a story worth telling. Being an immigrant child has been the most defining factor of my life; it has had the greatest influence on who I am—thus this story needs to be shared. I tell this story because I have been told not to. I tell it for myself and for all of the children who have been told to understand our struggles, but to move on, to not write about it in our college essays. I must tell this story because if I do not, who will?

About the Author: My name is Tehani Gunaratna. I was born in Sri Lanka, but I reside in New York City. I spend most of my time on trains, where I read too much and I don't write enough and I'm trying to do more of both.

High School Attended: Bronx High School of Science, Bronx, NY

The Process: The essay prompt asked students who have a background or identity so meaningful that their application would be incomplete without it, to "share their story." My upbringing is the largest factor of my identity and so I did exactly as asked. Ironically, I was told by many trusted adults that my essay was too bold. I am willing to compromise, but not when it comes to my writing. I left the tone of my essay in its original state because I am confident the message is clear.

Acknowledgments: I'd like to thank Isuree for encouraging me to use this topic, and Terry for dealing with my pickiness about editing.

ALIVE

Jiwon Jeon

Most everyone was in black, and those who weren't wore black ties or proper suits. We were standing in a single file, placing white flowers in front of Hye Lin's portrait as Korean tradition stated.

Hye Lin was dead.

They said she went peacefully, that she left while taking a nap. I never knew her; I didn't know her face. I never even knew she attended the same school that I did. To me, her death was a callout that she was alive, had been alive, breathing in the same space as me.

We sat in the gym, our heads bowed, listening to the deafening silence. It was heavy. It wasn't fragile, like the silence that descended when nobody knew what to say. This time, everyone knew what was going to be said. And it was precisely because we knew that the silence felt so heavy.

A group of Hye Lin's friends played music; someone else sang. Others shed tears, choking out words unuttered before, too late to be heard. Here and there, sorrows whipped around us like a heavy rainstorm on the sea.

Hye Lin's father stepped onto the stage. The heaviness of his sigh through the microphone dragged down my heart, drowned the words thrashing inside me. In that sigh, I could hear not only his breath escaping his body, but his joy, his hope, his life.

"Hye Lin was . . . a wonderful daughter."

He fought his tears.

"She was bright, she was kind, she was warm-hearted. She . . ."

Tears won.

This time, the waves drowned me, too.

What if I died? What would my dad say when I died? Would he talk about me? Would he cry wordlessly? Would he be like the father standing now in front of the microphone, choked but hollow inside?

I cried and cried. I didn't know exactly why tears fell from my eyes. But they did. It was as if something huge was choking my heart so that words couldn't come out. I cried because it hurt. The pain for those left behind to bear was so big that it splashed others standing on the dry rocks of the beach as well.

With tears still in my eyes, I looked around. The world that I saw then was sad. Everyone had a sharp fragment piercing through them, lodged in their hearts. It would melt down sooner or later. But it would leave behind a scar for all of us. For me, that scar opened my eyes and showed me something. It told me that we were not alone.

Hye Lin's death was not just a storm that whipped by. It was rain that washed into our hearts and flowed into our eyes, leaving behind the earthy fragrance of wet grass. We were not alone; Hye Lin's parents were not alone. We had divided the pain. It couldn't be equally divided, but we all took a portion and stored it in our hearts.

It would be a lie if I said I cried for Hye Lin. But I did cry because of Hye Lin. I cried because her death lit up so many things that I had not been able to see before. Everyone had different pains. Everyone had numerous scars in their hearts, burns from the crippling pain. And scars do not disappear, but they can heal. And because we all had the scar inside, we were together.

Someday, I will write about Hye Lin. When I am a writer, when I can sit down and recall this memory as one rummages through an old album, I will present her to the world. Her name won't be Hye Lin. But she'll be there, unchanged, just as she was for me, living on as the essential truth beneath the surface of our lives.

I will write about the girl whom I saw, first and last, at her funeral.

And I hope my writing heals.

About the Author: My name is Jiwon Jeon. I have spent twelve years of my life in an international community in Beijing. I have found a home here, and I hope to find more as I move on through life.

High School Attended: Western Academy of Beijing, Beijing, China

The Process: I decided on my topic by going through what impacted me heavily and geared me toward what I wanted to do with my life. After completing the draft, my counselor and literature teacher provided me with advice, which I referenced to complete the final version of this piece.

Acknowledgments: I would like to acknowledge Mr. Cifizzari and Mr. Johnson for providing me with guidance throughout the whole process, my parents for always supporting me and believing in me, and Hye Lin for making this essay come alive.

CRANIOSYNOTOZILIAN LAIS

Lais Conceicao

I think I have a little more in common with dinosaurs than most. Yes, I, like the *Dilophosaurus wetherilli*, have a crest rising out of my head.

No, my crest isn't a bizarre metaphor for strange sinuses. Mine came from the developmental disorder craniosynotosis, in which my skull fused prematurely. The surgical procedure left a ridge-like scar running from the front of my head to a few inches short of my spine.

I remember this every time I visit O Museo do Bosque in my home town, Campinas, Brazil. Since childhood, I have been enchanted with this museum, surveying the glass-eyed critters in their dioramas. I would walk slowly within the musty wood walls, each step agitating dust that already saturated the air. I wandered the antiquated exhibits and pressed my toddler hands on the unfinished railings, leaning forward to gaze at a two-headed calf amongst other preserved animals.

At that age, I stared in dumb fascination, perplexed and repulsed yet somehow drawn to these creatures. Growing up, I devoured books about animals, always returning to the museum with new thoughts, arriving three feet taller and loudly announcing that a sloth's greenish tint comes from the algae that grows in its hairs. As a young adult, I pass by the exhibits again, breathing in the dense air with a sense of nostalgia. I stop at the calf and ponder biology, considering conjoined twins and how they often die in infancy. It occurs to me that, I, too, am an oddity. I reach up and trace my scar delicately, carefully expose the sensitive area. By some miracle, I made it past infancy, although my condition could easily have killed me or given enough brain damage to make me, well . . . not me.

I consider: What if my mother hadn't gone through dentistry school? What if she didn't have OCD? Would she have noticed that something was wrong in time to save me? Would she have known a neurosurgeon? Would he have given priority to operate on me?

Would I have lived?

Contemplating this, I realize the significance of my life. Although I am one of billions of humans, I am only one out of three million—the rates for craniosynotosis. And, out of those, I am one of the lucky few who had access to treatment—and made it to adolescence as healthy as my peers. It's a miracle to me, and not one of life, but of science: of hundreds of years of neural, developmental, and surgical research.

I walk away from the exhibit, and return to class in Washington.

In high school, I found science classes enthralling, especially in the small stuff: DNA replication, disulfide bonds, atoms. I saw identities in molecules. I fell in love with chemistry, since it demonstrated that the tiniest changes can cause drastic alterations—from one chemical to my crest.

Like an enthusiastic science teacher, I guide unsuspecting but willing hands to my head and across my crest. I watch as their expression changes to curiosity and confusion, sometimes disgust and fear. Once, someone screamed. I don't mind. I take their interest and use it to inform them of the oddity on my head, telling them about the surgery, the science, and the dinosaur.

I love my similarities to my Cretaceous colleague. But I know I am more than just a crest: I am a lucky child, a miracle of a watchful mother, and, above all, a human who thirsts to learn more. I think I'll even get my own name: Craniosynotozilian Lais.

About the Author: My name is Lais Conceicao. I am a scientifically intrigued student living in Redmond, Washington, with great interest in the workings of the world and all the beauty in it and the desire to go into research in chemistry and pharmaceuticals.

High School Attended: International Community School, Kirkland, WA

The Process: I first wrote several drafts that approached the same topic but with slight variations in tone, style, narration, and precise content. I chose between the drafts after consulting with peers and then edited it based on their comments and recommendations. After narrowing my options, I revised and edited over the course of several weeks, checking in with the school counselor and college admission adviser to continue improving my essay until I finished my application and submitted the essay.

Acknowledgments: Thank you to my counselor and the essay counselor at school for reading and giving advice on my essay! Also a huge thanks to the classmates who read this and Mr. Plank, who had a college essay unit in his literature class.

EVER SINCE

Melissa Holland

As an eleven-year-old girl, I hung two things on my wall: an article that made me cry and a picture that inspired me. As I look back on it now, these pictures have shaped my mission and passion in life, guiding me in both my college and career choices.

Six years ago, my dad gave me a nature magazine which featured a picture of a Native American man crying, saying: "People start pollution. People can stop it." My heart broke; I read on. The article was filled with facts and stories of the awful conditions of mid-twentieth century Earth, from rivers on fire to oil-covered beaches. I was shocked! I knew these problems existed, but for some reason, that night, these facts struck me deeper. This article, however, did not highlight only the precarious position of Earth, but also gave hope for the future. This article shed light on the progress that has been made: Earth Day, Clean Water Act, and the Endangered Species Act. Perhaps this is why it struck me so deeply: the idea that there is hope for the future of our planet. This hope for Earth's future inspired my interest in conservation.

I was raised learning to recycle, to compost, and hearing my dad yell, "Turn out the lights; stop global warming!" As a little girl, I wanted to be an environmental engineer, my dream job. I wanted to halt habitat destruction, the extinction of vanishing animals, the smog hanging above cities, suffocating life below. I wanted to clean the rivers and the forests. This was and remains my dream: to make a contribution to sustaining and improving this planet.

I look over this article now and realize that it inspired my younger self to volunteer at the Cincinnati Zoo; to help my dad at the Edge of Appalachia nature preserve; to email restaurants that their Styrofoam take-out boxes are not environmentally friendly; to make a promise to donate 10 percent of my "income" to rhinos. I even pleaded with my parents: "Can we please adopt a rhino?" I had done my research. It was thirty-five dollars. My parents said yes! I chose a potential mother rhino named Rosa. This was the second item on my wall: a picture of Rosa, *my* rhino.

Every day, I wake up to the photo of Rosa on the wall next to the article that inspired me six years ago. These wall hangings are a constant reminder of the help our planet needs and our responsibility to care for it. It reminds me of my dream. It is empowering to know that I have the ability and resources to contribute to the solution of the world's problems. As I begin the transition from high school to college, I am excited by the endless opportunities for me to fulfill this dream of mine, to turn my adolescent passion into a career that will make a genuine difference.

In college, I want to continue helping the environment by joining or starting clubs with missions to help endangered animals. I am pursuing engineering as my major so that I can have the skills to solve the problems Earth is facing. After an engineering undergraduate degree, I am considering a degree in veterinary medicine, specializing in exotic animals. This will provide me with the skills to make my dream a reality.

About the Author: My name is Melissa Holland. I live in Cincinnati, Ohio, and attend Walnut Hills High School. I am planning on pursuing a major in engineering and a minor in either music or environmental science. I hope to be a part of helping endangered animals and the environment through college and my future career.

High School Attended: Walnut Hills High School, Cincinnati, OH

The Process: First, I took a very long time deciding what I wanted to write about. That often meant lying on my bed staring at the wall, thinking. But while staring at the wall, I saw that I had taped an article and a picture on it some time ago, and I realized it had been a long time since I read the article. Reading it, I remembered how much it impacted me and my life. In order to write a more personal essay and one that stands out, I decided to write my essay about these wall hangings. I quickly wrote out my thoughts and then left them to sit for a day. The next day, I came back and tightened up my thoughts. I reread the prompt and tried to make my essay sound like a story and something college admission officers would want to hear and would be interested in. I tried to show my growth since I was eleven years old and how I planned to continue my passion throughout my life. I then handed the essay off to almost every English teacher I have ever had and my father. After I used the feedback and edited my essay, I let it sit again for a few days. When I came back, I made a few more edits and then sent it off to the writing center at my school and my guidance counselor. They encouraged me to dig deeper and be even more personal. Afterward, I sent it off to an essay-reviewing website multiple times. This website helped make my essay sound more formal and more impactful in less words. The editors on the website are well-trained professionals and gave me harsh but outstanding feedback. After again letting it sit for a few days, my father and I did a final read through and sent it in. This essay took weeks to perfect.

Acknowledgments: My father, Jeff Holland, and the editing website EditRevise.com.

BUTTERFLIES

Yiran Xuan

Spirit animals, like Hogwarts' houses, are pretty arbitrary. Supposedly, for any personality, there's a perfect spirit animal match. However, people are able to look for similarities with a given animal symbol only to the point that they declare a perfect match. Thus, any creature can be anyone's spirit animal; people just tend to pick cool ones like wolves and dolphins. Nobody wants starfish or ostriches.

My spirit animal is the butterfly.

I'm a sarcastic teenage guy, and butterflies are dainty things that represent innocence, love, and prettiness. Butterflies are brilliantly colored while I wear drab shades of gray. Butterflies flutter; I walk like a predatory dinosaur. At first, the comparison seems to fall flat.

However, the most important aspect of the butterfly symbol is not appearance but metamorphosis.

Since elementary school, I've dreamed of starting and working on a brilliant secret project with a close team of friends. My fuzzier freshman self (I hadn't started shaving) mustered the initiative to make this dream a reality. In January that school year, I started a DIY innovation project with four selected friends. The plan: We come up with a genius invention, dedicate ourselves to inventing it for three years, and then unveil it to the public to be widely used and deeply appreciated. We named our team: "i like skyrim" (the popular game released that winter) and created a Facebook group, establishing the project as "legit."

Then we had to decide what to actually innovate.

While caterpillars have twelve eyes that can barely discern shapes, I had four eyes (including my glasses) that couldn't see two steps ahead into the project. I thought a genius idea would come out of a few discussions, and we'd start working very soon; instead, after our first batch of proposed ideas was tabled, we were caught in a trap of impulsive ambitions and hard reality. Ideas like instant-charging batteries, sidewalk generators, and punching bags that punched back were great even in retrospect but impossible for five high school freshmen.

The other members soon lost interest, but I was too stubborn to quit. This project was a matter of personal honor, so I stuck myself and my teammates in the deteriorating effort for three increasingly frustrating months. I believed the project would survive if I forced the group to stay and worked harder thinking of ideas. I was wrong. I deleted the Facebook group in April, marking the project's official end.

I doubt a caterpillar's time inside its chrysalis is particularly pleasant, especially while it grows its wings. I was sour for many weeks over the failed effort. Yet during the bitterness, I still felt proud for making the attempt. In addition, the memories of the better moments during the project, like the sparks of new ideas and the thoughtful exploration of new concepts, began to override the frustration. I was determined to rectify the mistakes I made the first time.

I had new wings of purpose, but I vowed also to be wiser; to plan extensively for each idea and be more perceptive; to be more practical than romantic regarding ambitions and ideas; to not waste time in bad decisions for "honor." Only then could I successfully create something to be proud of. "i like skyrim" was a start; since then, I have managed to *metamorphose* my efforts into several successful projects. I've written a book, started a school club, developed a (prototype) social network, and filled entire notebooks with ideas for more projects.

I'm currently working on the transcription of a famous concerto called the Butterfly Lovers Violin Concerto, based on the (melodramatically) tragic folk tale of two star-crossed lovers dealing with separation by dying, for my school orchestra. With 92 pages of score, it's a massive project that's spanned two years and given me half my white hairs. But when it's done, the Butterfly concerto will be the prettiest thing you'll ever hear.

About the Author: My name is Yiran Xuan. I'm a student at Dublin Jerome High School, and I get a lot of ideas. Learning how to make these ideas reality is one of my life goals, as well as becoming a better whistler.

High School Attended: Ohio Dublin Jerome High School

The Process: I started with a basic premise of "spirit animals," and designed a rough narrative around it and the concept of change. I went through twelve iterations, some improvements more major than others, before settling on a version that I was happy with (and too tired to further edit).

Acknowledgments: My parents, my school guidance counselor, Mrs. Russell, and Gabrielle Glancy.

My Home Team

Anna Meyer

In early May, my dad will come in from the deck waving chicken around like he has had an epiphany and he'll say, "This is our year, Ann." It's a common phrase, just like when he says, "Get some sleep, cowgirl," or "Tonight we're having poopy diaper sandwiches for dinner," but when he says it I know he believes it as much as he makes me believe it. About this time, there are at least one hundred games to go, and I can feel the summer creeping up under my light jacket of spring. School is almost over and our Royals are back on TV.

Around June, my mom will start complaining that there seems to be nothing else on TV and I think my dad pretends not to hear her because the channel never changes. The interesting part is since my dad is not a fan of some commentators the volume always stays on zero, and my dad commentates for me. It is actually better this way because then I get his undeniably biased opinions, complete with life lessons such as when the count is 0-2 you always throw the ball in the dirt. I also get his famous baseball quotes such as, "The beautiful thing about baseball is there is no time clock, everyone gets their fair at bats, and there is no reason to give up hope until the bottom of the ninth inning."

When the game started Tuesday night I was shaking. I'm not sure if I was nervous because I wanted the Royals to win or if I was nervous they would let my dad down. The first few innings consisted of all six members of my family, but about the sixth inning only my dad and I were left on the couch. I prepared to be disappointed as I watched a ball thrown by a Royal soar over the center-field wall. My dad looked at me and said, "You know, Ann, the beautiful thing about baseball is . . ." and I finished his sentence with "everyone gets their fair at bats." In the eighth inning, our rally caps came out. I started to perk up, but, being the superstitious people we are, neither of us said a word until the inning had finished. I learned long ago never to jinx a good thing. However, I knew this situation was more severe than commenting on how many green lights we had hit on the way to middle school. In the eleventh inning, our eyes started to droop. Nightmares of losing by sixteen in 2008 and being disappointed every year danced behind our eyes. In the bottom of the twelfth though, after eighteen years of "This is our year, Ann," it finally came true. Neither of us slept that night. We woke the whole family with our screams, and the dog was not happy with the shaking floor, but this is my perfect place and this is our year.

About the Author: My name is Anna Meyer. I live in Overland Park, Kansas, and someday I hope to write a law.

High School Attended: Blue Valley North High School, Overland Park, KS

The Process: At first, I sat down and I wrote. I wrote whatever came to mind. I did not filter myself one bit and I did not even include punctuation. Then, I read my essay and I thought to myself, "Wow, I think I got something here." When I read my essay to my dad, he teared up and that was when I knew that this came from my heart. I stuck with this idea because this is who I truly am and I thought that it showed an interesting side of me.

Acknowledgments: My dad, Joe Meyer, for giving me the place I am most content.

THE GRAYISH AREA

Breanna McMillan

In a world made up of seven continents, four oceans, and roughly 6,500 languages, it is easy to feel a lack of individualism. I am lost in a sea of personalities and second place to the newest trends, but most of all I feel tangled. Tangled in my untamed tendrils that I try to hide behind but that only attract attention. Some may refer to my hair as an Afro but I find nothing about that cool. Please do not pet me. I am not your pampered pooch. I will iron these curly wrinkles to be just like you.

Being Irish, Italian, and West Indian, I am considered mixed, a mutt. My mother originates from the Caribbean, and my father is Staten Island born and raised. As a child I was made aware by my parents of my culture. They would tell me I was black and white. Just colors to me at the time, I considered myself gray. I have an older half-brother who is fully black and two younger siblings that are mixed same as I. When I was young, I hadn't felt much different than other little girls. My baths were probably longer considering my mane swallowed all things that dared to go near it, but being mixed went unnoticed by my younger self until Christmas time. My black grandparents bought me white Barbies and my white grandparents bought me black Barbies as if they were afraid to show favoritism.

One year my father did what most men dare not to: he brought me to the American Girl Place. Home of the American Girl dolls. Thinking back, I grow nostalgic. The store was madness, lines unimaginable, crying, yelling, and spoiled rug rats filled the air. The idea of the American Girl doll is to find a best friend that looks just like you. We searched the store in hopes of finding a mini Breanna and the closest we came was a pale doll with dark hair and dark eyes. We basically had all the same features, aside from her straight, banged hair, and she was the one I wanted. I remember my father being so disappointed. He was more concerned with finding a doll that looked mixed than I was. Only now I can understand why this was a heartbreaking moment for him.

I remember so clearly the first day of my new school. We had recently moved from Brooklyn to Staten Island, now a family of four plus one baby boy. I was entering third grade and for the first time I felt different. My hair was too big and too frizzy. I hated it. I hated me. I began to refuse to wear it down. I would only go to school if my mother put it up and tight. So tight my eyes would turn into almonds. This continued for the next three years until intermediate school crept around. This was also the time I was introduced to the almighty flat iron. My hair was only ever straightened on picture days, and during that time I would stroke my hair infinitely all day long. I was in love. I finally looked like all my friends whose ponytails would swish when they ran. Little did I know how evil this flat iron was. The price of pressing each spiral into spaghetti is one I am still paying for. The damage done to my hair was so extreme. My desire to be like everyone else resulted in some serious hair therapy. I had to cut inches off my locks to resuscitate it. I felt like a boy, when all I wanted was to be beautiful.

My favorite thing about being mixed is the commentary. It's too shocking and unimaginable that I don't appear half black, so I must be kidding. I'm not. The question that gets me is "Are you offended if I say the n-word?" My opinion, everyone should be.

Discovering who you are is one of life's riddles. From all the crying and the brushing I've done, it was all necessary in my soul searching. I can't admit that I am confident that I have found myself, but I am able to accept what gives me my identity, no matter how big or how frizzy.

About the Author: My name is Breanna McMillan, I am a senior in high school awaiting college. I plan to study nursing to receive a degree to further obtain my ultrasound technician license. I hope to make memories along the way.

High School Attended: Susan E. Wagner, Staten Island, NY

The Process: I wanted to simply tell a story in this essay that reflects who I am. I sat in front of a screen one night with a pint of ice cream nearby and just wrote.

Acknowledgments: My parents.

RUN-ON SENTENCES

Regina Gretschel

I started strong, staying at the head of the pack, ignoring the discomfort that was slowly building in my shins. But I couldn't push away the pain for long, and I was soon falling off from the front pack and the ones behind it. Speed was no longer the objective of the race; it was finishing that would be my goal. The course meandered along in convoluted loops that never seemed to end, my shins burning and aching so badly that it was all I could do to not start walking, or worse, drop out of the race. It was at that point that I mentally exited the race, allowing my mind to focus on song lyrics to distract me from the increasing ache. I finished the race, the last one of my junior year of cross country, as second to last on my team. The year before, I was one of the top seven. My descent from varsity runner to junior varsity was a steep one and not something that I had been expecting at all. I attributed the slow times to my bad case of shin splints, but it hardly mattered. I was not the runner I used to be, and I was no longer the person that I used to be.

My injury forced me to reevaluate my life and method of expression—I could no longer run away from my problems, so instead, I wrote about them. Since I needed to take significant time off to let my body heal and rest, I was left with no place to exhale: Running had always been my way of dealing with problems. My life for the past two years had revolved around practices and meets, and I was suddenly left with no way to release my day-to-day frustrations and excess energy. I felt like I was going insane without having any goals to focus on. I needed a new outlet.

As my body began to rebel against me, I wrote pages of anger and irritation into my notebook. Even as I started to move on past my initial injury, I began to write even more, exploring corners of my mind that I had never thought to prod. I dove into writing wholeheartedly, trying my hand at any and all genres, but I soon discovered that I enjoyed writing poetry the most. One of my poems was published in my school's literary magazine, and I wrote a book of poetry inspired by nature over the following summer for my senior year capstone project. Writing has become an important facet of my life, so much so that I get urges to write like someone else might crave a candy bar. It gives me a place where I can express myself with no rules to adhere to, and no one ever has to know what exactly it is that I write, unless I choose to show them. When I write, I have complete control over what is happening— something that is rare and hard to find anywhere else.

I never expected to launch myself into writing as much as I did, and I especially didn't expect to enjoy it as much as I did. But then again, I never expected to be sidelined by running injuries all year, either. During outdoor track, I did manage to run my best 400-meter time and win a small tri-meet race in the event, but a few weeks later, my right shin got worse, and I was diagnosed with a stress fracture that put me in a walking boot for two months. I was disappointed, but it wasn't nearly as devastating as my initial injury in cross country. Maybe it was because I was used to being injured. But maybe it was also because I knew I had discovered my passion for writing and that it could sustain me through anything.

About the Author: My name is Regina Gretschel. I am a senior at Montgomery Blair High School and I live in Silver Spring, MD. I enjoy writing and would like to pursue a career where I can express myself creatively through writing. I also run cross country and track.

High School Attended: Montgomery Blair High School, Silver Spring, MD

The Process: I began writing my essay early in the summer before senior year, exploring different topics. After spending a frustrating few weeks trying to edit and perfect an essay that I didn't like, I decided to totally switch topics and rewrite one of my first drafts. That first draft became what is now my final product. My mom and older sisters were a huge help in the editing process and helped make sure that my essay is the best that it can be.

Acknowledgments: My mom, Regina Gretschel; my sisters, Johanna and Louise Gretschel.

LOOSE STRINGS THEORY

Madeline Woda

Superstring theory has revolutionized speculation about the physical world by suggesting that strings play a pivotal role in the universe. Strings, however, always have explained or enriched our lives, from Theseus's escape route from the Labyrinth, to kittens playing with balls of yarn, to the single hair that held the sword above Damocles, to the basic awfulness of string cheese, to the Old Norse tradition that one's life is a thread woven into a tapestry of fate, to the beautiful sounds of the finely tuned string of a violin, to the children's game of cat's cradle, to the concept of stringing someone along. Use the power of string to explain the biggest or the smallest phenomenon.

—Adam Sobolweski, Pittsford Mendon High School, Pittsford, NY (2005–2006)

My grandmother bought me a seamstress's mannequin for my eighth birthday. She scoured flea markets across the city until meeting Marianne, as she called her—rusty upholstery tacks, scarred wooden base, threadbare cream canvas. Neither my grandmother nor my mother knew how to sew, so I contented myself with draping fabric across Marianne and creating sketchbook after sketchbook of detailed fashion designs.

In middle school, I thought the only way to stand out was by dressing differently than everyone else. I so desperately wanted to stand out. I ripped the hems out of my Christian schoolgirl uniform skirt and stitched them back up with chunky red yarn, which swirled like flagella around my knees when my poor sewing job inevitably fell out. I stitched buttons and patches on my school sweater and let the strings hang loose, cobweb threads of my effort to be original. I still hadn't learned to sew; regardless, I did know how to make a scene with my clothing.

My aunt, noticing over sauerkraut and green beans at family gatherings that I wanted to be original, taught me how to knit. A compromise, she said. It's easier than sewing; it needs less material.— Come on, try again.—Hold the needles like you'd hold a pencil.—Try again.—Don't let that yarn trail across the carpet; the cat will have a field day.—You've dropped another stitch.—Try again.

It takes a village to raise a child; It took three women to fashion my view of family. My mother once took me to a local fashion show. Each piece seemed more resplendent than the next, if only because I could identify the designer. I asked her to explain the phrase "threadbare," watching the models strut in deconstructed pieces. To me, I said, threadbare sounds expensive, like the seamless garment the Roman guards cast lots for at Jesus's crucifixion. My mother observed the models, threads trailing from their dresses and denim. Strings, she told me, make up you and me: each string of memory and each string of DNA, every hair and every eyelash. I would rather be the unraveled sweater, she said, while nodding at the current piece on the runway, threadbare and well-loved. Loose ends are beautiful because they suggest history.

It is my grandmother's seventy-seventh birthday tomorrow and we will all, Marianne included if I have my way, be present to watch her blow out her candles. She has held lone status as head-of-the-table matriarch, teller of bedtime stories, and purchaser of special presents for as long as I can remember. Women, always wrapped up in clothing, have been an almost mathematical constant in my life, even when everything else seems to be unraveling. They—my mother in something cashmere, my aunt in a hand-knit sweater, my grandmother in fur—are the common thread. Creators of a natural phenomenon, they knit together a resilient daughter, a strong family.

About the Author: My name is Madeline Woda and I'm a senior at Columbus School for Girls in Columbus, Ohio. I will be attending Columbia University next year and aspire to be an editor and live in New York City for the rest of my life.

High School Attended: Columbus School for Girls, Columbus, Ohio

The Process: I underwent agonizing pain and stress. (Just kidding . . . it was actually pretty fun.) I reminisced about my family and my burgeoning career as a fashion designer.

Acknowledgments: My mother, aunt, and grandmother.

Revise

Martina Goda

Draft one: As an ambitious third grader, my life was established.

Draft two: "S-A-C-R-I-F-I-C-E," I articulated, anxiously awaiting the end of the torturous pre–spelling test rituals my mom made me do, ensuring that I could spell each of the twenty words correctly.

Draft three: Today is the day I've been waiting for. I stared at the computer screen at the three different versions of the same essay, feeling unfulfilled, knowing that starting over again would yield the best product. It is immensely difficult to open a blank page and let go of the past. On the other hand, like a fresh coat of paint, I am simply renewing who I am. And so I started my essay again. . . .

This is not the only time I pressed the restart button. In 2007, my family and I left Kuwait, where minorities were not welcome, and embarked on a journey. Stories buzzed in my mind of gruesome events that had occurred. My parents' hushed voices still linger, mixed with sniffs of concealed tears. Hours of eating seared lamb with hummus and playing intense soccer games while teaching my little sister to walk vanished, and my family relocated to Egypt.

Although the location changed, so much stayed the same. One afternoon, I learned the truth. In shorts and T-shirts drenched with sweat, we watched as the thick, gray clouds shrouded the sun. We rushed under the canopy of a mini-mart to shield us from the rain awaiting a taxi to pass by us. A taxi did pass by and twenty others, but no matter how much we signaled and shouted for them to stop, none of them even attempted to do so.

"Why won't they stop for us?" I asked.

"Because they know you are Coptic Orthodox Christian. You're not wearing a hijab," my mother answered. I finally believed with my eyes what my ears didn't want to.

A year later, my dad told me to say my last goodbyes to my lifelong friends. No follow-up questions were allowed. We were relocating to the United States. Five people walked into an apartment intended for two; I was forced to live there. We walked every day to school and back, years without a car, slipping on thin ice in harsh winters, and reminiscing about the feeling of the scorching desert sand in between my toes. My journey to America did not feel as victorious as riding off into the sunset so much as walking into five feet of snow, but I was still positive about starting over. I knew it was the best decision we could have made.

In middle school, though it was the dread of every fifth grader, I felt confident. I was relieved to see my friends, and felt I had finally adjusted to life in a new country. However, midway through the year, the principal of the magnet school we applied to called to say I was accepted. My mom, usually professional, gave shouts of joy, "Thank you so much, I truly appreciate it! You don't know how much this means to us!"

I walked into class the first day and shyly introduced myself. My teacher smiled slyly, and I knew something was going to happen. She told the class to go around and take a wild guess at my nationality. Still standing there, I listened to the answers as each student analyzed my features and tan complexion. Spanish. Greek. Portuguese. As each person attempted, I pushed aside feelings of embarrassment and finally exclaimed, "Egyptian!" All eyes widened and questions buzzed around me as my classmates asked if I had ever seen the pyramids or ridden on a camel.

I was in another new place, still a member of the minority, but I had decided to embrace my background and be proud of who I was. This life is not just about starting over, but revising the parts that came before to create the best version.

About the Author: I am Martina Goda, aspiring to become a physician. I will major in biology on a premedicine track in college and I live in Bridgeport, Connecticut.

High School Attended: Trumbull High School, Trumbull, CT

The Process: First, I brainstormed ideas and topics from my personal experiences and made an outline for each. Then, I chose to write about coming to the United States because it was the topic that I was most passionate about. I began to write about specific snapshots from my experience. After that, I wrote a draft, read it, and revised it. I also joined the Connecticut Writing Project's College Essay Workshop, which helped me finalize my essay. I let three people whom I trusted read my essay. Finally, I made the final edits and gave a title to my essay.

Acknowledgments: Connecticut Writing Project.

Blue Skies

Annabelle Lee

Why is the sky blue?

It's a question that every child asks at some point in time. It's a question full of imagination and possibility. But when the child grows up, does the imagination and possibility disappear? As children grow up, they learn why the sky is blue in science class, and when they become adults, they stop asking the question completely. They simply accept the fact that the sky is blue. Is this where it ends?

Why is the sky blue?

The molecules in the air scatter more blue light from the sun than red light. There is one simple answer, but is it a simple question? There are so many different angles that the sky can be seen from. So first we have to think, is the sky always blue?

No. I'm from Seattle, so the sky is often dark, gray, and full of clouds. My view of the sky is limited, blocked by the ominous shadows that loom over our heads. The sky is sometimes so evenly covered with a thick layer of clouds that I can't tell whether it's the cloud or the sky. But I've always liked that. I've never had to squint because the sky was too bright, I've never had to wear sunblock to keep from getting sunburned, I never got into traffic caused by bright sunlight obstructing the drivers' vision, and it certainly didn't stop me from asking questions. I knew that behind the clouds the sky would be blue. I still asked, why is the sky blue?

Every once in a while, the sky clears up and I see the sky behind the curtain of clouds. If luck is on our side, even we Seattleites get a glimpse of a colorful sky. During a sunset, I always think, wow, it looks like an upside-down rainbow. The darkness of the night always hits the middle of the sky first. Then as my eyes come closer and closer to the horizon I see every shade of color, blended down the sky. Between the dark purples and blues above my head and the bright oranges and reds at the horizon, I see a sliver of the light sky blue of the day.

Many adults stop asking the question because they know the answer, so they no longer care to question. They're too busy with their everyday lives to stop and wonder, why is the sky blue? I am a busy person. I'm busy getting an education, I'm busy trying to get into college, and I already know why the sky is blue. But, I can't help but stop and stare sometimes and ask myself, why is the sky blue? Not because I don't know, but because it still amazes me that it is blue and that we know why it's blue.

Even as I become an adult, I don't want to stop asking. Why is the sky blue? As I grow up, I will be able to have more experiences and change my point of view. So I will always ask. Why is the sky blue? Because the answer just might be different every time.

About the Author: My name is Annabelle Lee. I'm a student at International School in Bellevue, WA.

High School Attended: International School, Bellevue, WA

The Process: I asked my brother to play me some music when I was writing essays and he played "Blue Skies" by Frank Sinatra.

Acknowledgments: My brother, Andrew.

CONFIDENCE IS KEY

Christine Samaroo

After a long day of shopping, my mom and I boarded the F train. Tired and sore, we just wanted to get home as soon as possible. A few minutes after the second stop, a beautiful Muslim girl came and sat across from me, fully dressed in her Islamic attire.

Wearing a hijab is a requirement for all Muslim women, because it promotes modesty and encourages people to respect women for their mind, not their physical appearance. That same night I began thinking about wearing mine, but that thought was changed a few minutes after. I sat and saw ignorant people tease and mock her; I saw people try to pull the hijab off her head; I saw people being downright cruel to her. Inside, I knew she felt hurt, and as a Muslim girl I said to myself, "Do I really want to do this?" "Do I really want to wear a hijab and be treated this way?"

All the negative thoughts flowed through my head that night. Not one was positive, even though I knew wearing it was the right thing to do. The next day I woke up and got dressed for classes, and as I looked at the mirror, I saw the reflection of my hijab scarf just hanging there. And so all the negative thoughts came rushing back to me, like "No, don't, you'll get mocked, people are going to be cruel to you." But as the great Susan B. Anthony said, "Independence is happiness." I put on my scarf and I walked out of my house with my head held high. A few minutes later as I was waiting for the bus, a girl came up to me and asked me where I was from. She seemed nice, so I told her that I was from Guyana. She asked me why my head was wrapped. I told her I was Muslim and that it was a part of my religion. She looked at me with a nasty look. I didn't say or do anything because I didn't want to create a scene. I just let it be.

As I got onto the bus, I paid and took my seat. The same girl came and sat next to me. She kept pushing me and taunting me, saying, "Why don't you go back to your country, people like you don't belong in this peaceful country." I looked at her. I still didn't say anything. Throughout the bus ride, she continued to pick on me. Others sat and watched. They had nothing to say, even though I calmly asked the girl, "Please leave me alone." She didn't. It came to the point where she called me a killer. There and then I knew I had to step up and say something. I was not going to let that happen, I was not going to sit there and let her call me that. I stood up and said to her with courage in my voice, "You don't know me, and it's wrong to stand there and judge me by my appearance. Is this what this country is, land of the brave and free? Is that what it's all about? No, it's not. Don't ever sit and judge anyone by the way they look. If you don't even know someone, don't jump to conclusions."

From that day on, I've had the courage to wear a hijab in public and not care about what people had to say. It can be negative or positive, it doesn't bother me. I feel like Susan B. Anthony must have, fighting for women to have equal rights. I know that if I set my mind to it and show the world that a female in a hijab is not a bad person but just an average individual living a normal life, that can make a change in the world. And that change will be starting with me.

About the Author: My name is Christine Samaroo. I live in Jamaica, NY. My main life goal is to graduate with honors. After that, I will pursue my studies, showing hard work and determination, to earn a bachelor's degree in computer science.

High School Attended: Queens Collegiate—A College Board School, Jamaica, NY

The Process: I had no trouble writing this essay.

Acknowledgments: I would like to thank Ms. Ferris, my college seminar teacher.

TREE RINGS

Surya Nair

My life has grown outward, rings on rings on rings. If you were to take a cross section, you would see many consistent rings representing wholesome years and inspired growth. But like a tree, whose maturation can be affected by fire, drought, fluctuating temperatures, or other stressors, so my life too has irregular rings, darkened not by early frost or insect infestations, but rather, by family pressures and my own internal struggles.

My earliest memory is a fork coming at my face, as if my face is a dartboard. Sanath, my brother, is standing on a chair, laughing, pulling out more dinnerware from the cabinets. I was a year old and he was three. Knocked from my high chair to the ground, I remember being face to face with carpet the color of oatmeal. When my brother was three, it was discovered that he had a rare form of epilepsy, from which he suffered seizures attacking his left frontal lobe.

In the first part of my adolescent years, I began realizing how others saw Sanath: a lanky kid, almost 5'8", wearing an oversized T-shirt with a Disney character, preferring to talk to children rather than adults. Lingering in the front of a cash register at Target, muttering to himself, and sometimes waving his hands in the air, having an intense debate with himself, maybe reenacting a scene from Tarzan, I see the looks directed at him. Parents usher their children past him quickly, and glance at him over their shoulders, as if worried he will create a scene of epic proportions.

"Mom, make him stop! He's talking to himself again!"

"Why can't you just understand?" my mother sighed.

Photographs from when I was four or five show my brother and me swimming in pools of bright blue with webbed light reflections, clambering over train replicas at community parks in an area filled with wood chips, sharing space on the blue couch speckled with pastel yellow polka-dots, watching reruns of *Dragon Tales*, beaming up at the glowing screen. Polaroids of myself at three years old, nursing a sore elbow, tears running down my face. A tragic scene, until you note the skinny arm around my shoulder, providing a pillar for my childish sorrows. Time and time again, my brother is my champion, the biggest source of comfort in my life.

Recently, I read an article that describes how trees speak to each other. They interact, helping each other grow, by warning each other of environmental threats. I cannot help but wonder how my life interacts with Sanath's, and how his rings look, and even if I have helped in forming them. I wonder if, like the trees, my life force somehow speaks to my brother's, soothes him when he's upset, angers him at times, helps him survive. I wonder if you could read this in the rings of his life, as clearly as you could read it in mine.

I see, through Sanath, how we affect each other, how we create our environments, and it raises questions: From this point, how can I shape my life to help those like my brother? The road ahead seems unclear from this point on; however, it is mine to walk, and even if it is full of twists and turns, my stepping stones will be the roads my feet have already known.

About the Author: My name is Surya Nair. I live in Naperville, Illinois, and attend Naperville Central High School. Although I do not know exactly what I want from life right now, I plan to major in psychology.

High School Attended: Naperville High School, Naperville, IL

The Process: While writing my essay, I reflected on my experiences with my brother, and how the way I saw him changed over my years, while my mind matured, and how we both proved ourselves to each other.

Acknowledgments: Gabrielle Glancy.

HIDDEN LAKE

Kristy Beiles

My gaze was fixed on the trees flying by when I noticed what seemed to be the edge of a frozen lake concealed behind a cluster of bushes.

"Look!" I exclaimed, nudging my teammate, Jessica, in the arm.

A devious gleam crept into her eyes when she noticed the ice, and I knew we had the same idea.

"Let's skate," she said.

One glide forward on a silver blade and I had entered a whole new world. The usual commands "Extend your leg!" and "Tuck your arms!" were left behind as I slipped into this realm of beauty, exhilaration, and flawless simplicity.

Unlike the circular rinks I was accustomed to, the lake seemed to stretch on forever. For the first time while skating, I could hear the chirping of birds, feel the sun on my skin, taste the biting winter air. Something about the freedom of having no bounds and of being out in nature connected me to forces bigger than myself.

However, as we prepared for the world's competition the very next day, something was off. I could not keep pace with the music. Instead of the usual ease I experience when skating, I couldn't figure out where to place my feet. Maybe it was the nagging sensation of being trapped indoors after such a liberating experience the day before, or maybe it was the longing to be back at the hidden lake, but before I knew it, I was down. I was rushed to the closest hospital, where the doctor diagnosed the injury as a sprained knee.

As painful as it was not to be able to perform with my team the following day, watching them skate from the sidelines gave me a similar feeling to the one I experienced on the hidden lake. I saw synchronized ice skating in a new light. The arms of twelve girls moved in unison to the beat, every step mirrored to perfection by each skater. They did not seem to skate as individuals, but as one person moving with such serene grace. Watching my team, I imagined myself on the ice as well, our arms intertwined, performing as we had practiced for years. In that moment, I realized synchronized ice skating makes me a part of something bigger than myself and is more than the sum of its parts. When a group skates in unison with the same passion and goals, it becomes somewhat transcendent. Each skater moves not for themselves, but for the team as a whole.

Ever since those couple hours on the hidden lake, skating, and even the way I view the world, has never been the same. I no longer interpret ice skating as an obligation or even a sport but as a privilege and a way to be in touch with the natural forces of the universe. The experience also brought me to the realization that there is a hidden lake within me as well, in which I am free and in sync. I love ice skating so much because just stepping onto the surface brings me back to myself and my connection to the world.

About the Author: My name is Kristy Beiles, I have lived in Berkeley, California, my whole life, and my dream is to become a biotechnologist in the future.

High School Attended: El Cerrito High School, El Cerrito, CA

The Process: With Gabby's guidance, I followed a unique but successful list of steps to complete my essay. First, I did a free write, in which I wrote about all aspects of my chosen topic as they came into my head. This allowed me to pick out the most important points and use them to create my rough draft. Finally, I made some last edits and submitted my completed essay!

Acknowledgments: Gabrielle Glancy.

SHARKS IN THE LAKE

Erika Groudle

There are no sharks in the lake; the problem has always been my imagination. Imagining my future has always been scary. The fight has been long, but in the end it's always been against myself.

Imagine the scene if you will, a 4-year-old alone on a lake behind a behemoth of a boat, her parents sitting in the beast trying to teach her to water ski. She was successful for a while, until the third lap around the lake. Something happened, the lake was no longer her friend. The water was darker, colder, and she knew something was different.

(Dim the lights and cue the haunting music.)

She started to see the outline of the sharks swimming around her skis. They were chasing her and, no matter how fast the boat in front of her went, they kept pace. They grew with every twist and turn she took. The closest one taunted her by jumping out of the water and snapping just centimeters away from her little lifejacket.

(Red spotlight on the child.)

She began screaming and crying because she realized she was skiing with sharks and she was scared. This girl, breathing quite heavily, thought that if she let go of the rope she would get lost into the dark abyss below and get eaten by one of the many beasts that followed. With tears streaming down her face she began to chant, *There are no sharks in the lake*. Slowly, but surely, the sharks started to swim away one by one, until the very last one left her alone.

(Lights up, music softens and slows tempo.)

The girl starts to regain her breath and stops her mantra.

I was that little girl, and that day when I was waterskiing I learned something about myself, even if I didn't understand it until years later. My imagination was my worst nightmare and greatest asset. I refuse to let my dark imagination get the best of me. I have made my imagination work for me. I have used it to push me to make my dreams come true. With my GPA, as a kid in middle school I never thought I would get into a college, but my imagination has shown me that by trying hard I have the opportunity to get into college if I just push myself.

I'm able to use my imagination to put myself into any situation on stage to accurately portray a character from any time period, any age, or any walk of life. At one time the negative images in my head had gotten the better of me. Visions of people laughing at me for doing what I loved, being on stage. But after years of forcing myself to do it anyway, the visions changed, they were laughing at my character, my jokes, not me. I use my imagination to dream of a bright future for myself, one without any sharks.

Now I know there are no sharks in the lake.

About the Author: My name is Erika Groudle. I live in a small town in Washington. My goals are to break out of this small town and really make something of my life.

High School Attended: Monroe High School, Monroe, WA.

The Process: I found an old photo of myself waterskiing and it sparked the memory that became my essay.

Acknowledgments: I would like to thank my parents for teaching me to ski, and for everything they do, and Giles, for spending so much time forcing me to write.

CREATING MY PATH

Kaela Elias

"White privilege doesn't exist." *oh shit they're gonna fight*

I stared at my phone, sure I'd misread the text sent by my friend, Matthew, who lives in Georgia. Yet, there it was: a short sentence carrying immense weight.

At first, I couldn't comprehend how someone so intelligent could believe this statement. Then I realized many people in positions of power share this same view. *shit she right*

I cleared my mind and responded.

"Have you forgotten about slavery?"

"It's stupid to keep bringing up slavery because slaves and slave owners are dead."

"Innocent white people don't get killed by police officers just for being white. Racism doesn't just disappear because slavery was outlawed!"

"Are you kidding?? Dredging up the past with ridiculous ideas like 'white privilege' slows us down. We ditched that decades ago."

Unlike Matthew, I believe that history impacts the present. I am drawn to the Oberlin of today, but current day Oberlin would not be the same without its history. When I learned that Oberlin was the first coeducational college in the United States and a stop on the Underground Railroad, I felt loyal to the school before I had even visited. Like Oberlin's history, my interests are a Venn diagram where gender issues, politics, and social justice overlap. *she made this so seamlessly about oberlin.*

126

My friends from Berkeley don't understand why I keep in contact with Matthew.

"Why do you continue a dialogue that always escalates into an argument?" they ask.

"That's exactly why," I tell them.

Growing up in Berkeley has given me a skewed perspective on politics. People in Berkeley often consider "Republican" a dirty word. I don't want to be passively liberal because I'm from Berkeley; I want to form my own opinions by having my ideas challenged.

The most noteworthy moments of my high school experience involve heated discussions with teenagers like Matthew. We converse about topics that many people feel uncomfortable even thinking about. I live for that feeling. It propels me forward and forces me to clarify my direction. And that's not to say my path is straight. My path will have curves, winds, dips, and places where I just stand still, frantically checking my inner GPS for guidance. Sometimes I'll retrace my steps, attempting to find faded footprints from years past. Other times, I'll stride confidently forward until I trip over a rock. I welcome all of those experiences.

I don't know what my path will look like, but I know where I want to be when I'm on it—a place that has valued difference from its founding, a place where the administration trusts students with valuable artwork and the students embrace that responsibility, a place where students are weighed down by musical instruments rather than by cutthroat competition, a place where people want to have their opinions challenged, a place where I can feel comfortable being the Scrabble-playing, Harry Potter–reading, ACLU-supporting, trans-inclusive feminist that I am. In other words, the place where I want to follow my path is Oberlin.

Man I hope she was accepted

About the Author: My name is Kaela Elias. I live in Berkeley, California, and I'm interested in gender studies, law, politics, and social justice.

High School Attended: Berkeley High School, Berkeley, CA

The Process: I began by free writing, editing, and re-editing with input from and discussions with Gabrielle Glancy, my parents, and my close friends.

Acknowledgments: Gabrielle Glancy, Rachel Silvers, and Youseef Elias.

BECOMING A SPOKESPERSON

Kaela Elias

"As a cisgender teenager," a lawyer asked me during my interview at the ACLU, "How did you become interested in transgender issues?"

I was interviewing for the position of a teen spokesperson for the School Success and Opportunity Act, a recently enacted California law that allows transgender students to use the bathroom, locker room, and sports team that reflects their gender identity. I looked at my interviewers: the accomplished social justice advocates sitting in front of me.

I paused, thinking about the first time I'd heard the word "transgender." I thought back to my friend Rebecca from preschool. We played dress-up, concocted potions (under the watchful eye of her two moms), and drew mythical creatures only four-year-olds could create. I remember my mom picking me up from Rebecca's house one day, where she noticed a family photo of Rebecca with one of Rebecca's moms and a familiar-looking man. My mom looked closer, realizing that the man in the picture was Rebecca's mom before she transitioned. My mom was surprised; she'd never met a transgender person before.

"Did one of Rebecca's moms used to be her dad?" my mom asked me as we left Rebecca's house. I looked up at her, wide-eyed, attempting to wrap my four-year-old head around that question. Although my mom knew little about the concept of being transgender, she was curious about it rather than judgmental. My friendship with Rebecca connected me to the transgender community from a young age, and my mom's attitude toward it helped shape my view of people who are different from me.

Even though Rebecca and I attended different elementary schools, the memory of her moms, her house, and Rebecca herself has stuck with me. A social justice seed was planted in me, one that would later blossom into a flourishing plant and grow into a broader passion for celebrating difference. However, in middle school, my interest in social justice was often misinterpreted and even criticized.

"You worked hard," my eighth-grade humanities teacher wrote about my group project on the LGBTQ+ movement, "but you were too bossy."

I stared at the low grade scrawled next to her harsh words. *Too bossy?* I thought. I was excited, engaged, maybe assertive even. But bossy? I never believed my passion would be categorized as a flaw. For the rest of the year, I tried to distance myself from my supposed bossiness by being the opposite: passive and withdrawn. I began to sit idly by, silently working while waiting for others to take charge. Who wants to be bossy, such an unappealing quality, when every eighth grader just wants to be liked?

Now I realize the unfair double standard: Bossiness is a word only used for girls. Have you ever heard a boy being called bossy? We praise boys for their assertiveness, calling them leaders and commending them for taking charge. Those boys become corporate lawyers, CEOs, and presidents. However, girls with opinions are reprimanded for that very quality, cutting off their potential by criticizing them for an attribute that will help them succeed.

In my own case, despite my strength, my appearance often causes people to believe I'm the opposite. My skin is milky white, light freckles sprinkled across my nose and cheeks. Skinny twig-like legs attach to my slender torso, and dark hair rests above my blue eyes. I learned quickly that my small features and thin body type cause people to underestimate me. Whenever I make a controversial comment in class, people are shocked that the skinny, delicate-looking girl has strong opinions.

Looking back on that ACLU interview, I realize my supposed "bossiness" was the very characteristic that appealed most to the interviewers—they wanted a spokesperson, someone who wasn't afraid to speak up, someone willing to swim against the tide of social expectations.

Given who I was in eighth grade, it's remarkable that I've transitioned into just that.

About the Author: My name is Kaela Elias. I live in Berkeley, California, and I'm interested in gender studies, law, politics, and social justice.

High School Attended: Berkeley High School, Berkeley, CA

The Process: I began by free writing, editing, and re-editing with input from and discussions with Gabrielle Glancy, my parents, and my close friends.

Acknowledgments: Gabrielle Glancy, Rachel Silvers, and Youseef Elias.

UNDERCOVER TWEETY

Sarah Chung

My experience on April 16th would be considered to be a fatal blow to any self-proclaimed shy person. The first step into the grease-filled kitchen of Moy Kong Express became my catalyst for years of non-figurative sweat and tears. This experience of working at what society would mark as a lower level job would not be the first thing to come to mind when prompted for a "life changing experience." But, if you think about it, every experience, no matter how seemingly trivial it may be, has the chance to multiply into a domino effect. A cheesy example of this effect plagiarized from the pages of chick romance novels would be a chance encounter with a soul mate after a spilling of coffee on aforementioned counterpart. A more realistic example is this: my first day working at a Chinese takeout restaurant.

The job had been plopped onto my life like unwanted baggage, or more realistically speaking, an annoying ten-year-old cousin you're forced to babysit. On a delectable spring day after rejoicing about the purchase of my father's new restaurant that would save us from the pits of poverty, I was unceremoniously assigned the position of working as a cashier. The job came gift wrapped with a smattering of other small jobs such as bagging food and answering the shrill shrieks of the phones. An inexperienced seedling in the work force at the time, I didn't foresee the job as life changing. Similarly, when before riding the Raptor at Cedar Point, I also assumed the experience would be enjoyable. Anyhow, it doesn't take a nuclear biochemist to guess what happened next in both situations—a life was forever scarred.

Specifically, the experience of working as a Chinese carryout machine left me perfumed of extra crispy fried chicken all week long and the Raptor ride effectively turned my legs to the consistency of light density tofu that was used at the restaurant. After the first day of catering to the diverse range of customers, I quickly learned that speaking in my reserved murmur (my default speaking-to-strangers voice) led customers to resent me as the depressed, solemn girl behind the counter. Thus, what I like to call my "overly enthusiastic salesperson" slash "Tweety" identity was born. Like its predecessor of Best Buy workers, my derivative was just as grating on my nerves. My closest friends would have swore up and down that the person behind the perpetually sticky counter of Moy Kong Express was not me. Truth is, I probably wouldn't have recognized myself. The chirpy, teeth-flashing character I used was in no way a resemblance to my real personality, which was one embodying the laws of Stoicism and following the code of introverts, but it did the trick. No longer did old ladies huff disapprovingly at my "lack of enthusiasm," the hard-of-hearing ask me to repeat myself, nor my dad glare at me through the curtain of orders hanging on the steam table. Even my irritation from my brother's jabs about my "Tweety" voice vanished with my new appreciation of the persona.

To condense my metamorphosis succinctly, the act of working at the restaurant followed a well-known cliché. That is, what doesn't kill you makes you stronger. The domino fell and broke my hardened shell of introversion. Not to say that all traces of my pre-teen years of introversion have been wiped off the face of my personality map but rather that my more outspoken persona has undoubtedly entwined itself to my core. I'm proud to say that Tweety no longer lives only in the stuffy kitchen of Moy Kong but now thrives as a less frivolous version: a loudspeaker for thoughts and opinions that once went unsaid. What most introverts consider a catastrophe to their quiet lifestyle has ironically become my saving grace.

About the Author: My name is Sarah Chung. This is written by an awkward turtle who thrives on writing personal essays. I'm currently dwelling in the murky winter season of Troy, Michigan, but hope to one day to work in the medical field with an awesome college degree earned by becoming one with the mightiest weapon: the pen.

High School Attended: Troy High School, Troy, MI

The Process: The romantic setting for writing would probably be sitting beneath an elm tree while the summer breeze gently blows through, but my nemeses, the mosquitoes, make this dream an impossible ideal. But as I've learned from my grandmother, it's never good to force it. Well, actually, she was referring to constipation (she's a retired doctor), but I believe her advice applies to writing too. My essay's exoskeleton evolved from chicken scratch in a miniature green spiral notebook scrawled during a motion-sick July car ride back from the Detroit airport after picking up my relatives. It took four more weeks of peer editing, teacher evaluation and—I kid you not—SIX REWRITES, to hone the essay into something I'm truly ecstatic about. I'm not proud of its elegance but its capturing of my voice as a human being. After all, no matter how intellectually capable I could have sounded by making up a fake life-changing event (examples include but are not limited to: saving a three-legged monk on a climb up Mount Everest, becoming school president after a laborious campaign, saving an endangered panda mouse from being road kill) it would have become a stuffy third-person biography about someone else's life and not me.

Acknowledgments: First of all I want to offer gratitude to my Toshiba laptop for not giving up on me after the abuse you suffered when you froze for the fourth time. Also to my grandmother for always believing I could get into the "crème de la crème" of colleges and encouraging me to never settle for less. Lastly I'm thankful toward my benevolent English teachers for giving amazing feedback on all my essays. Thank you, Dr. Steltenkamp and Mrs. Liamini, for helping me become a better essayist.

Redemption Song

Isabela Caetano

Bob Marley once sang "One good thing about music, when it hits you, you feel no pain." My journey to understand what this meant started back in the second grade, when I had to learn to play the recorder. I hated playing that twelve-inch piece of holey plastic, but without it, I might have never discovered the secret powers of music.

It was not until middle school when I left the recorder and found the instrument to which my soul belonged—the guitar. I knew then that Bob Marley was right. Music never brought me any pain; however, that did not mean that pain could not touch me.

Over my practicing of simple diddles on the guitar, I could often hear my parents screaming in the background. Their fights were always the same: too much alcohol and not enough money. They always ended the same, too: the front door slamming followed by muffled sobs. And where was I during this? I was in my room playing a minor chord for every insult being tossed across the living room. The guitar was my only therapy, because at the time, it was the only thing in the house that would sing instead of scream.

Sadly, by the time I was in the ninth grade, I lost some passion for playing the guitar. My parents' bitterness and rage overpowered my reticent guitar strums and my relationship with music diminished. I felt that the brutally negative aura of my house impacted me in a way that my mind was no longer sharp and my life was flat. I looked at the guitar with some longing, but I did not have enough motivation to care about anything. Long solo sessions were replaced with sleeping or otherwise aimless living. My daily goal was to survive, not make it better.

Towards the end of my sophomore year, just as I was starting to feel like there was nothing in the world that could dig me out of my hole, the war was over. My parents finally went their separate ways. As a typical kid with a torn family, I was devastated that I no longer had my parents under one roof. On the other hand, there was a smidge of relief from the loudness and hostility of home.

It took another year to find my bearings in this new situation. I cannot explain the exact process of healing, but by the time I progressed into junior year, life started to look brighter. In the sweet silence of my room, I was able to hear my thoughts and realize that I was not destined to be a statistic about kids from divorced families. I instinctively knew that I get to write my own story and be the conductor of my life. With that, I found myself thinking of playing music again and making a final push to end my psychological friction. The pain slowly eased, like a shade lowered to block the sun.

One afternoon, I found myself reaching for my guitar again. As soon as my fingers found their familiar places on the strings, I knew I had found peace once more. That wooden box with metal wires became a bottomless receiver of my grief. It asked no questions and demanded no quick improvement. It was my secret way to feel soothed and loved almost instantly.

Now, music feels like an old, loyal friend. In a world that witnesses so much pain and suffering, including my own, my guitar is a choice I make daily. My experience taught me that no pain is ever wasted and that every big journey starts small at first—as small as a recorder or a college essay. These days I often wonder. . . . If I can survive the demise of my family and come out of it as a guitar player, what else can I do? Who else can I become?

About the Author: My name is Isabela Caetano. I live in Queens, New York, and I have grown up with music rooted deep in my bones. As I continue my musical journey, I plan to help other young souls heal their lives through music as I once did.

High School Attended: Baruch College Campus High School, New York, NY

The Process: First drafts are first for a reason. They tell the primary thoughts that the writer initially writes. So for me, during my writing process, it was important not to lose touch with my first draft. My first draft held the raw emotion of my story, and I was careful not to let that slip between my fingers when I went through countless revisions by my friends and family. So once all my core ideas and feelings were secured in place, it was just a matter of fine tuning my sentence fluency and word choice to make my final masterpiece.

Acknowledgments: My mom, my aunt, English class 401, Ms. Ross, Mr. Nourok, Maeve Cusack, and Bob Marley.

THE COUNTDOWN

Sarah Kaufman

I hadn't seen the sky in twenty hours. I hadn't slept in thirty. Maybe that's why I was crying. I wanted to believe that was why. Standing in that drafty hallway, I felt like a terrible leader and a worse friend. I had dragged my friends into this and now all of them, even Elise, were turning their exhausted anger toward me.

It was supposed to be fun. Theatreworks was holding their annual 1440 Countdown, where groups from all over the Bay Area compete to write, direct, and perform the best 10-minute play. In 24 hours. Other teams were experienced performers. Ours was a haphazardly gathered group of friends.

We started out enthusiastic and cheerful. Our play, *On the Right Track,* was about six strangers on airport shuttle, who, in the end, find a way to come together. It was ambitious, with conversations overlapping and intersecting.

But as the hours progressed, things got increasingly tense. Four hours before the performance, the emotional strain got the better of us and conflict broke out. Elise and Shayanne were having trouble with memorization. Bagby was confused about one of his lines, could we please change it? "Sure, cut that line, why don't you?" I thought. "Not like it took me fifteen minutes to come up with." Teagan didn't understand why the scenes were all intercut; why couldn't we do each story separately? "Yeah, Teagan, if you want to completely reformat the script, be my guest." I was being petty, but from my point of view, I had done most of the work while they sat around playing iPhone games.

"About that," Shayanne spat, "all the other teams worked together on their scripts, but you wrote our whole play!"

I suggested we take a break.

That was the only thing we could all agree on.

That's how I found myself combusting in a hallway. Maybe they were right. Most of them had never performed before, and my script was complex. I had failed my team and failed myself and I wanted to just give up. To turn in my crazy 1440 tie and go home. And maybe I could, I thought. I could walk right out the door. Or. Or I could wipe my face off and go back in. I could stop being so protective of my work and lead.

I straightened up and left the hallway. It was time to stop pitying myself and solve the problem. Gathering the team, I admitted that the script was complicated, and that was on me. I took on a challenge, and if we failed because of that, then my ambition was to blame. But I wouldn't have written it if I didn't think we could do it. And I still did.

As it turned out, Bagby was right about that line; it was too complicated. But even Teagan admitted that it was too late to totally restructure the play. Shayanne and Elise discovered that if they pretended to text on their phones, which would totally fit their characters, they could have the lines in front of them for most of the show.

When we finally presented our play, my heart was beating in my stomach. But then, everything just clicked. The audience laughed at all the right moments. People wiped their eyes as we recited the Mourner's Kaddish at the end. We bowed and left the stage to wild applause, blissful and united.

Our play won second place against some of the area's top drama schools. And I learned that being a leader isn't always holding your ground and it isn't always pleasing everyone. It's sometimes one, sometimes the other, and mostly somewhere in between. And it's never easy. But the only way to truly fail is to give up.

About the Author: My name is Sarah Kaufman. I live in San Jose, California, and I wish to study musical theater and/or playwriting in college.

High School Attended: Willow Glen High School, San Jose, CA

The Process: Theatreworks' 1440 Countdown had a major effect on how I deal with leadership opportunities. I am very much a storyteller, and I hoped to showcase that in my essay, because one necessary skill of a writer or performer is the ability to tell a story. I started by writing a personal, detailed account of the events and then went back and focused on the important parts of the story.

Acknowledgments: I'd like to thank my mother for not letting me quit and not falling asleep while we finished all 21 of my college applications.

GRANDPA STEPHEN

Skylar Powell

Could the person who's influenced you most be someone you've never met? Because my grandfather died before I was born, over the years I created my own legendary character from the pieces of information I was given. My mom often described her father's many positive attributes to me: She told me he was a great teacher, he was patient and generous, and that he loved math just as I did. What my mother told me about my grandfather became the seeds of my image of him, a figure larger than life.

My Grandpa Stephen was more than just good at mathematics: In my mind he had a mathematical worldview. He was someone who saw the numbers behind everything, and because he understood the numbers, he understood it all. My mom told me about their many adventures traveling and visiting foreign places. In my mind, Stephen was an explorer. He wasn't content to stick to what he knew; he wanted to find and experience the novel and extraordinary. My mom often said she admired his humility. My Stephen was humble, and through this humility he was profoundly charismatic, and able to win over all those around him. He could find success because he could relate to people. He could quietly establish that he was the most interesting person at the dinner party. And I felt like I wanted to be like him.

It was not always this way. As a younger child, I didn't want to know anything about my grandfather. My mom told stories which held great personal meaning to her, but at first seemed random and scattered. I was often frustrated because I felt that she was trying to manipulate me with her narratives.

"It really is too bad you never got a chance to know him," she often said to me. I thought she was trying to convince me be just like him and to follow in his footsteps. When she told me that he was brought back to life in me, I didn't know what she meant and I didn't want to hear it. At that time, the most important thing to me was to find direction on my own. But as I got older, I found myself wanting to know more about him. I wanted to better understand how my own story could resonate with this person whose name was passed on to me.

One evening I asked my mom if we could watch old footage of my grandfather's memorial service. As the tape rolled on, I found myself entranced. Occasionally, I looked over and saw my mom's eyes tearing up. I clearly remember watching the procession of his fellow professors and colleagues and former students come up to the podium and confirm what I had been imagining: his methodical and reasoned approach to every problem and his mischievous obsession with solving them, his generosity of time and thought to all those who asked for it, his warm and ironic sense of humor.

And I remember feeling certain that Grandpa Stephen could help me find the best in myself, to discover what I do well and how best to do it. So I continue to look toward my grandpa for inspiration and as a guide to follow. And sometimes it feels like I'm looking right at him.

About the Author: My name is Skylar Powell. I'm a student from Berkeley, California, hoping to find a career in business and mathematics.

High School Attended: Berkeley High School in Berkeley, CA

The Process: When I first saw Princeton's question, I almost instinctually responded "my grandfather." But after coming up with the topic of my essay, I had a very difficult time figuring out what should constitute the "meat" of the essay, and how I should express the ways he's influenced me. I spent a lot of time trying writing drafts about how I am similar to him, but I couldn't figure out how to convey the way he shaped me until I realized, almost all of a sudden, that my interaction with him has been entirely through story, legend, and imagination. After that realization, a first draft of the essay came easily. However, the subsequent revision and editing proved to be similarly challenging, but certainly rewarding.

Acknowledgments: My college counselor, Gabrielle Glancy.

FINDING MY SEA LEGS

Lucy Faust

I still had one-third of the race left to go. Out of sheer fatigue, I began to slow down. My arms felt heavy in the water; my shoulders ached from overuse. I lost feeling in my hands and toes. Worse still, doubts raced through my mind. Who was I, a teenager, to believe I could swim ten kilometers in the cold and rough waters of the San Francisco Bay?

Earlier that month, I had come home from practice just in time to pick up the phone. It was Mark Rosen, the director of the Bridge-to-Bridge race. "Because you're fifteen years old," he said in a hesitant voice, "before we create new legal documents for you, I want to be sure you've had enough training and experience." I heard the same doubt in his voice that I had heard in the voices of my parents. I knew this would be the longest race I had ever swum. I also thought I was ready.

As I dove into the fifty-eight degree water just outside the Golden Gate Bridge, I felt tingling sensations. A quiet numbness crept through the rest of my body. At that moment, looking up at the bridge above my head, my goals and my feet kicked into high gear. I quickly got my arms into a rhythm, to move forward and keep my body warm.

And then I was in the zone. When this happens, my mind wanders as my body does what it has been trained for years to do. I have been swimming competitively year-round since age eight. Long ago I became accustomed to intensive practices, daylong swim meets twice a month, and a constant smell of chlorine radiating from my body. The water is a private space that has kept me balanced when my life tips to either side of the scale. It is a place of mind and body where I feel confident and capable with a strong sense of purpose. And so when I heard about the bridge-to-bridge swim, I couldn't resist. Whenever I thought about the possibility of swimming this race, a fire lit up in my heart that I could not ignore.

The Golden Gate behind me, I caught sight of the Palace of Fine Arts on my right and Alcatraz on my left. Although I only touched one jellyfish, I was thankful of what I could not see below. My dream was becoming a reality. The sun, casting beams through the bridge's cables behind the towers, was beckoning me.

Yet the finish line was still a long way away. Those last three kilometers pushed me more than I had ever thought possible. I was on my own. I had to remind myself why I was here at this moment and why finishing was important. I had made the decision to race and had spent years preparing for this moment. In spite of the fears of my parents, the worries of the race director, and even my own doubts, I needed to test what I was made of and see what I could do.

Finally, as if I had suddenly found a hidden source of energy within, I powered through the last fifty strokes knowing how close I was to reaching my goal: a ladder attached to a boat—the finish line. The first female to finish, I was also the first finisher without a wetsuit, the third overall finisher, and the youngest participant in the race.

My heart was my guide throughout the swim. I grew up playing in San Francisco's Bay. It was here that I would come into my own. I could not let myself fail in the place where I learned to dream and soar. I needed to finish fast and finish strong in the waters from which I came.

About the Author: My name is Lucy Faust from Piedmont, California. I love swimming, smiling, knitting, laughing with friends, and taking full advantage of the outdoors.

High School Attended: Piedmont High School, Piedmont, CA

The Process: I did a lot of free writes and always knew in the back of my head that this experience changed me and encouraged me to dig deep, in and out of the water.

Acknowledgments: I need to acknowledge my parents, my junior English teacher Celia Rogers, Gabby Glancy, and one of my coaches, Rick.

MONTUNO:
LEARNING MUSIC IN CUBA

Benjamin Bock

My fingers roll across the piano. Curious faces peer through shuttered windows and applause erupts from the room. The Cuban pianist smiles. The din fades to silence, and a jungle bird screeches somewhere overhead. Hushed voices murmur in Spanish and English as my jazz ensemble shuffles papers, preparing for the next song. Snapping, I count off the tune and claves click. Rhythmically, I begin the montuno. The horns burst into melody, echoing throughout the halls, ringing out across the school.

I can hear the persistent rhythm of drums even as I sit in class. Cuban students surround me, asking about my life back home. I respond in broken Spanish, equally intrigued about theirs. Every musician here has been playing since they were four years old. The school feels somehow familiar, as if I have known these students all my life. Perhaps it is because I, too, began playing when I was four. Growing up, my house always had music; my grandmother's piano, my father's records, my mother's guitar. As I speak with the Cuban students, I wish to spend hours with them, understanding these musicians, my fellow peers. I am in the middle of a sentence when a teacher beckons toward me. I must leave the dust-filled classroom. The first private lesson has begun.

The piano teacher has a warm face, ancient eyes. Sitting at a flaking piano, I tell him I wish to learn about montunos, the rhythmic arpeggio intrinsic to Cuban son music. We start out simply with basic rhythms and modalities. However, an hour later I am panting, playing vigorously at breakneck speed. He shouts "Eso! No, eso!" (That! No, that!) Finally, drenched in sweat, I stop, hardly believing it has been only two hours since we started. I shake his hand despite the pain, smiling broadly. That evening, I sit at the piano as muffled drums thump through the walls, playing my montunos incessantly.

As I learn from the Cubans, they learn about blues from me. I show them Chicago boogie-woogie playing and "I Can't Stop Lovin' You," a Ray Charles soul tune. The students dance in the back of the room, listening to blues for the first time. That night we jam for hours. Immersed in heat, I try Afro-Cuban rhythms on the piano as they try the blues. When we finish, we talk for hours more, about music, about each other's lives. Night falls, and I return back to the hotel, thinking deeply. I feel comfortable here, with passionate students and music everywhere.

Outside the school it feels as if there are no real rules. Men in shorts sell cigars out of their houses and drive their '50s-era Fords as fast as the chugging engines can carry them. Yet I do not feel danger in the streets. Though I stick out in the dark alleys of Havana, people greet me warmly. That night our jazz band listens to rumba, the African side of Cuban music. We play in gigs and in the school, jamming for hours on end. We dance, which I would never do before, bathed in the unforgettable aroma of Cuban cigar smoke. We talk for hours with the students, discovering their way of life, trapped on an island looking back perpetually into the past.

Somewhere in the jungles of Cuba lies a Soviet prefabricated mess. It crumbles into itself from disrepair and negligence, yet inside its peeling husk the halls burst with life. Tropical plants shoot skyward from a lush garden, murals with bright hues explode off the walls, and music escapes from every door. Classical musicians clutch French horns and jazz pianists play in little rooms. Violinists pace the balconies, practicing endlessly. Drummers beat perpetually, echoes of congas and timbales ricocheting across the white courtyard. Somewhere in the jungles of Cuba is my home.

About the Author: My name is Benjamin Bock. I currently live in Berkeley, California, and play piano constantly. My goal is to follow music wherever it takes me.

High School Attended: Berkeley High School, Berkeley, CA

The Process: After returning from a transformational music trip to Cuba, I instantly knew I wanted to write about my experience. I spent much of my time concentrating of the energy I saw in Cuba and how to incorporate it into the essay.

Acknowledgments: Gabrielle Glancy, Jean Nudelman.

Am I a Vampire?

Brenna Costello

Day 12: The bats still haven't realized I'm human.

Day 26: I think they have accepted me as one of their own.

Nope, one just flew directly into my face.

Day 30: I'm trying to regain the trust of the bats by making them their daily diet consisting of bat mix, two equally spaced rows of peeled bananas, and three fistfuls, give or take, of chopped red apples to top it off. All of which will be devoured in point three fifths of a second by all my furry bat friends.

Day 32: I just finished setting the diets in the cave, I hit my head on a stalactite, and then proceeded to trip over a stalagmite, almost skewering myself like one of the three large hanging ropes of cantaloupe, honeydew, and watermelon that the bats absolutely love.

Day 39: C.J. the zookeeper taught me how to use the siphon to drain out the extra guano to ensure maximum sparkle in the bat cave's draining pools.

Day 40: Michelle, the head honcho in charge of the bats, gifted me with a compliment on how well I cleaned the cave, and Mark, my boss, proceeded to tell me, "You know she never gives compliments." Does this mean I could be a professional bat-poop cleaner?

Day 44: I was cleaning the cave when a mother bat dropped her baby, conveniently right into the puddle of water below. Thinking the poor helpless creature had suffered too great of a fall, I gently reached down to collect the neonate. Death is a part of the cave's natural order of life, and I'll often find up to six dead bats on any given day working in the bat cave, usually babies who have not yet learned to fly. When I examined the little guy I noticed it squirming around in my hand, so I did what any good surrogate mother would do—I dried it off with my shirt, making sure to spread its thin, delicate wings, dabbing them completely dry, and then putting my pinky finger in its miniscule mouth, allowing for maximum oxygen intake, and patting it on the back to dispel any extra fluids. Then, grabbing it by its miniature Skeletor feet, I hung it "right-side down" on the little patch of burlap sack on the top of the cave, for its mother to come collect it. I gave myself a figurative gold star for the day.

Day 51: I only heard the joke "That's a funny looking animal" and "Look. Here's the teenager exhibit" about twenty times today, and also found only two dead bats. That calls for a celebration in my book!

Day 55: Mark congratulates me on mastering the bat cave, and I get to move into the temple, working with a multitude of both harmless and venomous snakes from around the world. I couldn't be more excited!

Day 57: I was told to collect 35 large crickets from the bin in the back hallway. How does Mark know my one weakness? Not to disappoint my boss, I go ahead and stick my hand in the tub filled with thousands of the jumping nightmares; when I pulled my hand out I was expecting to see stark white bone staring back at me, but au contraire— my hand was miraculously still intact.

Day 60: Grasshoppers are still on my list of those-who-must-not-be-named.

Day 62: I am once again reunited with my 400-plus low flying, half blind, nocturnal, fruit devouring, furry aerial mammals. Even though one might classify it as impossible or downright insane to be completely comfortable and eerily calm in such a hectic place as a bat cave, I think I rock the mystery pretty well.

Bats + dark caves + human being = vampire.

Yeah, that's got to be it.

About the Author: My name is Brenna Costello and I live in Louisville, Colorado. I have volunteered at the Denver Zoo for four years, and I love reptiles, amphibians, and bats, of course. I hope to be a biologist and a filmmaker one day, making documentaries on my travels and findings in the natural world.

High School Attended: Peak to Peak Charter School, Lafayette, CO

The Process: I started thinking about what I was going to write for my college essay when my brother started the process two years earlier, and when I was finally a senior and we began the process ourselves, I knew I didn't want the stereotypical college essay. I wanted to make people laugh as well as get an understanding of what it's like to live a day in my shoes. I wrote my essay the night before it was due, around midnight, because that's when I am the most creative when it comes to writing. Then my AP lit and comp teacher and I edited it, to make sure it fit all the restraints and regulations for my schools I was applying to, and the rest is history.

Acknowledgments: I want to thank Ms. Letter for believing in my essay every step of the way, my parents for trusting the creative process and for all they do for me, and the fruit bats for being my furry flying companions at the zoo.

TRAVELING IS A PART OF ME

Mera Freeman-Gerlach

Not till we are lost, in other words, not till we have lost the world, do we begin to find ourselves, and realize where we are and the infinite extent of our relations.

—Henry David Thoreau, *Walden*

With my minimal Japanese skills, I attempted to bring smiles to the faces of people who had little to smile about. Minamisoma, a town of seventy thousand, was still recovering from the tsunami, earthquake and nuclear meltdown, which had befallen them almost three years before. Even though we had come to bring food, I had also brought a Polaroid camera with me. As I stood in front of a group of kids who waited for their photos to be taken, I heard them yell "見せて" (Misete! Show me!) and I gave them the 5.4 cm-wide film printed with their smiling faces. After I left, they kept the food and photos, while I got to keep the memory of a time when I felt perfectly content.

When I look back on that experience, I am reminded of the place inside me that is awakened when I hit the road. When I travel, I am able to become who I really am—adventurous and creative.

Luckily, because my parents love to travel—my mom spent the last year researching in Japan—I have had the opportunity to pack my bags and go abroad many times in my seventeen years. This past summer, I spent six weeks in Nicaragua running educational camps for local kids. Two summers ago, my first time traveling alone, I lived in the small community of Mogobane, Botswana with a host family. My time there was complicated, inspiring, and distinct.

One particular day in Mogobane, I went with my fellow volunteers and a few kids from my community to explore a marshland nearby. From a distance we saw a white shape sticking out of the mud. As we got closer, we realized that a goat had gotten stuck. Struggling with our slippery, mud-caked hands, we tried to save it. At some point, I fell backwards into the vigorous suction of mud—known by locals as "quicksand"—only to have my shoe swallowed up by it. With much effort, we finally pulled the goat out to safety. The next morning we hiked back at sunrise, but sadly found that our goat had not survived through the night.

As difficult and bizarre as this experience was, it still evoked in me the feeling I get when I'm traveling. It helps me see that life is not always about the outcome. Yes, the goat died in the end, which was tragic. But the experience made me feel more alive, which is what always happens when I leave the familiar world of my Bay Area home.

In my travels, I have noticed that too often we choose to notice the dissimilarities between ourselves and other people and places, instead of seeing how much we are all alike. For example, when I was in Nicaragua, I got to see a very different lifestyle, one where the women wake up before sunrise every day to make tortillas and four-year-old children walk home from school alone. However, the longer I stayed, the more I realized that these differences are trivial and the way we are connected is what really matters. This understanding makes me feel like I can be comfortable anywhere.

As a fourth-grader, I went camel trekking through the Arabian Desert in Jordan. Standing atop a red sand dune, ready to sprint down as fast as I could, I already knew, as I know now, that I was happiest halfway across the world from where I live. It is as if, living inside me, hidden and quiet when I am in my "real" home, is a spirit that yearns to be lost again in unknown places where new and different experiences await me.

About the Author: My name is Mera Freeman-Gerlach. I live in Berkeley, California, and my goal in life is to become a chemical engineer who has time to travel the world. I row crew, tutor middle-schoolers in math, and love photography, skiing, and the beach.

High School Attended: Berkeley High School, Berkeley, CA

The Process: I started off writing about specific events in my life that were meaningful to me. Then I narrowed it down to this topic and prompt. Then I wrote a long essay expressing all my ideas in too many words. Using this, I created a first draft of what would become my essay after a few months of cutting, adding, and changing.

Acknowledgments: Gabrielle Glancy (college counselor) and Laurie Freeman (mother).

BEHIND THE BARS

Anina Baker

I remember it was daytime. I was walking with two friends, and the sky was a beautiful blue. There were kids playing; all the stores were open and bustling. Then suddenly everything changed. The skies were gray and dark. It became nighttime; all the stores were closed and had huge black bars on the windows and doors. I saw random groups of troublemaking teenagers on the street. I had the strong urge to get away from all of the dangerous people so I climbed up a fire escape and sat on the roof of a building, contemplating all of the crime and poverty below. I remember feeling very anxious and uneasy. I climbed down to try to find someone who could help me. A storeowner who appeared both friendly and dangerous let me call my mom and my English teacher. Neither answered; I assumed they were asleep. I thought of other people who could help, but knew they wouldn't be awake or wouldn't want to help. I felt very alone and abandoned. It was just me against all of the hurt and corruption in the world.

When I recounted this dream to my teacher, she asked, "Have you ever been to this place that you dreamed about?"

"No," I said. "Not that I can remember."

"Have you ever had this feeling before? A feeling of being abandoned and completely alone in the world?"

"Maybe," I said. "Maybe before I was adopted."

I know from my mom, who has told me the story, that I was adopted when I was ten months old from China. Police officers from the village said that my biological mother brought me to the police station and sat with me for a while. Then she laid me down near a gate and left. I was told that I was only a couple of days old when I was given up. I don't remember that, of course, but I do have a memory of looking outside of crib bars and seeing another baby looking at me and reaching out her hand. Perhaps I felt the same sense of abandonment that I encountered in my dream. When my mom picked me up from the orphanage, my caretakers told her, "She is very expressive, always finding a way to make her needs met." It's helpful knowing that I had the instinct to make sure I was being cared for. It's possible the same instinct showed up in my dream as my urge to find a way to safety.

If I weren't adopted my life would be very different. People in China have limited opportunities, and many live in terrible conditions. Even though it's hard not being able to hear stories or see pictures from my first ten months of life, I am very grateful I was adopted. I have no information about my life before I was adopted, and I do not want to try and find my biological parents. I don't want to be disappointed or feel bad about myself as a result of meeting them, so I will leave it up to my imagination.

Although I don't have many memories from before I was adopted, the fact that I was born in China and spent my first ten months in an orphanage had a significant impact on me. When I was younger, I was shy around people I did not know and never wanted to be hugged or physically comforted. Changes and transitions were challenging for me. I've outgrown many of these traits, which I'm sure come from living as an infant in an orphanage, but in some sense, they make me who I am. I believe that even though I was not born into a loving family at first, my life is now very blessed with a great family and unending opportunities.

About the Author: My name is Anina Baker. I live in Alameda, California, and go to Alameda High School. My goals in life are to always continue learning and to engage in activities I am passionate about.

High School Attended: Alameda High School, Alameda, CA

The Process: I began the process by writing a free write on the topic I wanted to write about. This really helped in getting the creative juices flowing. Then I had as many people as I could read it and comment on it, which helped me develop the essay.

Acknowledgments: My college counselor, Gabrielle Glancy. My mom, Leslie Baker. My teacher, Miriam Lenhardt.

entriguing title

CROP TOP REBELLION: THE DAY I WAS ASKED TO CHANGE AT A FEMINIST CAMP

Alexandra Hansen

weird phrase

I donned balloon pants, a gold arm cuff, and a crop top that exposed about an inch of skin. I pulled my hair back, looked at myself in the mirror, and told myself I was relentless, empowered, and beautiful. I grabbed my useful books and necessary coffee, and walked to class. I was attending a Young Women's Leadership program, where we explored different models of feminism and men's reactions to them, but also how we thought about the world and its place for women. At the program, we were encouraged not only to explore social constructs created for women, but also to think critically about everything.

I knew in my choice of clothing that I had strayed from the safer, corporate-feminist look. While I reject the idea that a woman's wardrobe should subject her to social criticism and objectification, I know that these things still happen. But I was shocked when I was shamed for my choice of dress at a feminist institution. The program coordinator addressed me in front of my class and asked me to change, because my outfit was "totally not PCP" (practical, classy, professional, which, I may add, is a very vague dress code). A stranger's objectification paled in comparison to the critique of a feminist, whom I respected, especially in a setting structured around celebrating women's rights.

belief vs. rality

In my next class, we discussed how women are expected to present themselves in today's society. Using my recent experience as an example, I asked honestly whether I would be more successful if I dressed in a more conservative way. To my surprise, the class became enraged and eventually decided upon a "crop top movement." The fact that "PCP" regulated our choices in this summer program was troubling; how could other women be expected to express themselves freely, if we couldn't do so at a progressive program and in a liberal city? *good thinking*

The girls and I congregated later that night. We composed and signed a letter to the program coordinator. My signature seemed to say: I reject your judgments and critique of me. We slipped the letter under our program coordinator's door.

We wanted to promote a healthy discussion of how women are expected to present themselves. We expected the discussion to move beyond my issue and to a greater debate. But the program coordinator's response quickly dashed our hopes: "Wardrobe is not a feminist issue," she claimed. I wanted to ask, if wardrobe is not a feminist issue, then why are women being shamed for what they wear? How can the president of South Africa, Jacob Zuma, rape a woman because "her short skirt was asking for it," and get away with it? How is it that "What were you wearing?" is a valid question during rape trials? Why can women be stoned for showing too much skin in some parts of the world? Wardrobe is nothing if not a feminist issue.

I didn't want to be seen as a rule breaker, sticking up for bare midriffs. Covering up can be a strategic move, for instance for a politician such as Hillary Clinton, and I, too, want the attention to be on my words, not my clothes. I will continue to use clothing as a means of expression, but I am not willing to sacrifice respect from others and their focus on my ideas, rather than my body. This year, I am editor of my school's style blog. I plan to focus on self-empowerment and expression, rather than conforming to current trends—a perspective I wouldn't have developed if it weren't for my experiences last summer. For me, my colleagues this summer, and for countless women across the world, wardrobe will continue to be a feminist issue. The most valuable lesson I took from this experience is one with a general application: We need to think critically about everything, from society's treatment of us to how we respond.

The conclusion seems weak

About the Author: My name is Alexandra Hansen. I am a senior attending high school in San Francisco. I currently volunteer as a program developer for a nonprofit called Turkish Women's Initiative. I hope to major in political sciences and one day work in the foreign services or intelligence sector. Whichever it may be, I will always be a women's rights activist.

High School Attended: San Francisco University High School, San Francisco, CA

The Process: I attended a summer program at Barnard College, and I was inspired to write about an experience I had there. I started off with about 1,800 words, which I had to condense to 650. Thankfully, as I am an author who becomes very attached to her work, my college counselor mercilessly cut sections of the essay. It took me about two months to write this piece.

Acknowledgments: My college counselor.

It Comes, It Goes

Pedro Del Cioppo Vasques

A giant jacaranda tree, with its sweet purple flowers and dark thick branches, casts a shade on three old men. They are all wearing Havaianas flip-flops, khaki shorts, partially buttoned floral shirts, and white fedoras. They sit in silence around a red plastic table with lime caipirinhas and an ashtray full of cigarette butts. The deserted beach, the cool breeze, and the cloudy sky are subdued, letting the thundering breaking waves reign over the men's attention. The rolling motion of the waves takes them on a trip to the past.

The Arteiro finally breaks the silence and asks the others if they remember the times when they played hopscotch in the cobblestone streets. He doesn't wait for an answer, and while gazing at the sea, he recounts their childhood. They rushed out of school to climb the mango tree at the town's square. After eating the succulent red mangoes, they competed to see who could throw the pits the farthest, but it was in vain for the Quietinho always won. The Arteiro continues with a smirk: the night they camped on the beach. It took them hours to set up the tents and to start the campfire, but the radiant image of the full moon's reflection on the sea's calm waters made it all worthwhile. The old man shuts his eyes for a moment, smiles, and then opens them again. He searches around the table for the innocent faces of those children that are still imprinted in his head. Instead he sees wrinkly faces of men who have already journeyed through most of life. He then stares at a single delicate jacaranda flower, and confesses, "Ah, se vocês soubessem como eu tenho saudades daquele tempo!"

The Quietinho, inspired by his friend's remark, gazes into each of his friends' eyes. As a child, he was always surrounded by his entire family. Pai, mãe, tios, tias, primos, primas, avôs, avós, and even neighbors, came to his house every weekend for lunch. It was feijoada on Saturdays, and spaghetti on Sundays. He sets his eyes at the point where the sun meets the sea, and vividly watches his family sitting around the kitchen table arguing over Pelé's penalty kick, the mayor who was accused of laundering money, and the nauseating perfume of Tia Eva. His mother and Tio Caio joked that Tia Lúcia is strangely quiet, so the apocalypse must be near—they never found out, though, that she was having an affair with the mailman. Quietinho smiles and stares at a pebble of sand. He sees his grandpa's playing cards, hears his grandma's ear-piercing laugh, smells his cousin's stinky feet, savors the basil of his mom's spaghetti sauce, and feels his father's hand on his left shoulder. He then exclaims, "Que saudade!"

Moved by Quietinho, the Boêmio shares his story. His life was full of passionate meaningless encounters and one true love. He spoke, with his natural raucous voice, about the times he spent his nights at small bars, drinking beer, and making his way toward attractive women. He never had a fit body or an attractive face, but he seduced women with his beautiful poetry: his sensual flute playing. It wasn't hard because the flute is melodic by design, and Portuguese is romantic by nature. Despite his numerous romantic encounters, he only truly fell in love with a woman who had a pale face, carmine lips, and French blood. The Boêmio stops the story, observes the immensity of the sea, and admits that it was the shortest romance he ever had, for the woman is now gone forever, but it was infinite while it lasted. The Boêmio ends his story by gulping his caipirinha and muttering, "Saudades é tudo que me resta!"

All three men sit in silence reflecting on their stories. They wander into their past in awe and sadness. They taste the unripe kiwis and the honey that saudades offer them. *Saudade* is melancholic like longing, and soothing like hope. The Boêmio, at last, clears his throat. He pulls out his flute. The Arteiro, in response, pulls out his guitar, and the Quietinho pulls out his tambourine. The flute cries, the guitar smiles, and the tambourine dances to form a chorinho. They improvise rhythms and verses, and realize that *saudades* rhymes with *amizade* (friendship), *vontade* (desire), *simplicidade;* it sounds like *saúde* (health), but it comes from "solitude." They play with the word all night long, and they conclude it's a dramatic poet's absolute favorite word, because it's a romantic word from a romantic language. In the charming sounds of their bossa nova, and through their rustic Brazilian way of life, they pour their pasts onto the beach. They drown themselves in their own sea of *saudades*, until the morning sunshine reminds them that it's now the present, and not the past.

About the Author: My name is Pedro Del Cioppo Vasques. I live in New York City, but I'm originally from Brazil. I plan on majoring in neuroscience, or biology, while doing a premed track.

High School Attended: Eleanor Roosevelt High School, New York, NY

The Process: U. Chicago is known for its provocative prompts. In order to tackle the prompt, I had to think, think, and think, and read a lot of fiction to find inspiration. After really understanding the different facets of the word, I was able to come up with a way to craft those multifacets in a creative way.

Acknowledgments: Ms. Hsu.

IF CURIOSITY KILLED THE CAT, MY DAD WAS AN ACCOMPLICE

Gordon Downs

Some of my earliest memories are of ten-minute car rides to elementary school, when I'd ask my Dad how things worked. From the back seat and later from the exalted front seat, I posed every question I could think of.

"How do light bulbs work?" I asked one day, and my Dad shot off a description of how an electric current flowing through a tungsten filament produces light. My mental image of an atom—a "Jimmy Neutron"-esque cluster of CGI balls flying around in circles—began to transform as I learned what atoms and electrons actually were and what a positive or negative charge meant. It took me several mornings to grasp many of these ideas, but I always got there eventually. And as soon as I understood light bulbs, I asked how car engines worked, and then how nuclear power plants worked, and how the stock market worked, and why the sky was blue. I loved the warm, cheek-tugging feeling of looking at something and understanding how its components came together to accomplish a task, and I wanted to know as much as my seemingly omniscient dad. In middle school, when my mom started taking me to school instead, Dad read Google's science news to me and my little brother every day when he got home from work. We perched on the edge of our couch while he read about "invisibility cloaks" and how some can bend light around objects using carbon nanotubes, and he explained carbon nanotubes and properties of light along the way. I was bursting with so many questions that it took us half an hour to finish a single article, and my dad always answered each one.

I still ask my dad questions like, "If you were in a spaceship going close to the speed of light relative to, say, Earth, and you launched a projectile in your direction of motion, would that take more energy than launching the projectile at a lower relative velocity?" But more often than not, the answer now is "You know, I'm really not sure about this one. You'll have to look it up." And so I do, but not always at the best times. I'll be reading about King Lear in his iconic storm when it hits me that I don't really know how lightning works, exactly. So, of course, I have to read the Wikipedia article on lightning, and in that article there are so many links to so many other fascinating articles about hurricanes and harvesting lightning energy and rockets that trigger lightning strikes, and each of those articles has links to so many other fascinating articles . . . and suddenly it's midnight, I have 20 tabs open, and Shakespeare remains unread.

At school, my best friends and I discuss implications of special relativity or the theoretically best shape for a bridge given various constraints or what it would be like if the earth were rotating significantly faster or experiments with the "artificial atom." I'm more interested in biology than they are, so I probably bore them half to death when I tell them for the third time how tree frogs freeze solid every winter and simply thaw out and hop around again in spring because they store so much glucose in their cells that their cells stay rigid in the cold— and if we can figure out how to replicate this property then maybe we can improve the methodology of organ transplants or maybe even freeze people during space travel! It would be like science fiction.

Every once in a while, my friends and I talk about how light bulbs work. And when we do, I know the factoids weren't the most important things my dad gave me in those ten-minute car rides to elementary school; his real gifts were my curiosity and insatiable desire to learn more.

About the Author: My name is Gordon Downs. I'm a senior from Tucson, Arizona, and I want to do research in a STEM field, but I haven't decided which one yet. I play volleyball, intern at the University of Arizona in the summers, and am in my school's math club and Science Olympiad team.

High School Attended: University High School, Tucson, AZ

The Process: I basically wrote my life's story in 650 words, and then asked my friends what they thought of it. The majority opinion was that I should focus a lot more on a single theme, so I chose curiosity and just took the parts of my essay that were already about curiosity and expanded upon them. I think I've done eight revisions now, with feedback from friends, family, multiple English teachers, and my college counselor.

Acknowledgments: My essay never would have been written if my dad hadn't encouraged me so much to ask questions.

On Being the Oldest Sibling

Lucy Hurst

It's Christmas Eve. My three brothers are three years old and I am five. A Christmas party is in full swing as Santa arrives. Our parents round us up with the finesse of sheepdogs and send us down the red velour carpet to the large red man. William and Peter begin with wobbly lips. Christopher offers a strident shriek. A chorus of sobbing ensues! My cheeks burn a shade of mortification that helps me blend into Santa's jacket. My mind races. *How could they humiliate me this way?! But* why *was I humiliated? Could I have more at stake in the brothers than I thought?*

I accepted my role as older sister to triplet brothers reluctantly. I wanted nothing to do with the new pet mongrels. I was jealous of the attention they garnered; incessant grandmother coos at church, their matching outfits, and their triplet stroller—a cumbersome three-seater—with no place for a singleton sister. Being the oldest was isolating as the brothers constantly occupied my parents. I yearned for a delicate sister or a hamster. But, alas, I had to make do with three blundering boys who poured my prized sea monkeys into my prized tea set.

Eventually, I realized the brothers could be enjoyable in moderation. Hide and seek, for example, was a win-win scenario. The brothers always hid in the same spots and screamed if I walked by. Brother tag was far easier than school tag! I was no match for the rowdier boys of my second grade class. I finally warmed up to being older and wiser. I knew how to spell and could tell my parents how "D-U-M" I thought the brothers acted. I could effortlessly enlist a brother to gather supplies for "potions class" in our garage. In reality, the confidence that leading the brothers gave me was, more often than not, a fanciful illusion to cover my true bewilderment at the daunting prospects before me—learning cursive, getting field trip permission slips signed on time, and multiplication tables. Nonetheless, I gained a tentative sense of self-assurance leading my motley crew.

When I observed my friends' older siblings, I realized how much more I had to learn. Sarah's older sister knew *everything* about clothes and music and makeup and boys. Joanie's sister knew all of Joanie's teachers and disclosed endless academic wisdom. Frannie's older sister had already applied to colleges, so Frannie knew the art of pruning a prime résumé. I was jealous of my friends and their guides. What did I know about clothes or makeup or music or boys or teachers or résumés?

Now the brothers are sophomores and I feel more than ever that my guidance is necessary. I drop advice more and more frequently as I approach graduation. It's reminding them to make sure their dates have a ride home and a warm place to sit before leaving a dance. Or sledding a little longer even though I'm supposed to drive them to swim practice.

The brothers proved a tough audience for my rookie mistakes, like failing the learner's permit test and letting it crush my sophomoric ego or backing into a minivan in a carpool line. They will, nonetheless, probably make these same mistakes, too. But at least I've provided some precedent on ameliorating the repercussions. I learned this responsibility not by choice. But I have learned to relish Peter's messy science experiments, Christopher's incessant ESPN babble, and William's exhaustive knowledge of cars. I now realize that being the bossy older sister has taught me more about the value of friendship and navigation than I ever could have learned from any other role model.

About the Author: My name is Lucy Hurst. I enjoy writing and biology and Spanish and hope to study these in college.

High School Attended: DuPont Manual High School, Louisville, KY

The Process: In writing to this prompt I went through several phases of ideas. I wanted this essay to be the greatest and most interesting topic of all time. Eventually I realized that my topic was living in my house with me. Upon choosing my topic I found that it was exponentially easier to write than trying to contrive meaning from a "cool" topic that didn't really affect me on a daily basis. So writing wasn't as arduous as was editing with a fine-toothed comb.

Acknowledgments: I would like to thank my college counselor, Junius Scott Prince, for offering feedback on topics and drafts. I would also like to thank Mrs. Amy Ritchie for encouraging my writing.

THANK YOU, SHU-LI

Jakob Felty

I sat in a dark room alone for the fourth straight hour, staring at the familiar images move across the iMac computer screen. Shu-Li, with his small hand in mine, was leading me through the worn tile hallway of his home, an orphanage in the small village on the outskirts of Xian. I paused on a tight frame of his face, his joyous smile bringing a flood of memories back to me. He was proud of his new home, and he had volunteered to be the tour guide for this group of student journalists from the United States. Though the accommodations were meager by American standards, his home provided a safe haven from the poverty-stricken slums we witnessed on our bus ride to the orphanage. Row after row of decaying stone shacks dotted the landscape, each void of plumbing or running water. Like the other children, Shu-Li's story began with sadness and loss but now brims with hope and opportunity. He was one of the lucky children who claimed a precious spot at the orphanage rather than spend his childhood in the streets of his village.

The entire production process for the documentary short film we shot during our tour of China was a two-week-long emotional roller coaster of endless video editing and reminiscing. From the glistening metal and glass skyscrapers of downtown Shanghai to the winding rickshaw alleys of the Beijing Hutong, my fellow students and I were able to see, feel, taste, and experience a culture that was very different from our everyday lives. However, I kept coming back to the same piece of video, the same frozen image of a smiling boy dressed in his Sunday best tightly gripping my hand as he guided me to each room. I watched the children play funny games in the courtyard, and I understood their laughter even when I could not understand the words they spoke. I realized at that moment that these are the stories I want to share. This is the kind of journalist I want to become.

Being a journalism major at DuPont Manual High School carries the responsibility to produce high-quality professional content. I have been blessed with the opportunity to enhance my skills using industry-standard software applications and equipment. However, my personal commitment and work ethic within the program have provided me with additional opportunities to display my passion for journalism. I provided extensive live coverage of the 2012 presidential election that included the vice presidential debate, election night in Chicago, and the second inauguration of President Obama. I have covered the press conferences of congressmen, mayors, and school superintendents. I have enjoyed a front row seat for the teachings of the Dalai Lama and backstage passes for my favorite recording artists. My determination to become a professional journalist has opened doors to many great opportunities for real world experience. These experiences have become so central to my identity that they continually motivate my pursuit of higher education in the field of journalism.

As I reflect back on my high school years as a student journalist, I am appreciative of the instruction I have received and proud of the content I have produced. Following my trip to China, I served as the managing editor of our school's news website. This year, I am anchoring our daily news broadcast. We no longer compare ourselves to other high school broadcasts or publications; we strive to be competitive with local and national media. Regardless of whether I am writing an article, shooting a gallery or video, or delivering the news live on air, my passion and determination for journalistic excellence is rooted in the desire to tell a story that resonates with people on a deeper, human level. For me, this passion was sparked by a young boy with an infectious smile who lives half a world away. Thank you, Shu-Li.

About the Author: My name is Jakob Felty. I live in Louisville, KY, and attend DuPont Manual High School in the Journalism and Communications Magnet. I hope to continue my journalism education in college and become a broadcast journalist.

High School Attended: DuPont Manual High School, Louisville, KY

The Process: I was inspired by the documentary film that my fellow journalism students and I produced, which included a segment on Shu-Li's orphanage. I wanted to write a more personal account of this brief encounter with a boy who had such an impact on me. I initially wrote as much as I could remember about my feelings and experience, then I went through several edits to create an essay that would convey my experience within the word limit. I am very happy to have the opportunity to share it with others.

Acknowledgments: Jeff Felty, Rachelle Felty, James Miller, Marti Johnston.

GOING AGAINST TRADITION

Alondra Lucero

I probably made some random family relative in Mexico, one whom I never met before, gasp in shock when she learned through the grapevine I was not going to have a *quinceañera*. I thought my mother would react the same way when I told her, maybe shake my shoulders. But instead relief washed across her face, as if the Pope himself had blessed her. I did not realize my decision, a simple no, would cause such a reaction from my mom. But for me it seemed I had made the right one.

In Hispanic culture, a quinceañera is a special celebration of a girl's fifteenth birthday that signifies her transition from childhood to womanhood. It is a chance for a girl to feel like a Disney princess, to have all eyes filled with admiration for her. It is a chance for a girl to dance a graceful waltz for her captivated audience and publicly show she is no longer a mere child, but a woman.

I could have been that girl. But I did not feel comfortable with that tradition. The last time I wore a lavish dress was when I did my first communion. Even then I was uncomfortable. I had to sit up straight to avoid wrinkling my dress and eat very carefully to avoid staining the white fabric. I could not play outside with my cousins. Instead I had to be a "doll" for the photos. I knew this would happen again in my quinceañera.

The image of femininity that is represented by the quinceañera is a terribly narrow vision of what is womanly. Instead of encouraging individuality and passion in a girl's life, the custom encourages conformity. For many generations, girls have been fit into the same mold. This was something I struggled with until one day I realized that I could not force myself to conform to an image that did not truly represent who I was. There are many other ways for girls to express themselves—from ice-skating to sketching pictures to working as a neurosurgeon. It all depends on what the person is truly passionate about.

When I was a high school freshman, I always dressed in a comfortable shirt, jeans, and sneakers. It was my go-to outfit for every day. Back then I would have described myself as a tomboy. It was just a phase that I was going through. There I was, at age thirteen, in jeans and sneakers, wondering if I wanted to wear not only a dress, but also makeup for the first time. As the years of high school passed, I slowly changed my appearance. Now I am taller and feel more confident and feminine. But I did this at my own pace.

Although I have grown in the last four years, there are some traits of mine that have not changed and never will. I know I will always be too busy with more important things to spend much time worrying about high heels and makeup. However, I do sometimes listen to "Corazón de Niño" by Raul Di Blasio and imagine myself twirling on the dance floor in the beautiful, silky dress I would have chosen. I imagine being *that* girl at times, especially when I hear that song. But I do not mind leaving her behind because deep inside I knew she was not me. Instead I am still growing and transforming myself into someone I can be proud of. Someday I will be sitting in a research lab, observing specimens through a microscope and carefully taking notes. I will wear a white lab coat and study thousands of samples given to me in test tubes. I may or may not find a cure for cancer through my intensive research. Whatever happens, good or bad, I know I will be okay because I will get there. I just know it.

About the Author: My name is Alondra Lucero. I live in Astoria, New York. My goals in life are to become the first person in my family to attend a four-year college and have a career as a microbiologist.

High School Attended: High School for Environmental Studies, New York, NY

The Process: I decided to write about not doing my quinceañera. It was a decision that was easy for me since I never felt the need to do one, although it did break my father's heart. I am his only daughter and he hoped that I would celebrate my fifteenth birthday through this Mexican tradition. However, I did not want to and I thought I was going against my Mexican heritage. Instead I found a different way to show my family my transition from childhood to adulthood. And it did not cost my parents a single penny.

Acknowledgments: I would like to greatly thank Mona Molarsky, my personal college counselor. Without her, this essay would have not been possible to finish.

THE DOCK

Julia Schoeni

I knew the dock was dangerous. The wooden planks were sagging in places and, in spots, boards were missing completely. It bobbed wildly in the lake sludge as it tried to support the weight of four kids. As Grant, the oldest of us, dove in, there was a resounding crack that made me tense up, prepared to abandon ship at any moment. Zach quickly followed suit, and after waiting to make sure everyone was out of the way, I was next to cannonball off the landing. When I reemerged, I could see my six-year-old sister's silhouette highlighted against the darkening sky. She was shaking, with cold or fear I didn't know, and her arms were folded in a way that made her resemble a small, frightened animal. *Sounds like an actual story*

"What's wrong?" I taunted.

She hesitated before responding and in a small voice said, "I'm scared."

I was two years older. A decent older sister would have said, "It's okay. I'll come and get you down," or something like that, and maybe on any other day, I would have. But before I could open my mouth, I heard from behind me, "CHICKEN!"

A voice in my head told me that I couldn't contradict Grant, that I needed to be in complete agreement. After all, I didn't want to be the chicken in question. So I did the unthinkable. I told her to jump, and it wouldn't be long before I regretted the decision.

Grant was a bully and always had been. He had pulled her hair, called her a scaredy-cat, and chased her around the house on numerous occasions. And I had laughed and done nothing to stop it. I don't know what my problem was. I don't know why I let Grant walk all over me, and always at the expense of my kid sister. She looked up to me. I was *supposed to be her role model.* But I was far from a role model. I was a bully. And I had let her down on far too many occasions.

She hit the water and then was gone. She had disappeared like a magician's assistant. The ripples from her less-than-graceful entrance melted away, and the water became an unbroken mirror. In that mirror was the face of a monster: me. I taunted her. I cheated her. I betrayed my sister. What would she have been when she grew up? How many kids would she have had? Would we have been close? I couldn't think; I could only react. I took a deep breath and arched my body to dive into the water before me.

It was nothing like the movies. I couldn't see her slowly turning pale. I couldn't see her body drifting toward the lake floor with her arms raised above her head and her hair covering her face like a veil. Actually, I couldn't see much of anything. I thrashed around wildly and forced my eyes open, although it didn't make much of a difference. I had to make contact with some part, any part of her. I had to. Please.

Please.

I was unsure whether or not what I grabbed ahold of was a fistful of lake weeds or my sister. Whatever it was hung limp and lifeless in my hand, the temperature of ice. All I could do was pray as I propelled myself in a direction that I thought was up.

Two heads broke the mirror this time. Two dark-skinned, dark-haired heads. Two coughing, sputtering, choking girls.

I remember gloating and saying that I had saved her life. I also remember her telling me that I had almost killed her. I couldn't understand why she wasn't grateful. Now, I know. I can't remember if, back then, I ever said, "I'm sorry."

About the Author: My name is Julia Schoeni. I've always wanted to become a doctor, so as of right now, that's the plan. The causes of breakdowns in the delicate machinery that is our body is fascinating to me. Hopefully I'll be able to fulfill that dream of mine.

High School Attended: Newtown High School, Sandy Hook, CT

The Process: What really helped me get started was writing whatever came to my mind. I had already started the story, but I started it in a different place and what I ended up writing in that 15- to 20-minute period became the bulk of my essay. I had lots of help editing and revising sections of the essay afterwards.

Acknowledgments: Everyone at CWP Fairfield and my family.

BLOOD

Jared Newman

My mother won't let me get a tattoo. I don't particularly want one. But, nonetheless, the tattoo injunction is quite clear.

The storefront on the corner of 14th and P. blended 1950s ice cream parlor and Brooklyn hole-in-the-wall, complete with wild flavors: black sesame, cinnamon thyme, each listed in Readerboard lettering. I couldn't not stop by. Pausing the Bob Dylan in my headphones, I ordered Thai strawberry sorbet, and the woman behind the counter began to scoop.

Then—I saw her wrist. On the inner part of her right wrist, she had six words tattooed in a perfect circle: *they is they is they is.* An infinite circle of incorrect grammar.

"That's a crazy tattoo. What does it mean?" I asked.

"Oh." She switched the scoop to her left hand, pocketing the right. "It's the last line of a short story I like."

"Really!? Who's the author?"

"You might not know him. No one ever does."

"But it's so familiar." I replied. "I swear I've read it before."

There were customers behind me in line. Fat rain clawed at the windows; tourists ran inside just to be dry. And, motionless, she watched me dig at the recesses of my memory.

"It's about a bank robbery!" I yelled. "He's a teller. No! He's a book critic who can't stand the clichés...And they shoot him . . . Tobias Wolff . . . 'Bullet in the Brain.' That's it! That's it!"

She smiled.

As she rang me up on an iPad, she explained, "I got it after I graduated. I majored in creative writing and read the story in a workshop. I adored it. So, I got married to it."

Slipping under the counter, she joined me as I ate. We talked MFAs and Jonathan Franzen and how much we both hated microfiction—whatever that was. She was working at the store until one of her pieces got published. "So at this rate," she said, "I'll be here until I'm manager." I told her I had gone to summer programs at the *Kenyon Review* and Iowa Writers' Workshop, but currently I was selling my soul, working on the Hill. Laughing, she assured me writing wasn't the only valiant path.

Many artists lead these double lives—weighing reliable careers against pursuits of publication. As young and inexperienced as I am, I had trod that same balance: spending two summers first at writing workshops, then in longer stints on political campaigns. This summer, however, I had only applied for "real jobs" and got one in Congress—something for which I had spent months pleading my maturity and learning how to write cover letters. I felt guilty letting my writing slip to the side during those precious weeks when I usually got so much done. But licking my Thai strawberry, I wondered just how uncertain the writing life could be. Young writers tend to only consider the success stories, not the poets barely making it with two day jobs and fifty form rejection letters.

I often think of that tattoo. It's impossible not to be struck by its definitive assertion of selfhood—proclaiming that this woman was a writer through and through. And looking at the tattoo, I finally understood why I, too, needed to be a writer. Yes, I love my political work; I love that grassroots organizing means hearing thousands of stories like hers. But writing is a compulsion.

Tattoos are permanent because they go deep; your body responds to the needle like an infection, ingesting the ink until it remains permanently housed inside your cells. Writing is no different for me. Forces deep within my blood, deep inside my macrophages and fibroblasts, compel me to write. In my mind, there is no balance between professionalism and creativity, because I am not making a choice to write; I have to. It's permanent.

So now that I'm eighteen, perhaps I should get a tattoo . . . on my wrist . . . a circle:

I am I am I am.

About the Author: My name is Jared Newman, originally from New York. I was accepted SCEA to Yale, and hope to pursue a major in English while there, so that one day I could be a presidential speechwriter like Toby Ziegler.

High School Attended: Phillips Academy, Andover, MA

The Process: To write this essay, I first spent many days jogging and coming up with ideas on the move. I had always known the narrative my essay would present. I just needed to understand why that narrative would sell me as a candidate. In search of that answer, I spent a day or two writing down adjectives I wanted readers to conjure when looking at my essay. From this list of adjectives, I wrote the essay in one night in August of 2014.

Acknowledgments: I'd like to thank my mother and my best friend, Ellie.

Embrace the Rain

Talia Dolny-Lipsy

It starts to drizzle and everyone scrambles to get out of the pool. I hear thunder and inhale the fresh scent of rain in the distance. I carefully walk up the steps and onto the surface surrounding the crowded pool at the Breakers Hotel in Florida. I hear my mom sweetly calling my name and I lie down on her, my little toes reaching for hers. She lays a soft yellow blanket over me to keep me warm. I stay put, feeling the warmth of her body as the rain sinks through the blanket. I feel so content with her arms wrapped around me.

Instinctively, I knew something was wrong, although nobody had told me. I had noticed simple differences such as her loss of hair, getting sick by the side of the road, and no longer eating healthy and kosher food. During the entire trip, I never wanted to part from her for fear of something bad happening. At this young age, my perceptive nature uncovered a sense of ambiguity and fear. This was my last vacation with my mom because she died that February, when I was eight.

Every time it rains, I feel safe, the same way I did when I was wrapped up in the blanket in my mother's arms. My mom didn't want to give in to cancer. She never thought she was going to die, and I never thought so either. Many people say they don't want to give up, but her soul screamed strength and perseverance in an all-encompassing way. Even though she died, her fighting soul lives on. She wasn't just a strong-willed, opinionated woman; she was also very spiritual and connected to her faith. When she danced, it was like her spirit took the wheel and was in control. When I was about six years old, I used to ask her, "How

183

should I dance?" and she would tell me, "Dance as if nobody's watching." At that time, I took those words very literally. Now I look back and think there's a lot more to that saying than six-year-old Talia could grasp. Now it means: "Live your life filled with passion and curiosity and stand up for what you believe in despite how you are viewed."

Last winter, I was at a conference in Washington, DC with Girls Learn International. We had long meetings all day and guest speakers at every meal. During lunch one day, I sat and listened to a guest speaker attack Israel. When I heard his words, my throat tensed, and my heart sank to the bottom of my stomach. His words shook me to the core and stung my soul. My homeland was being violated; a piece of me was being violated. I felt thick, hot tears run down my face. I took a deep breath, inhaling positivity and exhaling negative thoughts. Then I explained to the people around me why I was so upset. This solidified what I already knew. Like my mom, my heart is, and always will be, with Israel. Protecting her and fulfilling Tikkun Olam (repairing the world) is what I'm meant to do.

My passionate loving mama taught me to fight for what I believe in, and that's exactly what I intend to do. The rain acts as a restart button to my crazy ambitions. It brings me back to that place by the pool of peace and tranquility. I feel as though it's cleaning the earth of all its sins. It relaxes me; the pitter-patter puts me at ease and makes me remember, one step at a time; the world can't be repaired overnight. For now, I can sit on the porch with my tea, a book, and just listen. The smell of the fresh rain infiltrates my lungs as I take in its beauty.

About the Author: My name is Talia Dolny-Lipsy and I live in the Bronx. My goals in life are to pursue social justice and activism through politics.

High School Attended: The Churchill School and Center

The Process: I started off by brainstorming topics that are meaningful to me and that describe who I am. I eventually decided on the rain, which I have loved ever since I was little, and I explained its importance to me in relation to other aspects of my life. Then I wrote a memory of being in the rain with my mother, which was the inspiration for the rest of my essay. After this, I wrote multiple rough drafts and had my college guidance counselor review it.

Acknowledgments: Ms. Hugger, my college guidance counselor, and my dad, Mark Lipsy.

TOUCH

Charlotte Knopp

Every day, I close my eyes and feel Khedar's respiration, feel his heartbeat, feel his ears pricking back and forth, feel his tail switching, feel the exact location and position and angle of each of his legs beneath me. I close my eyes and feel every detail of every stride, every dip of his shoulders, every flexion of his hocks. Bareback and bridleless, I feel the gentle give and take of his forehand with my seat, feel the gritty sting of sweat on my bare, thorn-scraped legs, feel my fingers tangled in his mane.

I can return to the barn, lie in his stall, and, with my eyes closed, describe his position and facial expressions as little, bristly whiskers brush longitudinally across my cheek, lipping along my cheekbones—simply by the sensations in that small contact point. His pony kisses are soft and gentle as he plays with my hair, flipping the frizzy red curls into my eyes, nuzzling me gently, and alternating with playful little shoves. There is nothing more lovely than feeling his forelegs buckle as he lowers himself to the ground and curling myself gently into the contours of his neck and chest, laying my head on his shoulder and closing my eyes, letting him wrap around me while my cheek rests there, absorbing the wonderfully sweet, musky heat emanating from his shoulder.

When I ride with my eyes closed or late at night when it's dark, the feel of Khedar beneath me informs me of my surroundings. I feel what Khedar follows with his eyes. I know the texture and firmness of the terrain by the length of his strides and the softness of his extensions. I know the slope of the ground as my hip angle opens and closes to accommodate his shoulders. I feel the approach of chevrons, coops, and coffins as he sets his weight back onto his haunches, and I know, from the exertion beneath me, the rounding of his back, and the weight of his mouth in my hands the height and breadth of the jump. When we crash through water, I feel the resistance against our legs, and when we are truly swimming, I feel his legs pumping and paddling—and I feel the toes of his front feet grab onto the lake bottom as we return from the drop-off.

On my horse, I'm inextricably connected to something other than myself, wound tightly into another body, perfectly calibrated with his movements, and intimately aware of every shift. On Khedar, touch is simple and pure. Reaching that equilibrium of give and take swathes me in the intensity of an entirely tactile world, carries my mind away from everything but the language of touch.

Khedar is everything to me. I've had him since he was a baby, trained him myself. He's ineluctably comforting. He's my passion and my hobby. He's my study-buddy, my shoulder to cry on, my best friend. When I'm with him, he's my eyes and my ears. He is all my senses but touch: that, we share. Allowing all external stimuli to dissolve, I can condense my emotions, consolidate my thoughts, just feel. Decompress. Recharge. Bask in my introversion. He's my eternal Zen, siphoning away all external stressors, stripping away everything but the present, making me drunk on closeness, inebriated by proximity, and intoxicated by the melding of our senses—beckoning me into the lucid and unadorned language of touch.

About the Author: My name is Charlotte Knopp. I'm a senior at Minnetonka High School in MN, planning to double major in English and biology. Ultimately, I'm interested in medicine—probably pathology or epidemiology.

High School Attended: Minnetonka High School, Minnetonka, MN

The Process: My thinking spot is atop my horse, because horses are my thing and the barn is my place. On my horse, Khedar, my mind wanders; I let it float around, branch out, pursue different avenues, and perhaps most important, I allow it to backtrack. During this stage, I dictate the piece in my head: I match the cadence of my sentences to the rhythm of his canter, punctuate them with his transitions, and become fully consumed by ideas, language, and the gentle movement beneath me. And then I write.

Acknowledgments: Ms. Susan Sinkler.

PENNY-COLORED OASIS

Yolanda Wadolowski

Copper-colored specks dotted my palms, collecting around my lifeline. They became smudged as my forefinger rubbed against them. Soon, the spots faded and then reappeared as I grabbed the dangling chains once more, their layers of rust bearing the toil of endless, frigid winters. Only slight breezes from the Baltic Sea would guide them, as a mother might sway the crib of her sleeping infant. I moved forwards and backwards on the swing gracefully. The hairs on my arm brushed the leaves that reached out toward the swing's stoic frame from the collapsing gazebo. I used to move away from these leaves, for they were hostile and sharp. Now, with their edges smoother than I remembered, I allowed my arm to touch them. The swing itself seemed to glide, and when I squinted my dark blue eyes, my feet soared above the apple trees. Their soft green tones and undertones beckoned me. I was warmly welcomed as one of them.

As I rose from the piece of wood that had carried my body, the rows of trees invited me into their embrace. The tall, thin blades of grass caressed my sun-kissed legs, allowing my feet to seep into the cool, moist ground below. Young apples, which had prematurely fallen off the trees for reasons unknown to me, lay in the dandelions. The apples' soft brown bodies marked weeks of growth. They now rested among those lavish weeds, which had miraculously survived the impact of the falling decayed fruit. I plucked the dandelions with my thumb and forefinger. Among the wishes I uttered, I wished for a glass of sweet lemonade. Countless thin wisps of seeds were sent away.

The sight of their bodies being lifted by the wind brought me back to the first time I journeyed to this land that bears the wistful red and stark white flag. I had once lain out on a plush, bright red blanket, upon which I felt a certain lightness and disconnection from all that seemed so necessary before. Beneath the shade cast by the apple trees, my two nieces' large smiles highlighted their deep dimples. Once we painted our nails because no one said we could not. The brushes sometimes missed our nails and embedded pale purples and vivid blues into our skin. Behind us, in our own little world, an apple fell, we shrieked, and laughed for no reason at all. The quaint town of Zambrów smiled at our laughter, allowing for a chuckle or two itself.

There I felt pure joy. It was the type of joy that made me wander under stubby bridges and between the luscious dandelion leaves. My nieces' Polish tongues uttered words that sounded like melodies, with their half notes and staccato beats. In the large garden of the doll-like home of my mother, every hour simply teemed with feelings of blissfulness and serenity. Later, there would be times when the home's hinges and crevices looked for me between the rusty chains, next to the bright smiles of those twins. Yet they did not find me for my visits became rare. So I made sure to encompass each experience fully, for during those pleasant late summer months, among the tall swings and lavish trees, there was an unspeakable displacement of time.

About the Author: My name is Yolanda Wadolowski. I live in New York City, and in my free time I enjoy playing the piano and guitar. In the fall, I look forward to beginning my college experience as a political science major and economics minor.

High School Attended: New Explorations into Science, Technology and Math, New York, NY

The Process: Writing my essay was a two-month process, during which I interchangeably filled out college applications and began answering supplement questions. I went through nearly fifteen drafts before I decided I was ready to submit this particular essay. It was definitely a stressful process overall but by choosing to write about a place where I felt at peace, I was able to focus my energy on completing my applications ahead of time.

Acknowledgments: Lindsey Palmer.

CANDLES

Elaina Walker

I remove a match from the small cardboard box, and, with a quick swipe across the sandpaper, wait for the tip to reappear in orange flames. Its warmth climbs up my hand while I decide which candles to light. The glowing flares start to illuminate my room, and I extinguish the flame before it can touch the skin on my fingertips. Reaching behind my closet door, I feel the wooden frame of the Van Gogh my grandfather painted for me before I finally come across a green, plastic plug, and insert its metal prongs into the wall. My room becomes brighter as the white Christmas lights dangle in the open air and outline the mirror nailed to the closet door. I lie back on my bed and close my eyes. The cold breeze sweeps into my room and absorbs the candles' strong aromas, as I lie, drifting into a different world, far away from current realities.

It is in this moment that I feel perfectly content. I feel free, relaxed, powerful. Earl Grey perfumes diffuse throughout the air and circle up into my nose. The scent brings me back to the Christmas Eve family dinners at my aunt's house; we would sit by the fire drinking tea, ripping open the Christmas presents under the tree. I breathe in again, this time inhaling the sweet, raspberry-scented candles, and it feels as if I am back at my kitchen table, surrounded by my best friends before they left for college. My grandmother's worsening Alzheimer's, my parents' brutal legal battles with my uncle, my father's alcoholism, and even homework assignments: They all slowly fade from my mind.

Every day, I expect myself to succeed in school, to succeed in sports. Maybe it's the pressure of going to a competitive high school, or maybe it's me pushing myself to reach personal goals. These pressures have carved out who I am as an individual, and I thrive on a fast-paced lifestyle. But they can also distract me from the simple happiness of life. From volunteering, sports practices, achieving good grades, and maintaining a social life, my days are jam-packed and hectic, with rare amounts of free time. I often feel a heavy weight mounted upon my shoulders. When I return to my bedroom at night, it is as if all these pressures suddenly disappear, no longer of such importance in my life. Lighting candles lets me retreat to a world away from my family issues and rather rigorous schedule. The candles provide a sense of calmness; I am able to find my inner solace.

But it is over too soon. The room starts to overheat from the candles' warmth, and the scents overpower the oxygen in the air. The wicks shrink into nothing; the candles' wax burns into liquid. I blow out the candles before they are completely gone and am forced to return to reality. Still, I keep the matches lying next to my candles as a reminder that I will be back to my private utopia.

About the Author: My name is Elaina Walker and I live in Marin County, CA. My main goal at the moment is to leave college and find a career I am most content with.

High School Attended: San Rafael High School, San Rafael, CA

The Process: It took me over two months and many, many drafts to finalize this essay to my pleasing. Reading the rest of my application, the admissions counselor would see I am extremely involved in sports, my leadership class, and the community. So in this essay, I wanted to share the other part of my life, the part aside from the chaos my life brings. This essay displays how my daily pressures and life events have shaped who I am as an individual, but also show the admissions counselor how there is a spiritual, peaceful side to me that is just as important and can be brought out by my nightly candle ritual.

Acknowledgments: None.

A ONE-INCH, PLASTIC STORY

Brynne Erb

Some people's stories are told through photographs, Facebook timelines, or even Twitter feeds. However, my story is captured in a one-inch long device that reads "Toshiba, 4GB." While it may seem like just an ordinary staple of every student's supply list, my flash drive is very important to me because it is a living record of how I became the person I am today through my writing.

My flash drive holds a record of every essay, every presentation, and every edit of my extended essay on Jane Eyre's innate morality, a ten-page paper necessary for the acquisition of my international baccalaureate (IB) diploma. It holds the poetry I experimented with for class in eighth grade, the memoir draft of the infamous tubing incident for seventh grade, and the first ever three-paragraph essay I wrote as a tiny, enthusiastic sixth-grader.

If I look through my folder labeled "Freshman Year," I can find my essay on *Romeo and Juliet,* where I discovered that Shakespeare was worth the buzz. It records my encounters with the characters of Steinbeck's Lennie and Lee's Scout Finch, whose innocence and keen understanding of the world made me shiver as I read. Under the folder named "Sophomore Year" I can re-create my indignant fury when I found out Tom Sawyer unnecessarily kept Jim in captivity when he knew Jim was a free slave and my disappointment when Huck stood by complacently.

In my flash drive, I can call up the first essay I wrote for Ms. Mosiman, who ripped the carpet out from under my feet by banning the five-paragraph essay structure for our IB Literature class and forbade us from talking about the "passage" (in reality, I learned, a passage is not a passage; it is a *moment*). There I can find the first essay I wrote for IB European history, realizing that as much as I love Elizabeth and Darcy's love story, Austen's novel wasn't a good primary source outside of examining family life at the time it was written. My flash drive is home to the only existing copy of my edited extended essay, the culmination of three readings of *Jane Eyre,* ten hours of writing, and five unnecessarily frantic emails to my essay adviser.

This small piece of plain, black plastic captures my story best because writing is an integral part of my identity. A lover of books since I was six months old as my mother let me peruse picture books in my crib for hours, I have always had a passion for all things reading and writing. Developing this passion in and out of school led me to become who I am today: our school newspaper's editor-in-chief, a third-year writing coach, and an IB diploma candidate student who can't get enough of Louise Erdrich and Annie Dillard.

My story, housed in my flash drive, is a record of my growth, not only as a student, but also my growth as a person. My writing through every age developed in skill but also in thought. What was most important to me, what angered, excited, or saddened me during those years is in this one-inch device that I bring around with me everywhere on my school days. It holds these past versions of myself, smaller, younger versions of myself that I will never be again, that cannot be captured with a camera or an Instagram "Throwback Thursday." While it is important to grow and look to the future, it is equally as important to remember how I got to this moment, this version of myself, my current identity, and that is what my flash drive does for me.

About the Author: My name is Brynne Erb, and I live in Chanhassen, Minnesota. Some of my goals in life are to travel to every continent, write my own blog, and do something professionally that involves writing and editing after college.

High School Attended: Minnetonka High School, Minnetonka, MN

The Process: I wasn't sure that I wanted to write about this prompt, but when I read the Madison prompt about something that goes unnoticed in my daily life, I thought of my flash drive and how it contains my evolution as a reader, writer, student, and person. That seemed to me the most appropriate way to give Carleton a glimpse into who I was, as my story (being someone who loves to read and write) just couldn't be fully told without involving the books that I read in school that made me who I am today.

Acknowledgments: I would like to thank my mom for her constant inspiration and her support of my reading habits.

THE LEFTOVER

Alison Levitt

On a recent episode of *Chopped*, lousy leftovers were the mystery ingredients. I felt badly for, but could not help identifying with, the first chef to leave as he echoed my own feelings about leftovers—he said he would NEVER use leftovers again. My own entry into this world, delivered remarkably and miraculously as the second twin relegated to a tiny cramped space, left me with the same violent lifelong aversion to leftovers.

I've always had a love-hate relationship with food. I love eating it, and I hate wasting it. It could be construed as a problem that I spend so much time on Buzzfeed looking for 37 ways to cook a chicken breast or an egg (whichever came first), but I like to think of my food connoisseurship as my duty to prevent leftovers from ever grazing our well-worn-in plates.

Coming from a "no take-out" family, I had to become creative if my campaign against leftovers could ever succeed. My favorite books have always been cookbooks, and I have been voraciously tearing through them since the age of three. First, pointing out pictures of individual chicken pot pies for my parents to whip up and later trying to reinvent mini egg soufflés to account for all of the taste palettes in my family. I ruled the roost. Switching from merely flicking through cookbooks to dutifully taking up my helm at the counter with a trusty chef's knife, I became the point person of my family on any and everything food related.

As I grew older and travelled to play dates, I began to learn that leftovers were the norm, and ten-year-olds didn't typically menu plan. However, since no one had ever defined "normal" in my life, I was given the opportunity to define it for myself. Normal became finding a new cookie recipe, and then finding a new friend to make them with. Normal became finding myself through the ambition and initiative I was able to exhibit in the kitchen.

I have always been inspired by the artful talent that chefs have used in creating their masterpieces, but I quickly learned that my fascination wasn't in my love of food but in the way I utilized it. I craved the freedom I had to organize both people and food when I was in the kitchen. As I became more comfortable in the kitchen, I learned to become more comfortable in other aspects of my life. I assumed the position of goalie on my varsity field hockey team with gusto, as that was a place where I was at liberty to use my leadership skills to organize the field. Each player was a part of the buffet that I tweaked and encouraged to brilliance.

I attribute a lot of my success, and the depth of my involvement in leadership activities, to my crusades against leftovers. The more leftovers that piled up in our refrigerator, the more rhetoric I had at my disposal to ensure that they never hit the plate. I learned how to speak with ethos, logos, and pathos, rallying against my mother, determined not to revisit last night's meal. My verbal prowess, constantly honed at home, continues to be my most valuable tool when speaking in front of a large group.

Though my relationship with leftovers has never been a mutualistic one, I have grown to appreciate their impact on my childhood. Had I settled for less, I would not be the advocate I am today. My determination and forthrightness are skills that I have sharpened alongside my knives, resulting in my never-ending quest for the ideal meal. And the satisfaction I have in knowing that I stayed true to my beginnings.

About the Author: My name is Alison Levitt. I am from New York, New York. I'm currently the student body president at my school, play three sports, and love being outdoors with friends. In the future, I hope to find a career doing something that makes me excited to go to work every day.

High School Attended: The Chapin School, New York, NY

The Process: I wrote draft after draft of my essay, obsessing over each word until I felt that it was just right. I learned so much about myself during the writing process, and I am very proud of what I have accomplished.

Acknowledgments: Thank you to my parents, siblings, and guidance counselors for helping me through the process.

ELEPHANT THEORY

Daniella Tang

Elephants are big, strong, smart, and beautiful. Elephants easily pull six whole tons of weight; they paint pictures of each other; they even slam-dunk. You'd think, at the end of the day, elephant owners would be hard pressed to keep them controlled—if it weren't for a small piece of twine. When those elephants are babies, their owners tie one hind leg to the ground with string. They kick and pull, but to no avail—and, over time, come to expect that they can't break free. They have *incredible* potential—but at the tug of twine, they let a lie overcome them.

That's my favorite anecdote from *Do Hard Things* by Alex and Brett Harris. It's the book that helped me realize I *am* an elephant, and so are so many other kids with huge potential, convictions, and passions. See, around my age, kids are barely expected to even have a decent talk with an adult or pay attention in school. The reality is, we can accomplish so much more, but often don't. As we grow, we're told that adolescence is a vacation, a get-out-of-jail-free card, an era of languishing and waste. And whole generations of kids have sunk to meet those expectations, myself included. But we don't have to. Low expectations and a false view of teenhood are our twine, stunting our potential, but we can break it so easily: by throwing the myth of adolescence and expectations to the wind and just doing the things we love. That's Elephant Theory.

I'm an ordinary teenager with a not-so-ordinary mission. If you ask me about it, I won't describe your stereotypical teenage dream. Boys (or girls, etc.) don't keep me up at night, fundraiser ideas do. Video games, concerts, and *The Office* reruns are fun, but they can't top directing a food drive. Ask me what fundraiser I have planned next and I'll talk faster than I text. The thought of spending my life in humanitarian nonprofit business is like waking up every morning to a wedding proposal. (Seriously, my heart rate goes up when I think about it. I've measured.) It rules me, and it can't be impeached.

But it wasn't until the Elephant Theory that I learned I don't have to wait until adulthood to start doing what I love now, big as it may be. And I don't have to let the low expectations of adults hold me back either. So why wait? If not now, then when? If not me, then who? Orthodox? No. But possible.

So in August 2014, I came up with a plan for a *big* food drive. The very next day, I recruited over 20 people to help me. In two weeks, we had a website up, and today, two high schools, a karate club, and a church are set to collect food for the 80,000 hungry citizens of my county—Hunger Games style. Yes, there have been bumps and mishaps. But it's also been the most fun I've ever had, hands down.

As I look back on the past few months (and explain them to others), I'm posed with a question: How'd I find the courage? To be honest, organizing a food drive wasn't scary at all. It was exhilarating. The scariest part of all this, I'd say, is how much I've learned. As I've drafted and delivered emails, calls, and proposals, as I've created a mission statement and a website and a points system, one thing permeates the rest: I'm not just doing this because I can, I'm doing it because I must. Would I do all this again, even with the many awkward miscommunication fiascoes and the bulky ulterior motives I've had to navigate? The answer is *heck yes*, because to me helping others in need is as intrinsic as blood. Something in me craves it. It's who I am. I would not have it any other way.

About the Author: My name is Daniella Tang, and I live in New Jersey. I'm a high school senior dedicated to unflinchingly defending human rights and empowering people to reclaim them via a major in international business.

High School Attended: Biotechnology High School, Freehold, NJ

The Process: To write this essay? I just sat down and wrote. I always find that my best writing—for school or for art—comes most natively and expressively when I don't try to outline or force my words into something they're not. I built my essay from the ground up, then went back and edited out unnecessary parts, added in more relevant concepts, and finally, when I was all done, went to friends, parents, and my guidance counselor to see what their feelings were about it.

Acknowledgments: My guidance counselor, Jamie Krauter, and my parents were so encouraging during this process and gave me really helpful advice during the writing.

MY EXPERIENCE WITH
SATANIC SOCIAL NETWORKING

Tyler Pugh

I send snapchats of Satan. Contrary to what may appear as a desire to satisfy a subconscious urge for diabolical spirituality, my satanic social networking is really just a product of forced monotony and an unorthodox sense of humor. However, I suppose this deserves some context and explanation. I'm an unconventional Texan. Born and raised within a stone's throw of downtown Houston, I will always be rooted in the southern lifestyle, but certainly not defined by it. I speak Chinese, make hip-hop music, and am soon to be an Eagle Scout. My wide array of interests and my approachable demeanor cumulates to an individual characterized by confidence and charisma—qualities noticed by everyone I meet. While that sort of appearance is nice, it leaves some of my favorite parts of my character to fall underneath the radar.

For instance, my tendency to push beyond the status quo. Equipped with nothing but my imagination and a cell phone, I converted a mundane part-time job to a factory for Lucifer-inspired snapchat art. I'd take a picture of a piano and draw a stick-figure devil sitting at it (presumably playing a rendition of Adele's "Rolling in the Deep"), biding his time waiting to devour a plateful of chocolate chip cookies, or on a park swing-set captioned: "What a beautiful day for human sacrifice."

When I got concerned comments from my friends about my mental well-being, I was rather taken aback, not in offense to the questioning of my sanity, but by the lack of appreciation for my personal perspective. While my drawings were just a silly way to pass the time, they were representative of something more. To me, pushing the envelope is not a vice, but a virtue. Moreover, I find that this value is an undeniable characteristic of innovation; one that I share with many great historical leaders and ideological pioneers: Siddhartha Gautama, who left his life as a prince to become a monk and found Buddhism; Nicolaus Copernicus, who first suggested that Earth was not the center of the universe; or, more recently, Elon Musk, who released all of Tesla Motors' patents in a gambit to challenge the dominance of the automotive industry.

Though ironically drawing a stick figure rendition of Satan on a social media platform may not particularly be worthy of the history books, I believe its symbolism remains well founded. It shows I am willing to step away from ideas of normality and acceptableness. It's a foundation for leadership and enacting change: the characteristic to shape society, rather than being shaped by it. While deriving all this from a trivial snapchat episode may seem erroneous, to me it is not. I find my controversial pseudo-satanic messages an unnoticed manifestation of an internal philosophy I continue to hold dearly—that willingness to step away from the status quo and challenge ideas of what is acceptable is necessary for innovation, leadership, and progress.

About the Author: My name is Tyler Pugh. Growing up, I had an unconventional answer to the hackneyed question: "What do you want to be when you grow up?" The answer always has, and always will be, simply: "Proud of myself."

High School Attended: Carnegie Vanguard High School, Houston, TX

The Process: I started with a challenge. A friend who already attended university offhandedly suggested I write about my Satanic social networking. I decided to give it a try. I wrote out, originally, about 1,600 words for the essay. I made sure I had a solid introduction and then just typed whatever happened to come into my mind. After I had all these ideas written, I sat down with a friend who helped cut it down to less than 500 words.

Acknowledgments: My friend, Cole Introligator. You're more responsible for me getting into college than you should be. So thank you.

HEARTHROB(BING)

Rayat Rahman

"What are you, some kind of teen heartthrob?" the officer asked me. My mother referring to me as her monkey-faced child came to mind. I shrugged. I seemed calm. Truthfully, I had never been so close to crying in front of a stranger, my first police encounter at that. My heart beating, I told him I had messages proving my innocence. "Do you realize that if these messages are incriminating, you can be charged and arrested?" Having been known throughout my life for being ugly, I couldn't have imagined a situation where my looks got me too much attention.

I've always been the nerdy kid. I recall a sixth grade phase where I sold potatoes with faces and short stories about my superhero alter ego. My nerdiness was nothing compared to my ugliness though. I was never ashamed of reading Wikipedia more than kissing girls, but being called "Shit-face" got tiring. It was pretty disorienting when I moved to NYC; not only did I lose a lot of face fat then, but I also learned how to dress and use hair gel. Strangely, I was now called "hot."

During this most confusing phase of my life, mirrors went from a reminder of my hideousness to an endless time occupier. I don't remember any trig classes because they were spent adjusting my hair. I experienced a surreal ego trip where I thought I could do anything; I learned that you didn't need character to be confident: A pair of skinny jeans and a mischievous smile were enough. I thought that I could stop showing up to tutoring, sacrifice homework for a starring role in the school musical, and worst of all, belittle the emotions of a girl I met on set.

I remember the awkward walk by the East River with her, our personalities mismatched and her interest in me superficial. Minutes after we parted ways, she had texted me, asking me about my feelings for her. I made the mistake of not responding, because one month later I was in school with three officers interrogating me: She had accused me of harassment. I imagined being sent back to Bangladesh, my dad's job and my future at stake. "Diplomat's Son Arrested for Molestation" was not a pretty headline. Trying not to let my hands shake too much, I pulled out my phone and showed them her texts. I was cleared. The administration, however, had to call home and report everything. When I got home, my father had gotten off the phone with my tutor, and report card in hand, he started a conversation that ended with my mother crying from shock, him from anger, and myself from guilt. This was my wake-up call. That my ego could cause so much harm and jeopardize my future scared me straight.

I spent the next year rethinking who I was. I decided to challenge myself, pushing myself into leadership roles in graphic design and Key Club. Learning three new instruments is humbling and six AP courses left me with little time to waste. I discovered my passion for teaching and worked at an after-school tutorial. Seeing students' eyes mesmerized as I told them about relativistic time or evolution gave me more validation than any mirror. I was now leading meditation circles with my family. I found that the world had so much more to offer me than the mirror ever could.

It took policemen and a cold, mahogany conference table to turn everything around. It's obvious to me now that my passions are creating, learning, and changing. I can adapt to anything. I could end up a plumber or executive and be content. But what would make me truly happy? If I could put my experiences, desire for improvement, and open-mindedness to use making a difference for those who've never seen the things I have.

About the Author: My name is Rayat Rahman, and I live in New York City. This is my fifth country of residence; my dad is a diplomat. I want to see the potential that Bangladesh, my home country, is absolutely brimming with become actualized, and I want to use my worldly experiences and education to play an active role in making this happen.

High School Attended: NEST+M, New York, NY

The Process: I knew what I was going to write about when I read the prompts. I sat and meditated for a few minutes before I just poured whatever I could think of onto the paper. I ran my first draft through my friends, and then my AP lit teacher, Ms. Lindsey Palmer. She gave me invaluable organizational and stylistic advice, which I incorporated into my essay.

Acknowledgments: Ms. Lindsey Palmer.

As Easy as Riding a Bike

Nicholas McLoughlin

I fall off again. I keep trying to ride down what seems to be this endless, narrow hallway. Each time I start riding again, I make it just a little bit further. The bike is big and almost impossible to steer. My physical therapist, Sara, is running right next to me the whole time so I'm never alone. The hallway doesn't feel quite as endless now because each time I get a little bit better and make it a tiny bit farther before I lose my balance.

It's scary riding the heavy bike all the way down the hallway but the thought of falling off or crashing into a wall is much more terrifying. Several times I almost slam into the wall, but Sara catches me just in time. The first time we went out to the hallway to practice I was really scared. She told me to get on and not to worry but I didn't want to because I thought I would get badly hurt. Sara promised me that she would give me a hundred dollars if she let me hit the wall. At first I thought about crashing for the hundred bucks, but as soon as she said that to me I knew that I would be safe. I trusted her completely and still do to this day every week at therapy.

This was the second time I learned to ride a bike. It turns out that I am the exception to the saying "You never forget how to ride a bike." I had learned with my parents years before, but over time I was no longer able to ride. My muscles had gotten much tighter and my foot turned out because of my cerebral palsy. It was really frustrating because every time I tried to ride my right foot would turn and fall off the pedal. The second time I learned I had to have a special boot put on the right pedal so I could keep my foot in place. I was much bigger this time, so my body had to figure out how to control the bike and not let the bike control me. It was harder to learn the second time because I was scared. My parents had always told me that I loved being on the bike and riding it around the playground but I had absolutely no memory of that. I guess as a little kid it had never occurred to me that I could get hurt if I fell off. I practiced twice a week for months, and eventually I did learn how to ride again, although I never really enjoyed it as much as I did the first time.

The determination that I had when I learned to ride a bike is the same determination I use in my everyday life for everyday tasks that I find challenging. There are times in life when it will be hard and I may crash into the wall, but I know that I will be able to make it down that long, endless hallway no matter how difficult it is.

About the Author: My name is Nicholas McLoughlin and I was born and raised in New York City. I am seventeen years old and a senior at the Churchill School and Center in Manhattan. My goal in life is to get a great college education and eventually start my own business. I also want to travel the world and experience different places.

High School Attended: The Churchill School and Center, New York, NY

The Process: The essay process went really smoothly for me. I knew what I wanted to write about from the beginning. I started the essay much earlier than I needed to, but it worked out very well for me in the end because I completed my college applications ahead of time. It took me a little while to get started on the essay, but as soon as I did everything flowed. The hardest part of this process was editing the essay over and over again until it was the way I wanted it.

Acknowledgments: I'd like to thank my mother and my guidance counselor for proofreading my essay and offering editing suggestions.

HELEN KELLER

Bianca Rico

She was regarded as a saint, a miracle child who defied the bleak future that had once lay ahead of her.

But somewhere along her journey in the public eye, Helen Keller witnessed inequality, so she (very publicly) became a feminist, a socialist, a pacifist, and a supporter of the NAACP. The FBI began to keep a file on her. She had become an independent thinker, and she dared to speak her mind. She had become dangerous.

Initially, when the world seemed to turn around and berate her, Keller stood her ground. However, when the American Foundation for the Blind told her that she had to either stop speaking so politically or end her work with the organization, she changed her mind. Keller's work with the organization had become important to her, so she made the decision to cease airing her famously radical beliefs in order to benefit her cause.

I admire Keller for daring to share her radical (and unpopular) worldview with a society that already didn't welcome the opinions of women, and I became upset when I learned of Keller's efforts to suppress her opinions. If I could speak to Keller, I would ask her if going "back in the closet" (vocally) later in her career brought back memories of being unable to communicate as a child. I would hope that she would reassure me that she made the decision from a place of power.

About the Author: My name is Bianca Rico. I live in Berkeley, California, and attend Albany High School. Empowering women is one of my life goals. Others include becoming more involved with nonprofit organizations and traveling the world.

High School Attended: Albany High School, Albany, CA

The Process: The process of writing this essay was difficult for me. I wrote several essays before this one about different women, but they just weren't quite right. I discovered my admiration for Helen Keller during a conversation that I was having with my mom and grew to love her more and more as I researched her for this essay.

Acknowledgments: Gabrielle Glancy.

MUDVILLE

Bianca Rico

I used to be the mayor of Mudville—a small town nestled among the roots of a dying tree in the yard of my elementary school. My own little utopia began when two friends and I were playing outside after a particularly intense rain and were delighted to find the ease at which the drying mud in the schoolyard could be shaped into perfect spheres. By the end of that wet recess, our orbs of wet dirt had evolved into tiny beings—each no bigger than one inch in diameter—with names and personalities. Soon, more and more girls joined in on our mud game, and we began to create a tiny, fairy-like city in the ground for our mud creations.

Mudville was a democracy—or so I wanted to believe. As founder, I called town meetings every day at lunch to vote on issues surrounding food supply, the latest materials that had come into bloom, and of course, our defenses against the enemy (boys).

At the time, I saw my rise to power as a natural sequence of events. At the first town meeting, when we set up the rules of Mudville, I suggested that there be a leader to keep the town organized. As I described the mayor's various duties, I markedly pointed out the "coincidental" fact that I had already begun to "perfectly" carry out some of the future mayor's roles (if I had to say so myself!). Unfortunately, I realized (and must now confess) that under my reign, Mudville may have been more of a dictatorship than a democracy.

My first abuse of power occurred when I took control of the town's aesthetics. I rearranged my friends' mudball houses when they were absent from school. Every time a friend took note of a slight difference in her house, I passed it off as an act of nature.

"The wind was vicious last night," or "There must have been a rain."

Once I tasted the glory of control, my appetite for power expanded, so I began to skew Mudville's "voting" processes by making up my own rules about each election.

"Anybody who doesn't share her dessert with the mayor today can't vote," I could be heard proclaiming. At the height of my tyrannical power-high—by this time, I was seven—I made the decision to control the population of Mudville by excluding one classmate, with whom I didn't get along, from participating in the town at all.

At the time, my second-grade self felt only a little uneasy about the way I was governing, but didn't quite recognize that I was exercising a dictatorship that cast a dismal shadow over the town. The moment that I realized the true nature of my governing style didn't actually come until my sophomore year of high school, when I was walking out of a class in which I had learned about dictatorships. I bumped into one of my previous Mudville friends. With dictatorships—and now Mudville—on my mind, my uneasy memories of the town suddenly made sense.

At the end of my sophomore year of high school, I had several opportunities to take on leadership positions in the various clubs that I was a part of, and I took those positions on with a new awareness. Now, I lead discussions with my school's Peer Help group and buildOn chapter by letting others talk, making sure that everyone's voice is heard, and making executive decisions only when necessary. My memories of playing with those little balls of mud at school have inspired me to want to influence people only in the most positive and equitable ways, but most important, they have ignited my passion for leadership and have helped me to realize that I am happiest when I am not basking in the glory of my power but, rather, guiding others toward their own dreams.

About the Author: My name is Bianca Rico. I live in Berkeley, California. My interests are education and climate change. My goals in life are to empower women and to work for nonprofit organizations.

High School Attended: Albany High School, Albany, CA

The Process: My mom and I were talking about my elementary school experience and when Mudville came up, we both realized that its story could make an interesting essay. Out of all of the college essays that I wrote, this one was the easiest. The words just flew out of my mind and onto the computer screen.

Acknowledgments: Gabrielle Glancy.

THE COLISEUM

Connor Bevan

Our unwavering belief in a cause so unlikely—a playoff run by one of baseball's most financially challenged teams—breathed life into a stadium and a city that were desperate for it. Watching shortstop Stephen Drew, a castoff and a spare part, yet so elemental to the enormous success of the A's, reminded me of everything I loved about Oakland and its coliseum. The rusty pipes in the ceiling, the cries of the vendors, the nooks and crannies of the antiquated pile of concrete— walking into Oakland's O.Co Coliseum is much like coming home. I kick back in the green seats and look out over the torn-up outfield grass. Nine exceptionally average ballplayers in white uniforms are succeeding in ways I never could have imagined.

As with the A's, the ballpark, located in a low-income, post-industrial neighborhood in one of the country's most problematic cities, is downtrodden, unsanitary, outdated, and ugly. Yet, no matter the exterior, inside the stadium resides a vibrant fan base and their improbably successful team. A collective, unifying hope radiates from the ballpark to the streets of Oakland. Despite the crime, mismanagement, and poverty, Oakland is still very much alive. Diversity, energy, and optimism power the city's thriving culture, and help give significance to the otherwise overlooked coliseum. Blessed with the fortune of growing up in an environment so enriching, I have interacted and bonded with people from all walks of life through the medium of the derelict stadium. Silicon Valley upstarters mingle with wage workers in what can only be described as a true reflection of Oakland.

Baseball has been a constant throughout my life, and with the A's practically in my backyard, I've found solace and a second home within the monolithic borders of their stadium. In recent years, I've been burdened with the load of a student-athlete, the expectations of a demanding family, and a multitude of other commitments. But once my ticket is scanned and I'm through the turnstiles, my worries and stresses melt away. For nine innings, I'm free to meet new people, enjoy baseball, and pour my heart into the team I've grown up with. When I was a kid, the A's were my role models: I tried to walk and talk and swing like they did. Now the coliseum provides comfort through its deep familiarity and the nostalgic memories of the victories and defeats of seasons past.

The stranger on my right puts his arm around me as we wave our towels and scream during Verlander's windup. Our scrappy, ragtag, but relentless Oakland Athletics are down to their final three outs in the playoffs, facing the star-studded Detroit Tigers and their MVP pitcher. No matter the six-run deficit or the talent discrepancy between pitcher and batter, every single one of the 36,000 green-and-gold bleeding A's fans refuses to surrender hope. I stand, hand clenched around the yellow towel, chanting "Let's Go Oakland," just as I have my entire life.

The coliseum has ingrained the fighting spirit of the "little guy" in me. From watching this team—a testament to all that is good in baseball, and in Oakland—I've learned how resilience can overcome any obstacle. The A's give me hope for this beleaguered city and show me what's possible with unity and hard work. Wherever life may take me, the Oakland Coliseum is, and always will be, my home.

About the Author: My name is Connor Bevan. I hail from Alameda, CA, an island suburb of Oakland. I am pursuing a career in either politics or economics.

High School Attended: Alameda High School, Alameda, CA

The Process: I began this essay in July, when, apart from a job in the mornings, baseball dominated my life. For a fleeting moment, the Oakland A's were the best team in the game; the team I had obsessed over my entire life was finally in the spotlight. Thinking about what to write my main common app essay on, I turned to Oakland's stadium, with all its quirks and imperfections. After turning out about 1,900 words of jumbled thoughts and stories, my tutor helped me crop and polish the essay into one narrative.

Acknowledgments: A very special thanks to Gabby Glancy.

A WHOLE NEW BALANCE

Crystal Low

"Is it raining?" I shifted my gaze upward, only to have scalding beams of light practically sizzle my corneas. My eyes darted toward the cement; there was not a single drop of water on the ground. I then realized that the "rain" I felt was just the sweat pouring down my back.

Summer. The fashion was hot, the air was hot, and I was hot. Yet it wasn't just the toasty temperature that made me exude liquid like a squeezed sponge. It was also because of what stood before me—a four-wheeled wooden deathtrap of a longboard that would ensure some brutal injury.

I recalled all of the instructions: right foot first, left foot back, and whole body forward. I also recalled that as a lefty, the opposite stance would be more suitable for me. But right when I began to change position, I felt my hands jerked forward.

I couldn't help but wonder why I was friends with the two grinning faces turned toward me—especially since they were dragging me around like a ragdoll. They glided down empty streets and concaved sidewalks, all the while roaring with laughter. I, on the other hand, incessantly screeched at the top of my lungs and clung to their hands for dear life. Unfortunately, my damp palms made said clinging rather difficult, and I inevitably lost grip.

Horror swallowed me whole, and I prayed for the first time in years. I was certain that I'd either end up as a pile of run-over mush, or as a brain-dead vegetable. But in the midst of my preparation for the worst, I noticed my feet were still grounded in a stable fashion. Still trembling, I began to realize that I was just fine.

It changed me. That day was certainly traumatizing, but I embrace it wholeheartedly. I experienced a newfound courage, and it permanently altered my perspective on life. Up until that point I've never truly felt anything other than weakness and insecurity; I was always that kid who was afraid of everything—even my own shadow.

At last, I understood that constantly avoiding risk would only keep a person static. Taking some chances, however, would be necessary in order to develop as a human being. I stepped out of my comfort zone and had become driven to overstep my limits, positively influencing my actions for the remainder of my life. Now as an ambitious individual, I continuously challenge myself while leaving my weaknesses farther and farther behind.

As I peer into the future, I see myself spending and enjoying many productive years enrolled at Clark University. Now more inclined to transcend my self-proclaimed boundaries, I plan to participate in the close and lively community offered, despite my social anxiety. I plan to challenge myself with the vast multitude of classes offered, regardless of how intimidating they appear. And with the help of Clark University, I will ultimately develop into the person that I've always dreamed I'd be.

About the Author: My name is Crystal Low. I've always lived in the quiet city of Ridgewood, NY. However, I aspire to one day leave, become more familiar with the rest of the world, and achieve ultimate happiness in my life.

High School Attended: New Explorations into Science, Technology, and Math, New York, NY

The Process: "Please recall and write about a defining experience you have had—it could be an achievement which has given you exceptional pride, an event that served as a turning point in your life, or something that in some way illuminates who you are as a person. Tell us how this experience has shaped your goals and expectations for your college years at Clark. (500 words maximum)" At first, I was at a loss about what I should write. Every idea I had seemed difficult to talk about, and I was at the point where I wanted to give up. I mustered all of my energy to focus for a few hours, really thinking about my life in the past two years. Yet, I still couldn't come up with anything. It was only after my mother demanded that I to go to Elmhurst and buy groceries that I realized what really influenced my life, and what I really wanted to write about. I was going to write about longboarding—my coping mechanism, my method of transportation, and my life's catalyst.

Acknowledgments: I'd like to thank my English composition and literature teacher, Lindsey Palmer, for helping me overcome my writer's block and for helping me gain confidence in my writing.

There Are Cows in the Story

Olivia Sterling-Maisel

"I'm hungry," I said.

That's when the cows emerged. They came trampling out of the bushes, all six of them very annoyed and very pregnant. Will shrieked and scrambled up a tree.

"What's wrong?"

"I'm afraid of cows."

And that's when the calves came out of the bushes.

The four of us had decided to go rafting in what became a very large flood and wound up stranded on an island.

I have always wanted to ride a cow, so I worked up my courage to approach one of the moms. Just as I tried to hop on her back, she decided to take a nap. After a few attempts to rouse her, I settled down, too. I woke up to one of the babies licking my face.

When we were finally able to swim back, we discovered a taco truck. After not eating for two days, the taco was incredible. Then I paused.

"Guys, look what we're eating!"

Following my gaze to the ground beef filling our tacos, Julian said, "You mean who we're eating."

I thought about the cows on the island and we all put down our tacos.

"That's the only thing that has ever stopped me from finishing a taco," Connor said.

We cast the tacos aside and walked back home. The moral of the story is that in the most unexpected circumstances, amid floods, rogue rafts, and pregnant cows, with a sense of play, there's always a "taco truck" at the end of the tunnel.

About the Author: My name is Olivia Sterling-Maisel and I have lived all my life in Berkeley, California. I am super excited to be attending Carleton this fall, and can't wait to join this amazing community.

High School Attended: Berkeley High School, Berkeley, CA

The Process: I started by writing free writes and then I would go back and edit and cut down my thoughts until I had a cohesive essay.

Acknowledgments: Thank you, Gabby, for looking at too many versions of this essay to count, and for your wise advice to "always roll out the dough before you cut the cookies." Thanks, Cec, for editing this essay down more than we ever thought would be possible, and to my parents for letting me write an essay about cows.

WHY CARLETON

Olivia Sterling-Maisel

I spent my five-year-old days playing the "Why" game, asking questions until there were no more answers. While this curiosity takes a different form in my life now, my eagerness for knowledge is still growing: Every answer simply reveals how much more there is to learn. I ask a lot of questions, so I get a lot of answers. When I asked myself what I want in a college, the answer came more easily than I thought.

I first heard about Carleton at a college fair, and in those ten minutes, the admissions officer captured my dreams for the next four years and put them all together in a small college in Minnesota. I had to find out more, so in the spring I visited. That was it for me. I didn't need to look any further to find an environment where students are open-minded and down to earth, where they love to learn and will give up their notes to let a prospective student (me!) follow along. I found a place where students don't take themselves too seriously, have silent dance parties, and play broomball at all hours of the night, a place where everyone has a voice and something important to say.

People ask me what job I want to have, what major I will choose, and what passions I will follow. I do not yet know the answers to these questions, but I have a strong sense that Carleton is where I will find them, and myself.

What empowers me is action, but before one acts, one must have knowledge. In my freshman year, a friend transferred out of our class because she was the only African American in it. I didn't see why it mattered. As time passed, the discrimination that I witnessed, both implicit and explicit, made me aware of the white privilege I had taken for granted. While in my ignorance I had good intentions, I now see the situation more clearly—a knowledge that both scares and empowers me. Change, however, does not happen without action. Recently, my youth activism group decided to bring in experts to speak to us on the subject of racism. Seeing the difference that increased awareness brought to us showed me the importance of having knowledge, and the power of knowing what to do with it.

About the Author: My name is Olivia Sterling-Maisel, and I have lived all my life in Berkeley, California. I am super excited to be attending Carleton this fall and can't wait to join this amazing community.

High School Attended: Berkeley High School, Berkeley, CA

The Process: This essay was one of the easiest I had to write. I already knew exactly what I loved about Carleton and so, unlike a lot of my other essays, I just sat down and wrote it.

Acknowledgments: Thank you, Gabby, for all your patience with this essay.

There's No Place like Camp Tuolumne

Olivia Sterling-Maisel

Within seconds, ash started raining down all around us, in the body of utterly flawless leaves. But that's not what caught my attention. The sun had turned into a fiery red inferno that looked like the menacing eye of a mysterious beast, watching idly as everything around it slowly burned. That eerie sight snapped us back to reality. We ran the fastest I have ever run into the main circle, usually the hub of activity, where we saw Lily, a staff member, talking furiously into a walkie talkie.

"You need to leave. Everyone's already been evacuated. If your parents aren't here, I'll take you myself. Now go get packed. Quickly!"

Moments before, I had taken my eyes off the ground for the first time since the beginning of our hike, expecting to see the familiar outline of trees in the distance framed against a brilliant blue sky.

"Max, do you see what I see?"

I searched for the playful smile that never seemed to leave his lips; the absence of it told me more than words ever could. Time stopped as we stood there looking at each other, frozen in place with the realization that something was very, very wrong. It was 1 p.m., the peak of our beautiful, summery Tuolumne day, but the sky was gray. It was a dark, thick and threatening gray that mixed with the reddish hue emanating from all around, a smoky cage that enclosed us. I held out my hand and Max grabbed it and pulled me close, as if we could protect each other from what was to come. Just then, a single leaf fell from the sky, a skeleton, every vein perfectly preserved in the ash of what had once been something vibrant and alive. That was my last year at Tuolumne. The camp burned to the ground hours later.

In all my years there, Tuolumne never lost its magic for me. I never got too old to sprint up the hill in search of my favorite cabin, or shriek and laugh as I jumped off Beaverhead, a rock in the swimming hole aptly named for its distinctive shape. At Tuolumne, I was able to return to the best parts of my kindergarten self. I could make a best friend before the end of the day, be impulsive and carefree. I could wander into the forest and come back hours later without having to worry about work to do or tests to study for. I was someone at peace. As I grew older, this became even more important to me. Tuolumne became my refuge, the place that I would close my eyes and think about when the world at home got too overwhelming.

The sum total of my seventeen years is wrapped up in the essence of Tuolumne, in every makeshift cabin, beaten path, melted ice cream snack. The physical place is no longer standing, but the person it helped me become is still going strong, as are the relationships that I built there. So even though camp is not physically there anymore, its spirit is alive in me and always will be.

But more than that, I have carried on the Tuolumne spirit and translated it into everything I do, and I am proud of how I have let it change me, both in its presence and absence. With the campsite reduced to ashes, I have found more meaning in the community that is still standing. My best friends and I can still go and watch the camp play with the same people we love, even if we are sitting on plastic instead of wood. We still sing the camp songs and go on adventures. We don't need the camp to be best friends. Through all of our late-night conversations, rafting catastrophes, and month-long trips to Europe, I realize that wherever I am, I can be carefree or whimsical or adventurous and at peace.

About the Author: My name is Olivia Sterling-Maisel, and I've lived in Berkeley, California, all my life. I am super excited to attend Carleton College this fall, and join their amazing community.

High School Attended: Berkeley High School, Berkeley, CA

The Process: This is the essay I spent the most time on. I started with many pages of material without a whole lot of focus, and throughout the months I was able to edit it down to this.

Acknowledgments: Thank you, Gabby, for teaching me so many valuable things about writing essays, and thanks to my family for all your support and help editing.

INVISIBLE

Madison Kahn

analogy

You are an airline pilot on the runway preparing for your very first flight. Think of the responsibility, the trust your passengers are placing in you, and the anticipation of pulling back on the throttle. That pilot was me after being appointed stage manager for the musical *Bat Boy*. Twenty-one songs, one hundred fifty light cues, eleven strobe lights, and fog every other scene all require the complete commitment of the tech crew, the actors, and the stage manager.

"Your goal is to be invisible," was the first piece of advice given to me by the assistant director. "If you do your job well, no one will even know you are there." My heart pounded in my head as I realized the success of *leadership* the show had been placed in my hands. The audience would never see me, but a single mistake would expose the backstage world. How on earth was I going to do this? *cool imagery*

Eerie green, purple, and orange lighting splattered the stage as I furiously wrote down light cues. The makeup crew huddled around Bat Boy, whose nose and ears kept slipping off his sweaty face. Someone from props sprinted across the stage dripping in what I hoped was fake *humor* blood. Theater works like a machine, with each part relying on every other, but sometimes, the machine malfunctions. Sawyer, a strawberry blonde crew-cutted sophomore, ambled on stage pushing the wheelchair a verse too early. The light illuminated his face perfectly as he understood his mistake, spun around, and hurried offstage. I was powerless and paralyzed as the sound booth fell silent. Static on headset. Then,

hella analogies

231

nothing is perfect

together, all of us exploded into laughter. As stage manager, I run the machine, but in theater, some parts have minds of their own.

"You can't leave in the middle of dress rehearsal. We need spotlight in two pages. You've *got* to stay here!" My voice ignited as the crew member in charge of spotlight protested. Opening night was two days away, and she wanted to run up to the local sandwich shop? What was she thinking? My voice had taken on a tone I did not recognize, a tone crucial for my position. My spine straightened against the back of the chair, my new posture reflecting the unexpected voice. I grappled with the idea of giving orders to my friends and classmates, many of whom I had known for years. Would they see or treat me differently outside of the show? Striking the perfect balance between stage manager and friend required my constant attention. Later, the crew member in charge of spotlight admitted to me that I made an excellent stage manager. I called my cues with a newfound confidence as I now eagerly awaited opening night.

With pitchforks thrown aside; fake bats soaring off into the distance; and a final, shadowy musical number, the actors formed a semicircle and grasped hands. The audience erupted, rose to their feet, and cheered for the actors. "I'm invisible!" Adrenaline coursed through my veins as I said my final lines: "Standby light cue #770. Go. Standby house lights up. Go."

I melted back into my chair as everyone let go of the machine. Theater is not just for the actors; it is a collective experience that extends through wired headsets, snakes behind velvet curtains, and pulses all the way up into the sound box. I can still hear the songs, still feel the headset pressed against my ears, and still see the play flying by. I like the view a lot better from the air. So bring it on: jets, cargo planes, hydroplanes, helicopters, hot air balloons, maybe even a blimp. I want to fly them all.

About the Author: My name is Madison Kahn. I plan on pursuing my passions in the writing and theater realms. I currently live in Los Angeles with my family and two dogs.

High School Attended: Brentwood School, Los Angeles, CA

The Process: "Some students have a background or story that is so central to their identity that they believe their application would be incomplete without it. If this sounds like you, then please share your story." My final essay contains only two sentences from my first draft. Coming up with my topic was simple, but accurately depicting the emotions I felt during my first real tech week as a stage manager was no easy flight. I started out with a free write, describing every detail. I then fell into a routine where I rewrote and cut the extraneous. I wanted the essay to be concise and poignant. I read the drafts out loud and printed them out to mark up with color-coded highlighters. After sixteen drafts, I read my final copy one last time and knew it was my best work.

Acknowledgments: I would like to thank my college counselor, Ms. Arora, my dad, and my seventh grade English teacher, Mr. Trivas. All three pushed me to pursue my passions and write an honest essay.

ENGINEERING MY FUTURE

Jennifer Kracha

The integral of negative time multiplied with danger comes out to equal stress, and through that stress comes strength and growth. Being a part of a family crippled by the disease of one member has forced me to become someone whom I never thought was possible: strong, independent, and able to stand on my own. Having a diabetic older sister has always meant that I have to be prepared for the most devastating circumstances. My necessary perpetual state of being prepared was made evident just this past summer when I was home alone for the week with my sister while my parents were out of the state. No book, no class, and certainly no person could have ever prepared me for walking in to my sister's room, seeing her on the edge of death. Her eyes almost rolled completely back in her head, her mouth slack, and her limbs twitching with the last evidence of life left in her body as she stopped seizing and headed toward a permanent coma. I had no time and no help, and I was forced out of my role as an observer and into the person in charge. Being put into a life and death situation led me to realize the importance of remaining the type of person who didn't crumble in a stressful situation, but rather to face it with strength that I hadn't even had the chance to uncover until that moment.

With the addition of the square root of failure added to observance, I have only expanded my ability to see where I can improve. Growing up under the shadow of two older siblings, I scrutinized their every decision and move. While they chose actions that affected them negatively, I saw every mistake that they made and was able to learn from them. From watching their failures, I was able to exceed their accomplishments, which only set the bar higher and higher for what was expected from me. What came from the square root of the sum of failure and observance was the suffocating feeling of pressure; pressure to get dean's list every semester, pressure to stay on the right academic and social track, and pressure to not make a single mistake. However, the pressure only motivated me to prove that I could achieve anything to a higher level than was expected. I was able to find the root of observing failure, that I witnessed in my siblings as well as myself, equal to pressure to be the ideal kid to my parents and teachers. This pressure only fueled my desire to step up and go one step further with everything I do, whether it be taking one of the hardest AP courses at my high school, AP physics, or pushing myself to take chances academically, socially, and mentally.

The change in my passion for physics and a career in engineering can be calculated by my initial passion from the beginning of junior year subtracted from my current and final passion. I was reluctant to embark in physics instead of a familiar science like biology or chemistry at the start of my junior year. Regardless of the increasing difficulty in the class, I became more and more enamored with the concepts and applications to the real world that seemed to come exponentially as the year went on in physics. While my initial passion for the subject came infinitely close to zero, my final passion for physics has soared, causing the change in my passion for engineering to be significant.

About the Author: My name is Jennifer Kracha. I intend to become a successful engineer to help solve large-scale dilemmas.

High School Attended: Peak to Peak Charter School, Lafayette, CO

The Process: I was initially inspired by my physics teacher to derive an equation that would accurately represent who I was and certain events that had shaped me into who I am today. Once I figured out a correct equation, I was able to detail each component of the equation into separate anecdotes. I chose to simplify the equation in the end to show how the most complicated of circumstances can become simple if you analyze them.

Acknowledgments: My AP physics teacher, Mr. Allen Hankla, gave me the inspiration to use an equation to describe myself. My outstanding English teacher, Ms. Kristie Letter, helped me through the writing process as well as molding my paper into its final form.

FINDING THE WOMAN INSIDE

Stephen Lee

[handwritten annotations: "LTWs books should stop misgendering her"; "I love reading this stuff"]

On my college application, it will say Stephen Lee, but secretly I have always really been Lauren; it simply took me a little while to realize.

As early as elementary school, I always felt that I was somehow different from my peers. I was too young to understand a concept like gender dysphoria, but in those pre-adolescent years, I always interacted with and felt more comfortable around girls, and as I progressed into puberty, I found it increasingly difficult to join my peers in embracing rowdy teenage masculinity.

I was raised in a very heteronormative, conservative community, and there is still a lot of ignorance surrounding transgender individuals, particularly among the older generation. My parents are social conservatives, sharing those traditional values. Homosexuality is not viewed favorably, and the transgender community is not discussed at all. *[handwritten: "no visibility"]*

It is very difficult to put into words what it is like to be transgender, or how one knows that one is trans; it is even harder for people who are not transgender to understand, because this feeling is not something that they could have experienced. For years, I felt that the male identity that I had constructed and my inner female were playing a game of tug of war over my future. I struggled to accept the reality that I was transgender, and I went through stages of feeling "male" at times, and "female" at others. Lacking a concrete identity exhausted me and left me indecisive, with an even greater lack of self-confidence.

I began to see a therapist, and while we discussed all of my thoughts, feelings, and fears, most of our time has been spent talking about my gender and sexuality. I began therapy in a state of flux, identifying as two-spirit, because I still saw male and female traits, but over time, I realized that I could never envision a future for myself in which I was truly happy as a man. Conversely, though shaky and ill-defined, I could see a future as a woman that would bring me a feeling of empowerment. It was then that I admitted to myself what I had known all along: I wanted to cast off the chains of my male identity and proudly live my life as a woman. I cannot fully describe how that revelation felt, but the best that I can do is that I had a feeling of being right, of being complete.

I have not yet begun to live this life publicly, but I have taken steps toward doing so. I have come out to my closest friends and have leaned heavily upon the support of the LGBTQ community, in which I have become increasingly active. I've joined organizations like GSA and community hotline, and those safe places have given me the opportunity to explore the person that I truly am, and have always secretly been. The moment that I am in their presence is like turning on a light bulb after wandering in the dark. A mask is lifted, my laugh is no longer restrained, and I can simply be.

Accepting my true identity has given me the tools to develop a deep personal intellectualism, driven me to study gender/sexuality studies, and prompted me to become an activist for LGBTQ rights, dedicating my life to combating intolerance and ignorance. More importantly, it has allowed me to be comfortable with who I am.

I still have a long way to go. I have only begun to confront my parents about transitioning, and I've yet to decide if sexual reassignment surgery is in my future. I am taking steps toward eventual hormone replacement therapy and creating tentative timelines for physical and social transitioning. I plan to begin this arduous but liberating journey during the summer before matriculation. College represents the opportunity to explore these endless possibilities, while growing into the woman that I was always meant to be.

About the Author: My name is Stephen Lee. I have resided in the coastal Californian community of Palos Verdes all of my life. I intend to study philosophy and eventually become a professor, or go into law and work as either an attorney or maybe even become a Supreme Court justice one day.

High School Attended: Palos Verdes High School, Palos Verdes Estates, CA

The Process: Writing this essay required coming to terms with and ultimately accepting my identity. At first, I wrote a draft that was stylistically very sound, but the details were lacking. I proceeded to write out a narrative with all the details of my struggle with gender identity and the emotions that accompanied it. Then, I began to blend the two together to create the synthesis that you see as my completed essay.

Acknowledgments: N/A.

TO MY FELLOW EMMAS

Emma Hunt

Nobody wants to be a clone.

Human beings are naturally inclined to differentiate themselves from others, to emphasize their own unique traits. We are told from a very young age that you should always be yourself, no matter what people say. Everyone is different, and those differences are important, so embrace them.

There's just one problem with this: I'm not really unique.

Shortly before I was born, my parents chose to switch my intended name from Julia to Emma, and my mom has always said that she changed it because she didn't know anyone with that name. She thought it was unique. But apparently many other mothers had the same idea, because ever since I was born my name has grown steadily in popularity. In 2014, it was the second most popular name in the English-speaking world. Over the course of my life I've met dozens of people named Emma—Emma Lukosy, Emma Arnold, Emma Tremblay, Emma Hasselbach. There's also celebrities like Emma Stone or Emma Watson. My friend Artem even knows a girl who has the exact same name as me, Emma Hunt.

So you can imagine, it's difficult to find a sense of self when your own name, the one thing that defines you as an individual, is similar to so many others'. And it's not like I have any particular dislike for my fellow Emmas. Some of them have actually been really great friends to me or are people whom I admire deeply. But you naturally feel a kind of ownership over your name. So when you introduce yourself to someone new and they immediately begin to associate you with the personality and traits of a different Emma, it can be frustrating.

This is why I've always been fascinated by the idea of a stage name. As someone who's hoping to go into the performing arts, it would certainly be appropriate for me to take on a different name to be credited with. Something special, that no one would relate to a different person. Maybe I'd be called something like Ruby and change my last name to Huntington. That way there would still be a bit of my old self present, but I would have a unique identifier for myself.

As I've grown older and looked into applying to various theatre programs at colleges around the country, I've considered this a lot. Should I change my name? Would it help me succeed later on? Would I still feel like myself? Or would it just be too confusing? I wasn't sure what I wanted to do. But after I thought about it for a while, I realized that I didn't want to go by a stage name. Despite all the negative connotations with being named Emma, I've always really liked my name. I think it's quite tasteful, and I love the way it sounds. When I really thought about it, I didn't want to be called something that wasn't my own name. Emma is who I am. I'm much more interested in being Emma than I am in being someone else, even if I have to share that with hundreds of people across the globe.

I was talking to my dad about this recently, and he mentioned that he'd always liked the name Emma because it reminded him of Emma Thompson, the famous British actress. At first I thought to myself, Great, another person who's just associated with my name. But I've always really loved Emma Thompson. She's a phenomenal actress and genuinely kind person, and I really look up to her. If she's one of the Emmas I get to share my name with, then I guess I'm okay with that.

About the Author: My name is Emma Hunt.

High School Attended: International Community School, Kirkland, WA

The Process: Once I knew that the essay was going to be about my name, I wrote and discarded several drafts where I explored my feelings about my name throughout the writing process. Once I had an idea I liked, the body and conclusion just kept flowing as I was writing, and I ended up keeping most of the latter half of that draft in the final essay.

Acknowledgments: Shout out to my AP lit teacher, Mr. Plank, for helping to make me the writer I am and encouraging me to get creative with this essay!

JESUS'S VACATION HOUSE

Jillian Rezen

As I walk out the door each morning, my mom reminds me that she loves me to J.V.H. and back because that is the farthest distance. It is farther than the span of my arms, all the way down the lane, and even farther than the moon and back. When I was a little girl, my mom would read the story *Guess How Much I Love You* to my brothers and me, and afterward we would try to imagine the greatest distance that illustrates the scope of our love. On a family road trip, we played our little game, and my brother called out with the confidence that he had won, that he loves us to heaven and back. After a few silent seconds of thought, my mom declared that she knew what was even farther. She reasoned that as vacation homes are farther than regular homes, Jesus's vacation house (J.V.H.) must be farther than heaven, and with that remark, the game was over. As a secular family, our conclusion was pretty ironic, but we happily stuck with it.

As I grew older, I would constantly ask my mom what was farther than Jesus's vacation house, farther than the stars, farther than everything we know. She would always say that she didn't know, but with my curiosity I would someday find out. Maybe I'd be an astrophysicist or a cosmologist. Ironically, I am pursuing a career in a field that some consider the opposite of science—theatre—but from my first exposure to it, I've always felt like a scientist.

At my first acting class, my teacher had me sit outside for five minutes, and afterward, write down everything I had seen, felt, heard, smelled, and even tasted. She taught me that one of the most important things for actors to do is observe. Because I was in the fifth grade, the only time I really consciously observed anything was in science class. The thought that I would use a scientific concept in a theatrical environment seemed quite peculiar to me, but as I continued taking classes I learned that science surprisingly has a very active presence in acting. I used parts of the scientific method during every lesson, such as observing, questioning, and analyzing a character's mind. The most exciting idea I learned when studying acting was that the depth of human emotions and thought was just as large as the cosmic realm I was curious about when I was young and that the exploration of it was just as fascinating.

I was honored to be accepted into the theater academy when I applied to my high school, but I continued to hold an interest in cosmology as well. I read books by Brian Greene and Bill Bryson and watched TED talks about the universe; I even wrote a play during my junior year about a mutual appreciation that grows between a cosmologist and a hippie artist on a late-night subway ride. When developing these characters, I began to understand and value the symbiotic relationship between the arts and sciences. This reminded me of the left-brain right-brain theory, in which left-brain people think logically and analytically, whereas right-brain people think creatively and emotionally. It would be assumed, by this theory, that scientists are left-brained and artists are right-brained, but the characters in my play prove that people are not nearly as rudimentary as this model. Scientists and artists do and must think logically as well as creatively to achieve success in their fields. Although I am pursuing a career in theater, I identify as a scientist as well, because I believe that the reach of those that can strike a balance between art and science, left- and right-brain thinking, logic and creativity, will always exceed their grasp.

About the Author: My name is Jillian Rezen and I live in Hillsdale, NJ.

High School Attended: I am currently a senior in high school at the Bergen County Academies, Hackensack, NJ, and I am pursuing theater in college at NYU Tisch School of the Arts.

The Process: While writing my essay, I was really nervous that it wouldn't be unique enough, and it would be just like everyone else's. I spent a really long time just trying to figure out what was an interesting topic or way to write my essay, but after a lot of different first drafts I decided to sit down and talk to my mom about it. We sat in my kitchen and she told me about what she thought I was going to grow up to be, and that became the basis of my essay.

Acknowledgments: Mother, theater teacher.

THE SHOW MUST GO ON

Katie Adams

Arthur Miller's words stare at me, mocking me, as I read them for the first time in the dim lighting of my school auditorium.

"He has lifted her, and kisses her now with great passion."

In the state of exaggerated disbelief I had regrettably sported many a time before, I turn to my castmate Jen. With my now sweaty upper lip, I let out a whimper. Thoughts race through my head, about how I don't deserve this, about the cruel audacity of Miller to give me such a fate, and about the fact that my grandmother will be subjected to watching this transpire. I have been cast as Elizabeth Proctor in my school's production of *The Crucible,* and the fiery kiss I have to share with my John Proctor has done less than enthuse me. This kid, whom I'll call Joe, is perhaps the exact opposite of the striking Daniel Day Lewis I had come to know and love from the movie adaptation. Joe is also younger than me and has an annoying habit of perpetually bragging about his job at Sears. Damn the phenomenal acting prowess that landed him this role!

Alas, I sink into my shallow fit of self-pity. Jen tries her best to comfort me in my time of distress. She reminds me of the unpleasantness of her stage kiss in last year's production, but I make some sort of quick whip back about Joe's detestable peach fuzz. The rest of rehearsal plays out normally despite my paramount misery, and I leave before it's dark. After I finish dropping off my castmates, I'm left with the risky fortune of being alone with my own thoughts. My stomach drops, but this time, not because I'm thinking about the kiss—I'm thinking about Joe. It occurs to me that he could have very well overheard me complaining about him and that I'm actually not really all that much better than him. Nothing separates me from him. His peach fuzz isn't disgusting; the fact that I can get so conceited and insensitive is.

My behavior can be rotten without me even realizing. I've crawled into my bed at night, with a warm body and a full belly, and let out a sigh because the school didn't call a snow day. Whenever I hear my manager say "for all intensive purposes," I smirk to myself and internally chastise her for her misunderstanding of the phrase. Every time the school asks for charity donations and I bring in a dollar, I beam for almost an hour, feeling like I'm Mother Teresa herself after feeding an entire destitute Indian village. If I was Joe, would I want to kiss me?

I needed my self-actualization that night. It's not okay for me to sit on a pretentious, hypocritical throne, pretending to love Woody Allen films. But the questions I asked myself didn't destroy me because I knew I was not alone. I was trying to rid myself of a behavior that was prevalent in most of my peers. In my parochial school, we were made to understand that we, the good, holy Christians, are the moral compass to the world. But I know we need work. And I recognize now that I'd probably be much happier if I looked for the good in others more often. That way, I can bring out the good in myself. So I'm trying to cut back on correcting people's grammar, to gossip less frequently, and to say "thank you" to my mom more. That being said, I'm still none too thrilled about this kiss, but we'll see how it goes.

About the Author: Katie Adams hails from Dearborn, Michigan and hopes to get a job doing what she loves while earning a lot of money. She's a real dreamer.

High School Attended: Divine Child High School, Dearborn, MI

The Process: I sat down and thought about what was most prevalent in my life at the moment, so I could write about something authentic. I was applying to college in the fall, like most students, so the fall play I was performing in was on my mind. I self-reflected until I had something meaningful to say and did my best to tell my story. I tried to make sure I had elements to my story that were unique and unlike other essays the admissions officers would be reading.

Acknowledgments: During my junior year, my librarian told me that admissions officers don't want to hear you boasting about how great of a person you are. I thought that was good advice.

THE GIRL WITH THE PAPER

Kayla Battles

Paper. It's thin and white. Comes in various shapes, colors, and sizes. On that paper are just ink smudges. When you think of it like that it sounds like a useless object, right? So why is it that paper with just smudges can dictate something as important as a child's education? As a child who can relate to this situation, I never really quite understood why either. Something that was designed to help students shouldn't be the very reason it is holding them back.

When I was in elementary school, I was a completely different person. She was called the girl with the paper: She was labeled an IEP to help her cope with the stress of school, and for the next eight years she had an extra teacher come in to help. There came a point when she didn't like the paper that followed her anymore. She then started studying more, worked on ways to relax in class, and stopped relying on the extra teachers to always catch her when she fell. At the end of eighth grade, she got an advanced pass on her standardized test and was able to handle the workload. Her mother and the paper girl decided then she would be okay without the extra help and forced the counselors to take off the IEP.

After arriving in high school, I became the person that I am today. A bird soaring through the sky, free to fly. I was determined to show not only my teachers but myself that I was able to handle my school work without getting upset or giving up. It's been a hard road. Procrastination, frustration, and laziness were the hardest things to get through, but I overcame them, becoming successful in school. College is all about having a heavy workload and getting through hard times. The skills I've learned, to show people that I am more than what is written on paper, is what I will bring with me to college.

Having the IEP is something I will never regret. It only sparked my interest in learning about how the human brain works. I now realize that mental illness isn't something a person can help or control. They were born that way and if they had a chance to be "normal" they would. I would like to study the behavior of criminals and study their thought process, testing if they are clinically insane or not. It is human understanding that allows us to see beyond a diagnosis and the person beyond the paper.

I will go above and beyond in college to be able to help others. We need to know that whatever is said on paper doesn't define anyone. I'd like to be one of the people to show them no matter what is wrong with someone, they can all be successful as long as they don't let anything hold them back.

About the Author: My name is Kayla Battles. I am a seventeen-year-old that lives in Brooklyn, New York. I would like to be a criminal investigator because I have always been interested in what makes a criminal break the law.

High School Attended: The Academy for Conservation and the Environment, Brooklyn, NY

The Process: It took me a few weeks to even figure out what I was going to write. I knew that I wanted to write something meaningful. I wanted to write something that colleges didn't know by just looking at my transcript. When I figured it out, writing the paper was easy.

Acknowledgments: I would like to thank my teachers for helping me edit the paper and Ms. Pushkin for helping me one on one with this paper and being someone I would always talk to.

NOT AS EASY AS IT LOOKS

Evan Shi

The heady rush and pride of standing there, in front of a crowd of over a thousand students and teachers at the Peace Memorial Park in Hiroshima, Japan, made all of the effort worth it. All of the long hours toiling over some minute detail of the circuit, all of the stress about parts shipping late or about systems not working, and all of the frantic planning and practice for the presentation itself came to fruition here on this auditorium stage. This was not a sightseeing tour. This was real. This was important.

My engineering mentor introduced a problem to me in the spring of sophomore year. A huge part of the dream of space colonization involves the harvest of asteroids for water, used to manufacture fuel and oxygen in space. The problem was the selection process. We needed to find the best way to detect asteroids viable for mining. In the end, my team and I, guided from afar by my mentor, found an interesting correlation in NASA data showing an inverse relationship between ferrous materials and water in asteroids. All we had to do was take some data and transmit it back to a computer for processing—more iron, less water. Easy, right?

The execution turned out to not be so easy. Challenges began to block us at every turn, and we all spent ever-increasing amounts of time after school in the lab. One solution to a problem would spawn even more problems, sometimes in unrelated areas. The setbacks piled up one after the other in an almost overwhelming flood. Something had to be done.

Frustrated, I eventually sought my mentor out to ask what could be done. At this point, we had not even been told that we would be presenting the results of our work in Japan (that more than pleasant surprise would come a little later), but I was determined to see this project through. The way things were going, our team would keep stumbling and eventually fall apart. The answer I found was so simple that it was a wonder none of us had thought of it before. We needed direction, to keep our goal firmly in sight, and we needed communication, to move from individuals working on separate parts to linked members of a real engineering team. I discussed this with everyone, and we made the slow changes the project needed to succeed, like careful documentation and regular meetings to keep everyone on the same page. After that, when solutions led to problems in an endless loop, we knew how to progress instead of simply floundering.

Sitting back several months later in my lab chair, solder fumes swirling toward the ceiling, I looked at our project with pride. A sleek purple circuit board, components neatly soldered to stylish copper traces, lay expectantly in front of me. Cheering as we watched the data stream in smoothly after months of constant issues and countless prototypes, we knew we had accomplished something amazing.

Engineering is about that shout of excitement when your creation comes alive. It is about the glowing feeling of accomplishment when a crowd of strangers cheers after your demonstration. But the true spirit of engineering is also in the minutia. It peeks its head out in the regular meetings with the team at the beginning of after-school sessions. It hides in the rigorous documentation that your team built up over the course of over half a year. It hovers closely around the crude diagrams drawn hastily on the whiteboard at the front of the room. This profound aspect of engineering has stayed with me long after my teammates and I stepped down from that stage halfway across the world. What I learned in the journey to that stage was the importance of focus and team communication—a lesson I will carry into the future in everything I strive to accomplish.

About the Author: My name is Evan Shi. I am an engineering student at the Bergen County Academies in northern New Jersey and plan to continue my study in college. After that, probably a career in engineering—but who knows?

High School Attended: Bergen County Academies, Hackensack, NJ

The Process: Typed up at around 1 a.m. during a school-sponsored trip to Lehigh University in June for a college admissions prep course. Revised based on feedback from the admissions officers there, and then revised over the summer. Slight tweaks were made based on comments from two of my old English teachers to transform it into the beast it is today.

Acknowledgments: Jake Talmage, Linda Campbell, Amanda Calcetas, David Wilson, Patricia DiAmico-King.

MIGHTY MINNOW

Leila Schneider

"Come on! Really? Yoga music?" a fellow coach teases. I can barely hear over the clamor. Even in my third summer coaching kindergarten swimmers, I am still taken aback by their boundless energy. Yoga music sounds like a perfect antidote.

"Put your hands on the floor," I say. "We're doing downward dog!"

Determined to bring order to the situation, I assume the role of yoga instructor, putting both hands and feet on the floor in an upside-down V. The kids start laughing. Then, silence. As I look backward through my legs, I see thirty little bodies following my lead. Like clockwork, each child, hair still dripping from swim practice, is struggling to keep his or her balance. Only music and infectious giggles surround me. As we move through our flow, the swimmers are intrigued by every pose. Adults look on, shocked and delighted by the sudden hush.

Just eight years ago, I, too, was a little swimmer running from the pool, ecstatic to be with the coaches for after-practice fun. Swim team was my home during summers growing up, and my love for swimming turned into a year-round passion. Now as summer team coach, I am immersed in the distinct smell of sunscreen and new latex caps, reminiscent of my early years at the pool. My role has changed. I'm an orchestrator of the team itself.

A window opens on the interval between the child I was and my young adult self. As I catch a glimpse of that younger me, I can see the metamorphosis. Just like my swimmers, I was once too consumed with negotiating each moment to see the big picture. So how did I evolve from being one of these young swimmers to the role model I am now?

My first year on the team, at age six, I was in a group called Mighty Minnows, named for the bursting energy inside our animated bodies. I paddled wildly down the pool, kicking with all my might, but barely moving forward. As an air-breathing human in a liquid environment, I had to become an amphibian. With countless practices and words of encouragement, I gained control and autonomy.

As my limbs grew, so did my attention to detail: where to put—and not put—my arms in the water, how to use my hands as paddles, my feet as fins. Steadily, my wild movements became self-directed. Practice, trial and error, until I found a way to glide effortlessly through the glassy blue. I was no longer splashing around in the shallow end, but navigating deeper waters, allowing my muscle memory to carry me forward—setting and achieving goals only previously imagined. Now I am the motivating force peering over the pool deck at my own minnows who are taking my cues through their foggy, goggled eyes.

Being a coach confers on me the responsibility of becoming a temporary buoy in the middle of the pool, a way station for tired legs. After sufficient rest and a quick pep talk, I am the wall they can push off of. On the deck, I become the jungle gym, as young swimmers beg for me to lift them skyward in backward somersaults. My supervisor, my fellow swimmers, and my own mighty minnows can count on me, and within the community that fostered my love for being a part of a swim family, I am now team yogi, team player, and team leader. No longer a tadpole, I emerge from the pool fully formed.

About the Author: My name is Leila Schneider. I live in the San Francisco Bay Area and hope to study cognitive science in college, and work with people.

High School Attended: Crystal Springs Uplands School, Hillsborough, CA

The Process: I was inspired by a revealing moment during my coaching experience last summer and began to put it down on paper. I free-wrote, and then stood back several times to examine it with new eyes and kept trying to find the most direct ways to express the feelings and sensations I had.

Acknowledgments: Gabrielle Glancy helped me identify what I was really trying to say. I learned so much about writing from her that applies far beyond college applications.

WORLD OF WORDS

Gaynor Norcott

I worry sometimes that, as a story, my life's overarching plot isn't truly relatable. That is to say, a lot of things don't come very easily to me: I'm not particularly accomplished at any instrument, I'm not the funniest guy you will meet, no sport more complex than Frisbee works with my uncoordinated body, and almost any other skill set requires some type of talent that I lack. The only thing that has ever appealed to my particular set of abilities is writing, which is to say that my words are the most important thing about me.

Words have always been my passion, ever since I was quite small. My family reminds me often of the many times I would, before I could even speak, yell and wave to people across rooms, attempting to get their attention. As I began to get a stronger handle on the English language, as many who grow up in English-speaking households do, and began to devour books at unnatural speeds, this need to communicate blossomed into a rapid-fire diction. I spoke like I had an urgent message, letting the words flow out in bursts and streams. I never stopped talking, and I refused to let go of my newfound love of endlessly speaking to those around me. I spoke and I loved it.

I came to rely on the words as a form of consistency, something that the rest of my life lacked. My father, being self-employed and constantly looking for new ways to put food on the table, led my mother, my three brothers, and me on a seemingly endless road trip, moving every few months or years, never getting too attached to any one place. While we made many friends and made great memories, nothing was truly constant. I loved the words, if only partly because they were always there.

I never stopped loving words, but the world I lived in wasn't as fond of letting me speak as I was. As I progressed through elementary and middle school, it was the apparent thought of my teachers and peers that I needed to be "taught a lesson about when to speak." My third-grade music teacher decided that, if I was not singing, I was not to open my mouth in his classroom. In fifth grade, the tall boy said I talked too much and punched me in the stomach. In seventh grade, my English teacher told me that English was for writing, not for talking. My world and my words were not compatible.

So, in order to avoid persecution from my surroundings, I transferred my love of words to a quieter medium: writing. The characters in my stories were always like me: capable of something special, but never extraordinary enough for the world around them to believe in them. I found my escape from the silence by creating the loudest, boldest stories I could imagine, filled with the adventures and excitement that my reality left me craving. Through this, I told people my story, and I discovered that the easiest way to get people to listen was by making them read.

My life progressed intensely from there as I began to express myself through written word. My family settled in a house in Kingfield, Maine, where I am writing this essay. I was accepted to and started attending the Maine School of Science and Mathematics, where I began taking advanced classes and making some of the most amazing friendships of my life. My youngest brother was born, raising our family's number to six. I was able to work through some of my hardest times by turning my writing ability to slam poetry, using my words to convey my thoughts and emotions surrounding the themes that plagued my psyche, such as my family's financial situation, mental illness, and my own experiences with sexual assault and gender stereotyping. I learned to use my words to help myself and others, writing not for escape, but for expression.

What I have found about growing up as a lover of words and an aspiring writer is that words will permeate every speck of your being. As a writer, I find myself focusing much more on the small aspects of my experiences and the individual characters and story arcs that populate my life. I've become more appreciative of the journey, rather than just focusing on the destination. I am more personable, and yet find myself with an ever-growing ability to balance this acceptance with my own values. I wish to change the lives of those who hear the words I have to say and read those that I write and to let others into my world of words, if only for the length of the story.

About the Author: Gaynor Norcott talks far too much, but he hopes that one day his love of words will lead him toward a better life. Though he has lived in many places, he currently resides in Kingfield, a town in rural Maine whose citizens do not take kindly to strangers, and attends the Maine School of Science and Mathematics, a school in a place that is, seemingly impossibly, more rural than his hometown.

High School Attended: Maine School of Science and Mathematics, Limestone, ME

The Process: I decided my best bet for college was to be completely honest with any college I could be accepted to. After all, why would I want to attend any college that wanted me to attend based off of a lie? So, I decided to tell them about what truly mattered to me: words. I told them my history, my plans for the future, and more about who I am as a person, while stressing that it is all eternally connected to words.

Acknowledgments: My family, for letting me talk even when I should have been quiet. Mike McCartney, for teaching me how to use my words for the betterment of both myself and others. Sarah "Ms. Wag" Goletz, for being my "adoptive mother" and for teaching me that the things I kept inside were more important than the world told me. And to all of the mean peers and abusive adults who tried their hardest to put me down: I hope that you can one day let go of the things that haunt you, just as I let go of you.

MIND, HANDS, AND VALUES

Irene Sakson

When I exited U.S. History with a 76-page Word document comprising my textbook reading notes, my friends were astonished, wishing they had worked as hard. To the contrary, I found myself quite uncomfortable, even ashamed: I wouldn't have wished my course of action on anyone. My colossal document stared me down with accusing eyes. I never thought "doing my best" would be my downfall.

Ever since I can remember, I have worked diligently in school, not because I am a perfectionist, but because delving deeply into my studies allows me to engage with my professors and peers on a level of mutual respect. However, upon entering high school, I found that being a good student had become a full-time job. I was crushed by the realization that I couldn't continue the activities I loved if I maintained this level of work. Success in school became an increasingly large part of my identity as I became reliant on my own continued performance, fearing I would fail those around me if I didn't perpetually present my best work. Although I continued to advocate exploration and self-discovery among friends, I became afraid of trying new things myself. My personal standards were in direct conflict with the values I held most dear, and I was confused and contrite.

Disillusioned with my own habits, I strove to reconnect with my passion for learning and exploration. When summer arrived, I wound up at the Bush Theater Department constructing the set for *A Midsummer Night's Dream*. My work at the theater was liberating. Our set designer recognized my bizarre affinity for power tools and brought me projects that confounded him. I loved brainstorming wild ideas together and executing them to solve problems. This creativity and innovation contrasted greatly with the isolating overwork I had subjected myself to, and I was elated and inspired.

One day, another technician and I were tasked with cutting driftwood pieces to exact lengths of six inches. The project required the blade of an enormously large chop saw to be within those same six inches of my hands. Despite my usual ease around the saw, I was nervous. However, for each particularly small piece of wood that made my body tense, my partner soothed my nerves by guiding the saw extra carefully and delicately. Without speaking a word, we had fallen into rhythm with each other. By the time the workshop was so full of smoke and sawdust that we put "Keep Out" signs on the doors, we had developed an unparalleled trust in one another.

Reflecting on my experience at the theater in contrast to the end of the school year, I realized I had lost my love of learning for learning's sake, and this felt like the greatest failure of all. My curiosity motivated me to work hard, but my fear of letting people down disengaged me from my work so the hours I spent were no longer fulfilling. The visceral discomfort of working for the wrong reasons had sucked the joy out of learning and out of me. I fought to earn good grades, to foster beautiful friendships, and to help others, but I had forgotten to fight for myself. At the theater, I became reacquainted with how partnership and mutual effort sustain and fulfill me. Although this internal change may not be instantly evident, since I still work diligently, it has restored my delight in all that I do. Instead of needlessly studying material I am comfortable with, I choose to take a walk with a friend to dive into conversation that inspires me and grounds me in my surroundings once more. Refreshed, I can refocus, to take on the challenges of the day with enthusiasm and a spirit of adventure. To use my mind, hands, and values to solve problems is invigorating, and I delight in the connections that help me become the person I strive to be.

About the Author: Irene Sakson is from Seattle, Washington, and will be joining the Harvard College class of 2019.

High School Attended: The Bush School, Seattle, WA

The Process: I knew I wanted to write about the transition I'd undergone in high school. It felt very relevant to whom I had become and how my interests had transformed me. Combining these factors with my aspirations and values yielded a story that felt very me, and so I wrote it.

Acknowledgments: Thanks to Alice Huang and Debbie Schmidt for helping me draft and edit this essay.

THE VIEW FROM BEHIND

Patrick Kane

It is December 24, 2013. I am sandwiched between my two sisters on the couch, paging through our old family photo album. We are seeing the same images beneath the shiny cellophane but from divergent perspectives. They remember these captured moments, while I recall nothing. "HA!" my sister exclaims, pausing on a photo from the same date sixteen years ago. Two teenage girls—one with a broad grin, the other too cool to smile—pose in matching red plaid skirts in front of the decorated evergreen tree. They hold up the year's best gift for the cameraman to see: a five-month-old baby in scarlet pajamas and a matching pom-pom hat. That Santa-clad boy is me.

Here I am once again, between my sisters, in our childhood home on Christmas Eve. My sisters' reactions to the photos reveal the joy they felt when my mom delivered me at the age of forty-three after numerous false alarms, complications, and heartbreaks. While my sisters reminisce about my late arrival, I reflect on what they, in turn, gave me. Rita, on my right, is turning the pages of the album, leading us down the path of our shared history. As the oldest, she is accustomed to being in charge, providing advice to my sister and me. In fact, she has made a career out of it; she is a human resources professional now. Continually asking, "Who do you want to be?" she instilled me with a goal-oriented mindset, encouraging me to pursue my passions and a fulfilling career path. Meanwhile, Laura is sitting quietly on my left; she is the middle child. A new book waits for her under the tree. It will be added to the stack of half-read books in her tiny Manhattan studio, where she squeezes in a few minutes of her favorite pastime after working long hours. Throughout my childhood, Laura would carefully select books from her treasured box in the basement for me to read. *Matilda* and *The BFG* filled me with wonder in my youth; *The Catcher in the Rye* ushered me into freshmen year; *Ordinary People* taught me about family and forgiveness. Through their example, my older sisters taught me the importance of sharing one's gifts with another. Inspired to give back, I have continually sought ways to share my contemplative, diligent nature with others in my community, whether through mentoring, tutoring, or fundraising for charities.

In the midst of the season of giving, I am sitting between the two people who gave me the most important thing: a feeling of home. During this annual moment of respite, upon the cusp of a new year, I am grateful for this place. My sisters have lived in various places over the years, whether Boston, Ithaca, or New York City, but they always come back. Soon, I will leave for college, but I know the memory of this place, between my siblings, will be the root from which I explore the world. Looking out the bay window, I see icy rain coating the grass with sparkling frost; it is close enough to a white Christmas for me. Though we are too old now for an awkward family Christmas picture, a photographer standing on the other side of the glass would capture a familiar scene: a boy nestled between his two older sisters on Christmas Eve. The only difference is someone else is wearing the Santa suit—our French bulldog, named Wiggs.

About the Author: My name is Patrick Kane. I live in Fairfield, CT, the suburbs. My goal is to live in a way that strays from the boundaries. I have many interests and aspirations: My English teacher recently told me I should become a writer; my sister thinks I should become a doctor; my parents think I should become an entrepreneur. I long to live a meaningful life, one that will be remembered and appreciated. I am a bibliophile at heart, a lover of the Beats, Faulkner, Genet, and Denton Welch, and regardless of what I do, I hope only to do what will allow me to see, as did they, the beauty in the world. I want to always be inspired, motivated by the unrelenting desire to better myself, regardless of whether my pursuits will earn me money or approbation. I want to explore with abandon, never losing sight of the prodigious expanse of what the world has to offer.

High School Attended: Fairfield Warde High School, Fairfield, CT

The Process: My identity as the "late-born" child in my family is paramount to who I am. I knew that my college essay would need to center around my sisters and how they have served as my role models throughout my adolescence. I focused my essay on a single moment, that which is my favorite in any given year: sitting beneath the evergreen Christmas tree with my sisters, paging through old photo albums. I revised my essay considerably, trying to make it as concise as possible. It was important to me that the essay be very personal, a candid reflection of myself.

Acknowledgments: Dr. Jeannette Faber, Laura B. Kane.

The Princess Party

Lauren Robinson

I was thumbing the pages of an old photo album the other day. The cover had the word FAMILY written in black block letters. The pages were ripped at the corners and every few stuck to one another. There were photos falling out the back: a picture of my dog and me on the porch, and my neighbor smoking in a lawn chair in his front yard. I imagine my life as a stream of moments that have slipped by. They have been placed in chronological order, documented, hole punched, laminated, and stacked into glossy sheets.

My mother always says that everything ends the same way it begins, with the truth. My mother's truth lies in actions. She believes that words are simply that: words. My father has a more provincial definition: a comfort in the Bible verse, John 1:14, "and the word became flesh, and dwelt among us." He likes to read the scriptures to me sometimes, to imagine that I'm slowing down with him, gathering the pages and turning them over in my hands. My father's truth has always been rooted in scripture, in words whose meaning never translate into action.

I flip the page and I'm seven again. Here I am buck naked, wearing a navy blue apron, and holding a whisk in my right hand. There is cake batter stuck to the floor and plastered across my face. My father is next to me laughing, holding a silver spoon, preparing to lick the frosting off his fingers. In a kitchen with floral wallpaper, whitewashed counter tops, and green kitchen chairs. Here is my first day of school. My first kiss. My mother when she was seventeen. The only time I felt snow tickle my skin on Christmas Eve. Here is the picture of the day I smacked into the gravel and twisted my arm in two. The first time I realized that the only thing I could control was myself.

I imagine the moments in the cracks. The ones not captured by a flash. The ones that slip by silently unnoticed. In this scene my parents prepare for my birthday party. I don't remember them fighting so I must be six. It's a princess party. We get to dress up.

The flurry of pink scarves and tutu dresses fills the room. My friends wave their wands and rummage the room for the most ornate crown. The best part is the cake. It's four feet tall, covered in pink icing and looks like a castle. I almost didn't want to eat it. They line us all up for a picture and say, "Say princesses!"

I made that up. It didn't happen that way. My parents prepare for my birthday party. I remember them fighting so I must be six. It's a princess party. We get to dress up. My mom hands me a light blue dress and it's covered in silver sequins. She puts her arms around me and strews a boa across my neck. My father shows up late. He has the best part, the cake. I didn't want to eat it. They line us all up for a picture and don't say anything.

It didn't happen that way either. I'm not exactly sure how it happened, but I know the reconstruction, the approximation of the moment. My comfort lies in days that have gone by, in places I can continually revisit. If you can imagine the mind as a world behind the eyes, a city lost in time, you'll find me there; shining the moments; putting them back into place; documenting the ones that need to be remembered. There is a part of me in these pages, in the creases and binding of the book. My truth lies in the action of putting the memories back together. The comfort I receive from building my life one moment at a time.

About the Author: My name is Lauren Robinson and I am from Houston, Texas. I hope to become a pediatric oncologist. I want to open a pediatric oncology home care company and provide affordable care in the comfort of one's home.

High School Attended: Carnegie Vanguard High School, Houston, TX

The Process: The novel *The Handmaiden's Tale* was my inspiration for my essay. I wanted to mimic Margaret Atwood's ability to trick the reader as well as make the reader an active part of the essay. I wanted the reader to be able to see the continuous reconstruction of memory work and take part in it while they read. My process included digging through a lot of photo albums. As I looked through the albums, I would write my immediate memories from the images. It was actually a wonderful experience. I am proud of what I was able to create and I enjoyed the process!

Acknowledgments: I would like to thank my parents for their help throughout this process.

RAIN AND RUST:
MY SOGGY CHILDHOOD

Eliza Hesselgrave

When I was younger, I was afraid of the rain. I had the unfortunate habit of leaving my toys outside for days on end, and the rain had the unfortunate habit of ruining them. I was convinced that thunderstorms were a force for evil, destroyers of worlds and other equally cherished things, like my purple bike with the iridescent tassels. The rain rattled our ancient windows, and the wind tossed my creaky door against its hinges. I used to run to my parents' room as soon as I heard the first drops hit my roof; my mom and dad would squish me between them in their bed, and I would cry while lightning splashed dark shapes against their walls. Watching from the window, I could see my dad run outside between lightning strikes, trying to save my cardboard box filled with plastic jewels. My mom would sit with me on her bed and tell me stories to try to calm my nerves. The next day they would laugh together, finding it adorable when I told them that the rain made me "queasy." They thought it was sweet, the way such small troubles loomed so large in my mind.

As I grew older, I started to realize that there were much worse things in the world than soggy toys. I lost pets and then family members. My best friend came from more challenging circumstances, and, through her, I learned about pains that were more serious than anything I had ever known. Middle school snuck up on me, and then there were days in which I would wake up to the sound of rain on my roof and just lie quietly, listening to the drumming. Eventually, I realized that my ladybug notebook would last longer if I kept it inside. I started to drop off my skateboard in my garage instead of leaning it against my steps. Slowly the sound of rain on my windows started to sound less like gunfire and more like a bedtime story. When I was seven, I thought that rusty handlebars were the end of the world. The realization that I had left my bike outside during a storm would keep me awake for hours. Then suddenly I was seventeen, trying to balance the pain of my first heartbreak with the stress of high school courses, waking up late in the morning and falling back to sleep to the sound of rain on my windows.

Now when the rain pounds on my walls, I don't imagine our trampoline corroding on the lawn or my scooter crumbling at the brakes. Now the rain means a fresh shine on my car and a brighter day than the one before. I've learned that summer showers can be sweet and refreshing, and that thunderstorms can be the best excuse to just curl up and read. It's been a long time since I climbed into my parent's bed when drops fell against our roof. My door still rattles during thunderstorms, but it doesn't scare me anymore. The things that I truly care about can't be damaged by sudden downpours or sharp gusts of wind. When hurricanes shake our coastal town I know that no matter how many trees fall down, my family will keep each other safe. The rain is a steady reminder that no matter how bad things seem to be, current troubles, like the rain, will ease with time.

About the Author: My name is Eliza Hesselgrave. I live in a small town on the Connecticut shoreline. I hope to graduate from college in four years with a degree in English and then either continue on to graduate school or work in the editing or publishing business.

High School Attended: Branford High School, Branford, CT

The Process: I procrastinated for as long as possible when writing this essay, citing my inability to choose a topic as an excuse. Eventually I got to the point where I couldn't put it off anymore, and I just began to write. Everyone had told me that once I started my essay it would just come out of me, and they were right. It composed itself in one sitting, though it took many rounds of editing to get it right.

Acknowledgments: Parents (Mark and Lisa Hesselgrave).

THE GOOD LIFE

Lahari Manchikanti

Lahari Studios is a rising animation company conceived by Lahari Manchikanti during her undergraduate education at the University of Florida. Throughout her life, computers and technology have surrounded her, leading her to the engineering path, until she experimented with the unique Digital Arts and Sciences program at the University of Florida.

I met Manchikanti in her colorful Bay Area apartment, where we talked in her living room filled with pictures of her loved ones, Amrita Sher-Gil paintings, and proudly placed University of Florida memorabilia. Not to mention her sketches and large storyboard, standing behind the sofa. We discussed her influences, focusing on her family and her time in college.

Manchikanti's vision for creativity in a STEM-dominated world has allowed her company to evolve from a meager animation studio to a multimillion-dollar company. She credits the start of her company to her parents, for instilling their values in her and supporting her ambitions, and to her education at the University of Florida.

"My dad, a software engineer at the time, would bring back all these new gadgets that I would mess around with for hours on end." Manchikanti was so often seen on computers that her father taught her how to code. "While other dads sneaked vegetables under their kid's noses, mine sneaked coding." However, the visual arts caught her attention more than coding and her father noticed this. He nudged her toward computers again, this time toward Photoshop and Adobe

Illustrator. Though she credits her father for supporting her interests, her mother gave her motivation.

Manchikanti's mother was taken fresh out of college to be married at the young age of nineteen, eventually giving birth to her a year later. "I would always joke around and call her a teen mom," she chuckles. „Because of her story, she has always stressed the value of education and financial independence to my sister and me. Because of my mom, I pushed to become successful and decided that the University of Florida would help me reach my goals."

The University of Florida offered a unique program that allowed Manchikanti to experiment in the digital arts and computer science. "At the University of Florida, I was welcomed by people who had similar ambitions and struggles. Thanks to Dr. Rong Zhang, one of my introductory lecturers, I became hooked to three-dimensional modeling and animation. Dr. Zhang, along with the other faculty members, ultimately inspired me to create my own animation company."

Manchikanti remains a proud alumnus of the University of Florida and plans to go back to the university to give lectures to aspiring animation students. She is still young and has much to learn in the mercurial world of business, but her mother's strength resonates within her. Her next project is a movie called *What If,* a story about a University of Florida admissions officer who has the tough job of accepting or denying a potential animation genius.

About the Author: My name is Lahari Manchikanti, and I am from Jacksonville, Florida. I hope to one day own or work for an animation company and contribute to organizations such as Girls Who Code and He for She.

High School Attended: Stanton College Prep, Jacksonville, FL

The Process: By the time this essay prompt came out, I was itching to write my college essays in a creative and eye-catching way. I realized that the perfect way to talk about my goals and to catch a reader's attention was to write as if I were interviewing myself. I had a lot of fun writing this essay and even researched famous interviews to understand how to structure my essay. I also researched UF's digital art and the sciences courses and professors to make my "interview" even more realistic.

Acknowledgments: Ms. Ibasco, my guidance counselor, and Mr. Knight, my teacher.

GRAVEL, CACTI, RAIN

Ilan Davidowitz

Gravel. Cacti. Rain. Welcome to Tucson, Arizona: home of the bitey and the furry and the scaly and the poky. Welcome to Tucson, Arizona, where I was born and where I grew up; Tucson, Arizona, where you need sunscreen in January and a water bottle year-round. In the summer, people slump down exhausted after twenty minutes of driving while cookies bake to perfection on the dashboard. But if we wait it out long enough, through the sauna of May and the oven of June, July brings our reward: gravel, cacti, rain.

Gravel stretches as far as the eye can see. From street medians to expansive deserts, little stones crunch underfoot and roll gently back into place, leaving nothing but dusty hints of boots gone by. In the heat, walking on gravel feels like walking on thousands of burning tacks. Remember, kids: shoes were invented for a reason. In June, you can smell the shimmering heat as it radiates off the ground, and an earthy, burning taste fills your mouth. Then come the clouds, rolling in over the Rincon Mountains. In July, gravel takes on a new scent. It seems to say, "I am parched and I am ready," and we all agree.

Cacti reside wherever they want in the Sonoran Desert. They rule the landscape of the Tucson Basin year-round with a spiny, up-raised fist, all the way from "Summer's Over" to "Summer's Here." They have shriveled to survive the oppressive dryness of late spring. July arrives, the clouds begin to form, and the cacti are ready. Their pleats begin to swell, a cactus's only way of retaining the water it will desperately need.

When the monsoon clouds form over the basin and the rumbling begins, we all breathe a sigh of relief. Finally, the heat lets up, the winds gust, and the sky goes gray.

Faster and faster, the droplets begin to fall. Above each cloud's patch of earth, the thunder rumbles and the lightning flashes, and we all beg the teacher to let us outside to dance in the glorious downpours.

It is now that the cacti, the gravel, and the rain find their harmony. The gray of the sky brightens the waxy greens of the cacti, throwing an otherwise dull-colored landscape into sharp relief. The rain and the gravel mix, and the smell of wet dust fills the air, turning us all giddy, unable to sit still and unable to focus. We no longer need to justify why we love the Sonoran Desert. The universal excuse of "But it's a dry heat" is replaced by a smile and gesture out the window, as the skeptics behold the sight we so look forward to.

Gravel. Cacti. Rain. A trifecta of beauty, peace, and excitement. It is a naïve northerner who scoffs at an elated Tucsonan at monsoon time.

"Gravel? You have loads of that!"

"Cacti? They're spiny and ugly!"

"Rain? Try living in Chicago for a week!"

"Our cacti," I reply, "can survive anything."

"And our rain," I reply, "makes Tucson come alive."

About the Author: My name is Ilan Davidowitz. I attend University High School in Tucson, Arizona, where I have lived my whole life. I hope to become a high school psychology teacher as I find the subject absolutely fascinating and important to understanding our lives and world. It is vital for students to understand and have fun learning such an important subject.

High School Attended: University High School, Tucson, AZ

The Process: In mid-August, our English teacher had us try out a few of the essays we were going to write for applications, and I could not figure out what to write. However, I looked out the window while we had a monsoon rain and decided that I had to write an essay about how beautiful it was. It sounds cheesy, but that really is what happened. I wrote a rough draft then and slowly edited it over the course of several months.

Acknowledgments: My mother was extremely helpful in her minor editing suggestions to make the essay sound and flow better.

A MEMORY OF MY FATHER

Cameron Cook

On a hot day in August of my junior year, I stood next to my mother as we buried my 450-pound father. I sat in a chair on the dry dirt on the outside row of the aisle, next to my little sister. Countless waves of complete strangers came up to me as they passed by to visit my father, telling me stories of a man that I had never known. I did not know the same man as those strangers did.

I had spent the last year and a half of my life living in a moldy and mildew-infested basement, isolating myself from the tyrannical horror of my father. Our house was like a battlefield. People slung hurtful slurs at each other on a daily basis; my father would spit them out like bullets flying out of a machine gun. I never saw the purpose of combating my father or challenging his authority. Instead, I would retreat to the basement, my fallout bunker. I disconnected myself from the war zone upstairs and evolved into a pacifist.

I remember painting a smile on my face every day so that my little brother and sister wouldn't forget what being happy looked like. Smiling helped; it made the mud I dragged my feet through a little less viscous. Some days I didn't have to paint on my smile; after all, I still had a mother who loved me and made me peanut butter and jelly sandwiches for lunch, and I still had a little brother to throw the football with in the front yard.

Over the past six years I had watched as my father's life deteriorated into relentless anger. I watched him go to a very dark place, and he never came out. The atmosphere of my house felt like everyone had a ball and chain around their ankles. The dynamics of my family would change as soon as we entered my house. My mom would tense her shoulders into a tightly curled mess as she walked by my father's chair in the living room.

I did not drown myself in tears when my family watched my father die in a hospital bed in Louisville, Kentucky, because I had been watching him die for the past six years of his life in a brown felt chair in our living room. When he died, I felt relief. I no longer had to come home to a verbal beating every day. I could touch the walls of my bedroom and they wouldn't be ringing from the intensity of my father's yelling. I did not cry because I missed him or because I wish I had grown up with a different father; I cried because I was so glad I had prospered in my situation. My situation wasn't a horror story; I knew my father for 16 years of my life, while some people never know who their fathers are. I had learned more from my father in 16 years than most dads can teach their sons in a lifetime. During those years I learned what kind of person I wanted to become.

I wanted to be happy. The most important lesson I learned from my father was that frustration and anger have no purpose on this earth. Life is too short to waste penning up anger and hating the world. Even in the darkest situation, happiness can move anyone's feet to a better place. When I smile, I feel young and innocent, like nothing in the world was made to hurt me. Most people may view the world as a dark and lonely place, but I view it as a chance to find one's self. I am glad I did not spend my childhood hardening myself to the corruption of the world, but instead embraced the world as the beautiful creation it is.

About the Author: My name is Cam Cook, I live in Evansville, Indiana, and my greatest passion in life is exploring religions. Although I myself do not belong to an organized religion, and I do not worship according to the practices of any one religious code, I consider myself to be a very spiritual person who is constantly searching for answers that only lead to more questions.

High School Attended: Signature School, Evansville, IN

The Process: This essay was written at the beginning of my senior year and was one of the most difficult essays I have ever written because of the pain I went through as I had to visualize the thoughts that had been cultivating in my mind throughout my entire childhood. To actually say I started writing this essay at the beginning of my senior year would actually be a false statement because I had been thinking about how I wanted to convey these emotions for a long time. It wasn't until my senior year that I wrote my thoughts down.

Acknowledgments: My English teacher, Ms. Gregg, and my mother.

FEMININE FEMINISM

Nadia Saleh

When I was five, my mom signed me up for both soccer and ballet. On Saturday mornings, I'd jump out of bed, put on my black leotard and pink tights and have my mom put my hair into a bun—a ritual we'd come to repeat hundreds of times. I'd pack my dance bag with my pink leather ballet flats, and my mom and I would walk the two blocks to the dance studio hand in hand. When we got there, my friends and I would practice what we'd learned the week before, and eagerly await the start of class.

Once class ended, my shoes would go back in my bag, my hair would come down, and I would walk back home with my mom, arms crossed, tears already building up in my eyes. The battle would soon begin: to go to soccer or not to go to soccer. I hated it. I hated that stupid sport. I've always been a small kid, and there's nothing I hate more than being in close proximity to large groups of larger people who are actively trying to knock into me. I hated that the other kids got so competitive; I could not care less who was better at kicking a ball into a net, though it still hurt my pride that I couldn't do it as well as the other kids could.

But damn it, my mother was raising a feminist. Even if said little feminist, to my mother's dismay, refused to wear jeans if they didn't have butterflies embroidered onto them, insisted on growing her hair long, and genuinely loved ballet. As long as she could hold her own on the soccer field, too. In the end, my mom did succeed in raising a feminist; we just have vastly different definitions of the word.

My mom believes that feminism works best when not mixed with femininity. She loved my fifth-grade English teacher for the posters she had hanging on the walls ("Yes I DO throw like a girl!"). She sighed every time I twirled around in a store's dressing room wearing another skirt I wanted to buy. To this day, she reminds me of the math contest I won in sixth grade, not the award I got from the library that summer for reading so many books. I received many science kits on birthdays, usually with a boy playing with it printed on the box. All of my beloved possessions that were pink, frilly, satin, or glittery, were purchased reluctantly and with an eye roll.

Typically, masculinity is seen as strong, and femininity is seen as shallow and weak. I believe that fighting sexism should involve fighting that connotation of femininity. My mom, however, believes that to earn respect, women should just be less feminine. But I'm a feminine person. It's part of who I am. My mom tried to change that about me because she thought it might hurt me in life. And maybe it will. Maybe it has. But I don't want to change it.

I'm proud to be one of four girls in my physics class, one of ten in my system level programming class, and one of twelve in my software development class. I love that my (female) friend and I are in charge of a computer science tutoring service after school. We celebrated when a woman was finally hired in the Comp Sci department. But I wish my mom had bragged about my accomplishments in ballet the way she does about my accomplishments in CS. Both are important to me, so my gender shouldn't make one more impressive than the other. Placing more value on my more traditionally masculine talents reinforces the idea that my femininity really is weak and shallow. All I want is to be able to walk into my physics and computer science classes and be taken seriously, even if I'm wearing heels.

About the Author: My name is Nadia Saleh and I live in Brooklyn, New York. I hope to earn a degree in computer science and enter that field after college.

High School Attended: Stuyvesant High School, Manhattan, NY

The Process: I started with a personal essay I'd written for my English class and modified it until I felt it reflected me well and was short enough to submit as a college essay.

Acknowledgments: My English teachers, Mr. Garfinkel and Ms. Schechter.

I'M A TEACHER

Michael Nguy

Pok. Pok. The ball popped every time it bounced off the towering wall in front of me.

"Get it, Cesar!"

Cesar whiffed and missed the small handball whizzing over his head. Another point for me as I played against the two sophomores. I prepared to serve again. *Pok.*

"Hey," said the sophomore. *Pok.* "When are you going to teach us chemistry again?"

I faltered, taken by surprise at his question. This sophomore whom *I* didn't know . . . knew *me*?

"I taught you?" Cesar served the ball. *Pok.*

"You taught me and you don't even know me?" the sophomore teased.

"Why? Do you miss me teaching chem?" I teased back. I finally remembered how I met this sophomore. *Pok.*

"Yeah. It was fun when you taught us," he replied. *Pok.* I smiled as I hit a corner shot.

The three weeks prior to this encounter, I visited the chemistry teacher during my free time. As a previous student of his who excelled in his AP chemistry course, sitting in on his classes should have been boring. I knew the material like the back of my hand, but I still got a thrill from watching him teach. After sitting in on several more classes, my teacher asked me to teach small lessons to the class. One day, I started by going over a Do Now question, explaining what a photon was.

A couple days later, I was reviewing Hund's Rule and Pauli's Exclusion Principle with the class, literally spinning left and right to show opposite spins. I admit, I wasn't perfect. I made mistakes. I couldn't count the number of valence electrons of oxygen properly because I was so nervous! *Yes, I know it's six.* I finally got into a rhythm though, and continued by showing the odd electron configurations of gold and silver. The students woke up from their daydreams, and their faces of boredom were replaced with looks of excitement and anticipation to learn. By firsthand experience on the other end, I knew that engaging students wasn't easy to do and it gave me such a rush knowing that I succeeded.

Despite being nervous from that first chemistry lesson, I've actually always loved teaching—I've tutored, worked at summer camps, and even taught classmates in my grade. As a child, I said that I wanted to be a math teacher when I grew up. I always thought it was just because I loved math, but the real reason was that I've always loved to help people. Once, I didn't finish my preschool classwork on time because I was helping a classmate's with theirs. The massive burns on my arms came from trying to help my cousin get hot food from the stove when I was just two years old. A self-proclaimed expert on the subway system, I've helped numerous lost tourists get to Times Square. I love helping, so it's only natural for me to want to teach.

That sophomore, whose name I still don't remember, made me smile in a way that made me feel appreciated—something I hadn't really felt before. I've been thanked for the help I've given before, except I never felt like I did anything significant enough to warrant gratitude. When I tutored and helped classmates, I simply clarified what a teacher had already taught. However, teaching students something they had never known before made me feel a new sense of accomplishment.

When I peruse the hallways of my school, going from class to class, I look like any other student. But school is more than just a place to learn. It's a chance for me to help others. That unnamed sophomore made me feel appreciated for the help I give and made me realize the passion I have for teaching. I'm not just a student at school. I'm a teacher. Anywhere.

About the Author: My name is Michael Nguy. I live in New York City and I attend NEST+m (New Explorations into Science Technology and Math) high school. I love helping others, and I aspire to become a chemical engineer to help solve energy crises.

High School Attended: New Explorations into Science Technology and Math, New York, NY

The Process: I was writing my common application essay for an English assignment. I did some brainstorming with my mom the day before the first draft was due, and reminiscing upon my past with her made me realize my passions I had as a kid are the same as my passions today.

Acknowledgments: I'd like to acknowledge my mother for helping me brainstorm for this essay, and my teacher, Ms. Palmer, for helping me make this the best essay I could.

WHERE OLYMPIANS RULE

Julia Spiegel

I want dirt under my knees and the sun burning my back. Dust in my hair and hands no amount of soap will ever get clean. I want to be waist-deep in a hole and digging deeper, knowing that somewhere beneath me lies the ultimate prize.

I want a small shovel in my hand, scraping the ground. The racing of my heart as the shovel hits something solid. I want my hands to tremble and my lungs to struggle for air as I brush the grains of earth off an unknown object. I want to lift a clay pot no bigger than my hand out of its earthen grave and let it kiss the sunlight once more.

I want a land where the Olympians still rule and wars have been buried by centuries. Where marble goddesses dance and satyrs play panpipes while chasing nymphs through olive-tree forests. Where trees are young women and Artemis roams freely among them.

I want a place where the language is almost as dead as the people who speak it. Where Julius Caesar gives a speech with far too many verbs and ten variations of the word "to kill." Where wars are fought with elephants and won by boys who are barely men. I want to learn every day. For my professors to share their wisdom and experience with me and for me to build my own: both in the classroom and in the field. To study Rome, why it lasted so long, and what brought the great empire to its knees.

I want a classroom where the dead talk and the living listen. Where scarred marble tells the story and I, behind a desk, know how to understand.

(*In the style of "What I Want" by George Bilgere*)

About the Author: My name is Julia Spiegel. I live in Benton Harbor, Michigan, and I plan on earning my PhD in classics and becoming a professor and archaeologist.

High School Attended: Saint Joseph High School, Saint Joseph, MI

The Process: For this essay, I took a poem I had written and expanded upon it, turning it into a college admissions essay.

Acknowledgments: Essay based on the poem "What I Want" by George Bilgere. My teacher, Ms. Eileen Klusendorf. My parents, Mary and Jim Spiegel.

N/A

Shi Chang

On July 12, 2012, at Beijing capital airport, my father hugged me goodbye. An odd feeling flooded my heart. In my country, hugging is not common, even within families. We've gone through routine breakups due to our diplomatic background, but this was different. He'd been appointed as the Chinese ambassador to an unstable Arab state, Yemen, while my mother and I headed to America.

The Middle East is in constant chaos. Working there not only involves great stress, but also mortal danger. I learned to worry when I was seven, studying at an international school in the United Arab Emirates. One of my friends, Nadeem, was a dark, brown-eyed Iraqi. I helped him with mathematics and, in return, he brought me fancy wrapped chocolates. One afternoon, I found myself alone because something had come up at my father's job. I turned on CNN's breaking news, which was airing a brutal war scene. At that time, I could barely understand English, but the tone and images of soldiers, guns, and tanks alerted me that something unpleasant had happened. The next day, the usual smile on Nadeem's face disappeared, as he and his mother had lost contact with their family in Baghdad. He told me that today was his last day of school. We promised each to keep in contact, but after parting, I never received his reply. Even now, I wonder what happened to him and what his life is like now.

I've been to 16 countries throughout my 18 years, and I've learned much from my travels. As I have become more mature and have spent time studying in an American high school, I've learned to synthesize these experiences and have begun to form my own opinions about the diplomatic issues my father faces at work. Despite objections from my family, I decided to visit Yemen this year. I knew of Yemen's ongoing civil war and understood the risks, but my passion for diplomacy and my eagerness to see my father drove me to take the trip. I wish to apply the knowledge I learned in school to practical questions of politics, religion, and quality of life.

When I landed in Yemen, it was different from what I had expected. The locals were friendly, and the scenery was truly admirable. I learned that each country, no matter how different—or threatening its reputation—has its unique culture and definition of beauty. However, the tension brought upon by civil war undeniably affects civilian lives. Every night I awoke in awe from gunshots, imagining the horror that takes place there. Flashbacks brought me back to the day when I saw the war scene of Iraq in 2003 on TV.

Although I consider it lucky that I did not experience any kind of gun battle during my visit, tension lies in the citizens' words when we had conversations. The homeless people had nowhere to go, and the people who had jobs were worried about the rebels' actions. Rumors spread that the conquest of Sana'a by the rebels was inevitable (which is the case now: The government began to fall with the resignation of the prime minister). As for myself, it is impossible for me to imagine how harsh it would be for the people who have to go through this every day. Every night, I think about my father and Nadeem, praying for their well-being along with everyone who lives in this kind of environment. Every night, I hope to bring a change.

On August 2, at Yemen capital airport, I hugged my father good-bye, still worried but proud. I promised myself to become a hero like him, to inspire friends and family, to help and achieve global prosperity. My experience in Yemen confirmed my desire to study international relations. Ultimately, with much still to learn, experience brings me one step closer to helping those in need around the world.

About the Author: My name is Shi Chang. I live in New York City, and my goal is to become a diplomat for the Chinese Foreign Ministry or the UN.

High School Attended: Columbia Secondary School, New York City, NY

The Process: I started this essay over the summer, and it has been done with great effort, taking more than ten drafts.

Acknowledgments: Professor Ari Rubin, mother.

Running Free

Nicholas Amato

Deep within the woods, I move at the earth's own tempo. At first it's hard to keep up as my body rebels against me with stiff knees and a 21st-century instinct that tells me not to push myself. But step by step, I transcend the stubborn joints and weak mindset, adopting a compulsion to push onward, fulfilling a more primal instinct. Encompassed by the nature around me and the total eclipse of the sky by the tree canopy, I settle into a pace. Nothing can stop me now. I am at peace with the world. I am a runner.

It is an amazing feeling when I can shut out the pain shooting through my body and let my mind drift into the rhythm of the run. There is only one true euphoria for me, and that is the "runner's high," fueled by a self-driven motivation and desire to roam free. I cherish how simple it is to do what I do. I never read an instruction manual and never studied a playbook; I just bought a pair of shoes and tread on the earth beneath me. I taught myself how to do it, placing foot after foot in an awkward frenzy when I was just old enough to walk, until now, when running is seamless and no longer a struggle.

This journey to embracing running came through self-discovery and determination. I remember playing baseball as a young boy and being pushed to run for the very first time. It wasn't natural then. The crowd was always stunned at how slow I was when I would nearly get passed by the batter on my way to second base. I realized from those days that running for speed wasn't my forte. It was only when I tried cross-country, a sport in which I could pace myself, that I developed my love of running. It became a release for me. When I was bullied in middle school and felt the world caving in on me, I ran. When I lost my beloved uncle from his depression, I ran even farther. When I was misdiagnosed with complex regional pain syndrome and was told I could lose my leg, I kept a positive attitude through physical therapy and was able to run once again. Who said it's unhealthy to run from your problems? Though running cannot fix everything, it lets me escape the burdens of the world, and gives me the clear mind I need to navigate life's obstacles. Through running, I have been enlightened to the virtues of patience and persistence, learning not to act on a problem within the time it takes to traverse one hundred meters, but rather to consider the issue over many miles and discover within myself the answer I seek.

I just have to keep moving, knowing the more ground I cover, the more likely I will achieve my perfect peace and contentedness with the world around me. Approaching mile eight, I first start to feel the runner's high and I know that the best part of the run is yet to come. Now with ten miles behind me, my body stops aching and the only thing I am consciously aware of is the visual perception of the pathway or road, and it's barely enough to keep me on course. Once I hit mile thirteen, I have got "it." My soul is removed from the flesh, and while my body is the earthly machine that inhibits my seamless run, I am a separate being. My footsteps and heavy breathing are gone, and I hear the wind whistle gently through the trees, the squirrels' chirps and scampers, and if you would believe me, I would swear I can hear even the conversation that the birds are having in the tree above me. They say they are at peace with the world, and I respond, "So am I."

About the Author: My name is Nicholas Amato and I am a high school senior in Traverse City, Michigan. I was recently admitted to the University of Michigan Ann Arbor and will be attending starting in the fall of 2015 to become a biochemistry major.

High School Attended: Traverse City West Sr. High School, Traverse City, MI

The Process: Writing essays used to be a dreaded burden of mine and it always took what seemed like eons for me to transform an idea into something substantial. With this essay quite the opposite held true, and I learned the value of writing from my heart. As a result of my passion for the subject matter, my new challenge was not to fill up the page but to actually limit my essay to a brief 650-word maximum. In painting this picture of what running means to me, I learned that essays that made a significant personal connection were the ones that ended up the best.

Acknowledgments: I would like to thank Duane and Vicki Amato (parents) and Mary Kay Trippe (college counselor) for encouraging me to always write from my heart.

THE WEIGHT ROOM

Lydia White

"This is Giacomo, the person not the place," I said, introducing the Italian man to my parents. The man laughed heartily, and my parents looked at us curiously. I met Giacomo when I stumbled upon his world. My school's main building has a side door that opens to a stairwell that when followed leads to a small auxiliary building. Inside is a room lined with mirrors. The room could be mistaken for a ballet studio, except the only barre in the room is a pull-down bar. This place, better known as Giacomo's, is a sanctuary where strings of conversation accompany a symphony of clinking weights. The burdens of the day melt away; life becomes a simple task: Pick up weights and put them down. The very mindlessness of the tasks brings lightness in a world of heaviness.

I was never the athletic type. I avoided anything that required hand-eye coordination. I would spend every gym class listening to the pitter-patter of my thoughts, my eyes following the grain in the floorboards rather than the basketballs flying past my head. Then, my freshman year, I discovered cross-country. I found my niche and I ran with it. I fell in love with running as deeply as a 14-year-old could, but running along the winding paths of Van Cortlandt Park, I looked and sounded like an old man, wheezing as if my lungs were clotted with cotton balls. I improved though, sheer stubbornness propelling me forward even as the other runners disappeared ahead of me. My body adjusted. My shoulders relaxed. My breaths evened out. My movements became perfectly mechanized like the hands of a ticking clock. But then I hurt my ankle and I fell out of step.

This led me to Giacomo's. Weight Room is not a mandatory class but a personal commitment. As such, it draws an eclectic group of people. I made friends with these oddities, becoming an oddity, a part of Weight Room culture. The jokes, nuances, and zealous debates edging on absurdity, were a part of my life almost every day from 3 to 4 p.m. I did not look very tough hobbling in shorts with a cast that went up to my knee, but I went from pushing 15 pounds to 90 pounds on the chest-press. It gave me purpose as I watched the running seasons pass by.

Giacomo's not only eased the restraints of immobility but was also a reprieve from the stresses of the day, such as creeping deadlines, and papers that weighed more than dumbbells. I sometimes overthink things, stressing over details, but in Giacomo's, I became weightless, my thoughts quieting with the mechanics of lifting. I seamlessly became a part of the machine, the repetitiveness soothing my thoughts into a lull. Performing the same task over and over again was not monotonous but meditative. I believe in free will, but giving myself over to the machine allowed me to retain my humanity. I stayed more parts human than parts overheated machine.

I began senior year. My shoulders relax. My breaths even out. My movements become perfectly mechanized like the hands of a ticking clock, as I fall back into step. Even though my ankle has healed, and I'm starting cross-country, I still continue to plug myself into the Weight Room, where I disconnect with my mind and connect with the buzzing energy of the room. Everyone is so focused on breathing when they're running in cross-country, there is no room for conversation, but conversation flows like sweat in the Weight Room. I would never enjoy therapy because the focus would always be focused on "my feelings" and me, but Giacomo's allows me to disappear and reappear, as I desire, becoming either a part of the machine or an extension of the teenagers laughing and lamenting.

About the Author: My name is Lydia White. I am an 18-year-old living in Greenwich Village, New York City. I have attended the Churchill School since I was seven years old and, with anxiety-tinged excitement, I am looking forward to attending Kenyon College next fall. I have no clue what I want to do, but I hope to stumble upon it.

High School Attended: Churchill School and Center, New York, NY

The Process: It took me a while to figure out a direction for my paper, but once I settled on an idea, I spent two weeks writing, rewriting, and editing several drafts until it resembled an essay. I had to kill many "darlings," sentences that I grew attached to and inevitably had to delete. My final draft arose from this carnage.

Acknowledgments: My ninth and tenth grade teacher, Mark Haslem.

An Unbroken Embrace

Arthi Bharadwaj

I wake to the sound of rusty wheels scraping metal tracks. Dazed from my interrupted sleep, I slouch against the wall of my bunk. Through the window, pollution clutters the landscape—never ending, as if the train weren't moving at all. Twenty minutes later, the train screeches to a halt. A green sign, scribbled in worn paint reads *Madurai*—the hometown of my mother, the life of my grandmother.

Fatigued and hot, I crave the chilly tile floor, the thin saris we used as cover in the heat, and spicy curry at my grandmother's house.

"Amma, how much longer till we reach Patti's?" Shaken, she answers, "By auto, we will reach in 25 minutes." The two of us, accompanied by my sister and father, squeeze into an auto rickshaw and prepare for the potholes.

Riding through the dirtied streets of India, I witness 25 minutes of starving dogs, roaming cows, beggars, and venders. In the center of this village lies the jewel of our visit. Pulling up to the pale pink house, I stare in silence. In my head, I could still hear her: "Yen Paathingala! Yen chellam. Ulla kula va! Ah, ne osandhite!" (My granddaughters! My dearest. Come inside! Ah, you've grown!) Arms waving, hugging my sister and me.

We push open the creaky gate, stepping on the tile pathways, avoiding garbage piled against the house. The bushes, untamed and neglected, spill over the sides of their holders, as if running away. Mold and feces fill the air.

I looked at Ama in confusion. "It's okay, Arthi. It looks like no one has maintained the house. Patti's gone. But garbage or no garbage, this is still her home."

Tearing the cobwebs off the door, Ama pushes through. She stands motionless. Her head swivels over her shoulders, taking in the horror of the house. White paint peeling off the corners of the walls, families of lizards hiking about the ceiling, mosquitos swarming the dulling lights. I follow her path, eyes focused on the ground. Ants rule the floor as if they were the current owners and I refuse to remove my shoes. In the adjacent room——my Patti's—disheveled saris shield the infested floor. Hesitantly, I enter.

It has been an entire year, yet I still expect her to be waiting inside.

Eyes darting around the room, looking for some form of comfort, I notice her favorite sari, masked in her cluttered wardrobe. Tiptoeing through the mess, I reach the material and wrap myself in the cloth like a cocoon. I can feel her again as I inhale her scent-—incense and sweet, sweet *Jangree*. Tears run free as I grasp on to the piece of her that remains. In this moment, trips to the sweet shop, watching Indian soap operas, and shopping for *salwar kameez* resurface.

I don't want to let go of the material. I don't have to. She will always linger as long as I consume Indian food, speak the Tamil language, and dress in traditional attire. Those actions cannot peel off the walls. As if she herself is embracing me, I trust the chilly tile, wrapping the sari tighter, sinking into its comfort.

About the Author: My name is Arthi Bharadwaj. Currently, I live in St. Joseph, MI. In college, I plan on pursuing a degree in biomedical engineering, then furthering my education as a physician.

High School Attended: St. Joseph High School, St. Joseph, MI

The Process: I have not always taken pride in my Indian heritage. When my grandmother passed away, I struggled with embracing my culture because she was such a great part of it. When I visited her house, however, I was reminded that I don't have to let go of her because she lives on through our culture. I wanted to share this vital piece of myself and this moment with the University of Michigan. With the help of an English teacher at my high school, we drafted multiple ideas but ultimately chose this scene to explore in my essay.

Acknowledgments: Mrs. Klusendorf.

COUNTING ELEPHANTS

Iris Rukshin

When I was little, I was scared of what I thought were elephants. The elongated black trunk, pliable green skull converging to a metal snout, and oversized emotionless eyes all terrified me . . . and there were four at home! An inquisitive child, I was easily distracted, but never enough to completely forget the silent, looming presence of the elephants. They came out and ate my head when the sirens sounded during an attack. And when the whole world was loud, but only I was quiet, the scary elephants and I would count: by twos, by sevens, by halves . . . until I fell asleep and the din diminuendoed to silence.

Fourteen moves and eleven years later, I now know that these were gas masks kept in almost every Israeli home at the time. Between the masks and violence and the abject poverty and anti-Semitism my parents suffered in Russia, my family moved around a lot in search of what I later realized was the American Dream. To date, my life has spanned three continents, three countries, four languages, and fourteen houses. With change as the only constant in my life and so many different aspects contributing to my identity, I struggled to "identify a culture" for myself.

But I could always console myself with the familiar logic of mathematics. Though I grew to relish inconsistency and thrive in chaos, the predictability of math was a safe haven I could retreat to when it all got to be too much. In a way, it was my rock until my freshman year in high school when my rock transformed . . . into a boulder.

With more questions than I could find answers to, I thrust myself into projects, papers, and hospital protocol. It's curious how retrospection exclusively lends realization and reflection. Only looking back do I realize that that was when I discovered my passion for applied math and epidemiology. In research, I found everything that I loved about both the variability of my life and the consistency of math. My life became an effort to quantify and predict the unpredictability of life, and numbers gave meaning to what I cared about. I still remember when bagging was exclusive to the grocery store, randomness was just a term to describe the unexpected, and probabilities were dull entities to be despised in word problems. I never would have imagined that these concepts would become beautiful mathematical techniques central to my definition of self. Suddenly, my identity wasn't a mysterious choice I had to make any longer.

My culture, I decided, would be defined neither by my past nor by my present, but instead by me. The duality of variation and constancy is a captivating part of research, tempting me to discover, for I revel in the elegance and fragility of the singular moment at the conclusion of a study when there is a pattern that only I know of. And for just that moment, the whole world is gray scale, and I am in color.

The more mathematical research has become a part of my culture, the more I have learned about myself and the professional world I hope to be a part of. Everything that goes into an investigation (paperwork, collaboration, perseverance, struggle, confusion, revelation, communication) has influenced who I am today. But, more than anything else, research has opened me up to something I have known ever since I was little: my simultaneous love of chaos and order, of life and math. For as long as I can remember, I have counted what I couldn't understand. Together, mathematics and my heritage make up the definition by which I interpret my life. That's the thing about culture— it demands to be recognized and valued, for it transforms rocks into boulders, formula into novelty, and ultimately, bland existence into dynamic life. So, the scary elephants and I will never stop counting: by twos, by sevens, by halves.

About the Author: My name is Iris Rukshin. After fourteen moves over the course of my life, I now live in New Jersey. Through all the change in location, language, and environment, I have always loved mathematics and medicine. I now hope to find a career in applied mathematics and computational biology.

High School Attended: High Technology High School in Lincroft, NJ

The Process: My background is a significant part of who I am and what I wish to do with my life, education, and career. So, I tried to convey how my academic passions have become a part of my culture due to my lifestyle.

Acknowledgments: I am very grateful to Mrs. Bufis, my parents, sister, and friends for their support and help.

Mud People

Jacob Cantor

I'm not a clockmaker, but I feel that they are as philosophical a group as any. They quite literally manufacture and quantify time. Their design decides our movements, our whereabouts, our communication patterns, and when we withdraw ourselves from the world for eight hours or so. Scary stuff.

What clockmakers know is that no matter how tamable humanity's perception of time may seem, it is unpredictable. Sure, we name the days, the months, the years, and act like we crafted these precious chapters in our lives, but what is truer than truth is that the universe doesn't care. When it comes down to it, we have been and always will be mud people. I say "mud" to symbolize our existential connection to our planet. Far more literally, we are hairless organisms atop a big, blue rock circumnavigating hydrogen. We came from the mud, and so we must, and will, return.

A development realized in recent centuries is that humans now have the ability to extend the time we hurtle around. In an unprecedented fashion, we've invented some highly sophisticated tricks to fight, cure, and dodge disease, which previously knocked us right back into the mud. We have had generations of people who were living way past their expiration dates, generations of people who from birth were destined to perish. Living among us are the products of Western medicine, able to walk, talk, love, and hate when they weren't even supposed to be living at all!

As clichéd as it is, I am a member of that prestigious club that nature never intended to exist. Luckily for us, this predicament has anointed me with all the exciting tropes of a college essay.

Besides being a blessing of "collegeboardian" proportions, there's a truly helpful aspect of having never been supposed to survive infancy. I've seen how incredible it all was. I'm a product of what mankind has labeled "progress," and I'm really a fan.

After this initial phase of recognition, I got to thinking about it. That part is tough. A truly introverted session with the topic of why you exist and how you probably shouldn't will lead you unto many a twist and turn, a forest of roundabouts, paradoxes, and ugly self-alluding truths upon the nature of humans.

What quickly became clear was that I am undeniably "unalone." Nope, I'm not as special as I'd like to be. I figure that, every day, children with equally valuable minds, hearts, and souls are saved by angels in scrubs. Their contributions are unquantifiable, and though I share an innate belonging to this lucky, lucky club, I am not its center, its president. Heck, I didn't even make the board!

But what's infinitely more upsetting and infinitely more important is to remember that where a child is saved, there are more who weren't. There were more people who, because of circumstances, were unable to arrive in such a brilliant institution of medicine and have their curable ailments cured. At which point your mind makes a final turn and arrives at a most dubious question. Why me?

Dumb luck.

I was born with congenital heart disease. Although I believe that all people have a responsibility to their fellow person, it is clear that mine's greater. Whether it's owing something to what many have labeled "human progress," or even proving myself and my nearly fatal peers worthy to have lived on this rock, there's work to do and I'm undeniably in a place to do it.

We needn't be a grand mason of time itself to see just how darned important the thing is.

Though it may do us all some good to think like one.

Now whether we received oodles of life-saving surgery, an important limb or the love of a fellow human being, we are all from the mud. And just how humbling of a commonality is that?

About the Author: My name is Jacob Cantor. Hailing from West Hartford, Connecticut, I am interested in politics and language. Currently president of my school's student government and an active member of the Human Rights Coalition, I plan to retain a sense of community and better my environment through activity and civil discourse.

High School Attended: Hall High School, West Hartford, CT

The Process: At the start of this process, before reading any prompts or choosing any colleges, I knew this essay was coming. At the end of junior year, I began racking my brain for unique events and facts concerning my being. Ideas and motives dear to me, but nothing would stick. Finally I remembered a poem in Kurt Vonnegut's book *Cat's Cradle* that expressed an idea of people being made from mud. This incited me to think about my own mortality. I was born with congenital heart disease and was saved by a series of genius technological breakthroughs. I'm lucky beyond measure. And it became clear that this question I was grappling with is what I had to write about. So I sat down and did it quickly before the ideas all left. I found a fitting prompt afterward.

Acknowledgments: Mrs. Blejwas, my AP language and composition teacher, showed me how to write and made me love it.

DISASTER IN THIRTY MINUTES OR LESS

Mitchell Gorman

The summer before sophomore year, I spearheaded a glorious disaster, a project that was almost doomed to fail from the start. I tried to make a movie. The production problems we encountered were phenomenal, and our knowledge of video production was next to nothing. Maybe if I was not persistent or stubborn, I would have given up on filmmaking, but it was too late for me. I had the bug.

"You can't be serious," my younger brother exclaimed when I told him of my plans to direct a movie. "I thought this was just a joke!" He was right, *Delivery in Thirty Minutes* started out as a joke, and it probably should have stayed that way, but when I set my mind to accomplishing a task, I throw myself into it, and *Delivery* was no different.

The problems began as soon as pen hit paper. *Delivery's* script was an incomprehensible twenty-seven-page conglomeration of characters, tones, and plotlines. Despite the glaring issues with pacing and focus, I began gathering a cast and crew for the movie. The crew consisted of my friend Will and me; I was the director and Will owned the camera. For actors, I enlisted friends and acquaintances from all over the city. In my hubris, I had written ten major characters, so I looked for actors among a diverse group, recruiting students from my high school, students from other high schools, students in middle school, my brother, and some of my former homeschool classmates. I took the successful completion of casting and writing as a good sign and forged ahead with production.

"What do you mean, you haven't read the script?" I exclaimed, shocked, to Jerry, the star, whose preparation was only matched by his acting ability. "We only have the pizza parlor for two hours, we've been planning this for weeks, and you haven't read the script?" Jerry looked down at his feet as Will and I began attempting to solve this problem.

"Hey, maybe if . . ." I began.

"You guys should really be shooting the whole scene twice," our lead actress, Vivian, interrupted. "My friends always shoot the whole scene twice, that way you can do better cuts."

Frustrated, I misguidedly turned my back on this problem and stepped outside to talk to the five actors who were waiting to shoot the next scene. An hour later, they were still waiting, and it was time for us to leave.

After that, when I tried to schedule *Delivery* shoots, the cast and crew were increasingly busy. One sweltering Houston afternoon, as my brother and I were returning home after a particularly tiring day of shooting, I realized that school was starting in a matter of days, and the chances of finishing the project were slim to none.

The lofty goals I had for *Delivery in Thirty Minutes or Less* were left behind, and I turned it into a trailer. While everyone seemed pleased, it was nothing like my original vision. But that no longer mattered to me because I had become fascinated with making movies. Working on *Delivery* had been a crash course not only in filmmaking, but also in organization, leadership, and setting realistic goals. I was able to take advantage of these newfound skills by improving my academics, making new friends, and creating a film club at my high school.

Delivery, like other failures and obstacles I have faced, remains a somewhat painful memory. But what it taught me, more than using a camera, directing actors, or getting permission to use a location, was to never let failure get the better of me. It is easy to let negativity consume one's feelings after facing failure or rejection, but if I had let the problems I encountered making *Delivery* stop me from pursuing something I was interested in, I may never have discovered one of my greatest passions.

About the Author: My name is Mitchell Gorman. Born in Honolulu, Hawaii, I moved to Houston, Texas, in 2010, and will graduate from Carnegie Vanguard High School in May. I drafted this essay last summer while attending the University of Houston's Wonderworks film production program—the course of study I intend to pursue in college, in order to achieve my professional goal of directing and editing films— and polished the essay in Mr. Holloway's English class in the fall.

High School Attended: Carnegie Vanguard High School, Houston, TX

The Process: First, I brainstormed many ideas based on the prompt, then I eliminated them until I had the best one. I wrote the first draft in one night, then spent several weeks revising it off and on.

Acknowledgments: I would like to thank the Wonderworks program at the University of Houston for holding the free writing workshop where this idea was born.

YELLOW

Morgan Gebhart

I have to see her again. It has been weeks and I swear that I am going
into withdrawal; I see her everywhere—in windows, out of the corner of
my eye—and I think about her constantly. I'm not sure that I'll survive
another day. We met, she and I, as summer waned and the leaves turned
and I knew that it was love. It built slowly as we got to know each other
better, as I got to know her personality, her interests, and as I was able to
see more of myself in her. Sorry, that's a lie. I saw who I want to be in
her. I do that sometimes, mix up who I am with who I want to be.

It seemed like we would be together forever, but now it is near
Christmas, and she's gone. There is nothing new to talk about, nothing
new to see together. That is, until today. Today she came back to me,
revamped. Gone are the old faded covers, the musty sheets, the worn
fabric edges faded to a nondescript gray—now she is here, framed in
bright yellow, her home laminated in all its shiny plastic glory. I hear her
calling to me from within these prison-like covers, whispers held within
the black letters on creamy paper, fresh from the press.

But I'm scared to run out again. What will I do when Nancy Drew
no longer comes to the rescue? What will I do when there are no more
tales praising her independence, her courage, her brilliance? Who will I
look to to answer my questions, to tell me how to navigate this large and
confusing world? Who will tell me how to solve the puzzles that the rest
of the world doesn't see?

In spite of that, I can't bear to keep her waiting another minute, but
first, we need to be alone. Somewhere no one can reach us or disturb us,

312

somewhere where the straight lines and unforgiving right angles of the room will no longer choke me. I know the perfect place. Slithering like a wyvern with her golden treasures, I make my way to the corner, dodging presents and low-hanging branches and the metal supports of our Christmas tree. Reaching my nest, I relax against the corner, smoothing out its rough edge with the rounding of my shoulders and legs as they fold into a soft, bowed shape. Finally, *finally*, I take the first book from the pile and listen to the soft sigh as I ease open the front cover. I have done something that cannot be undone. I have started the book for the first time, and now I am that much closer to ending it. I mirror that sigh of release-sadness and slip into my new world surrounded by the drama and love of Nancy and Bess, comforted by the unwavering knowledge that everything will be all right.

About the Author: My name is Morgan Gebhart. I attend the International School in Bellevue, Washington. I plan to major in Biomechanical Engineering.

High School Attended: International School in Bellevue, WA

The Process: Upon reading the prompt I immediately thought about snuggling up with a book. No matter what was going on in my life, books gave me a place to relax from the stress from everyday life and lose myself in another world. From here, I remembered how amazing it was to slip away from my family by finding a nook to read in.

Acknowledgments: Susan LaRosa and my parents.

FOOD FOR THOUGHT

Frank Boudon

My cousin and I exchange knowing glances as the unmistakable aroma of a Boudon family lunch permeates the air. Hearing the customary "À table!" we hurry down the hill, across a garden of plum trees and potato plots, under an arch entwined in blackberry vines, and through the kitchen door. My Uncle Laurent's home isn't the largest or the most beautiful, but its sprawling backyard and ancestral value make it a treasure tucked away in bustling metropolitan Paris. Paul-Eric and I scuttle into the dining room. We're moments late—an often inexcusable crime in European households—but thankfully, with the entire family present and chatting, we find our seats, relatively unscathed.

Words can hardly describe the quality of Boudon family meals, a delectable cross-section of the world's best foods. At the center of the table lies a traditional French appetizer platter adorned with hearts of palm, to its left a plate of fine *saucissons*, and in front of each person plenty of fresh baguette (this goes without saying). My mom contributed several Chinese staples, including handmade dumplings and an enormous bowl of steamed rice. Aunt Victoire's dishes are to die for; a native Ivorian, she prepared fried plantains and chicken covered in Côte d'Ivoire-style peanut sauce—my favorites. And, of course, ubiquitous American Coca-Cola fills all of our glasses.

Raising a fork to my salivating mouth, I pause and survey the table. Here we are, the most unlikely group of people imaginable, a family from four continents that, in a rational world, shouldn't exist. My parents met on a train in Germany, my aunt and uncle at a rest stop in

Africa. Perhaps it's because the universe has a strange way of favoring chaos; entropy, it was called in my chemistry class. Yet, we're scarcely chaotic. We're one of the closest families I know, brought together, paradoxically, by differences. We enjoy one another's company, discuss an endless array of (literally) foreign experiences, and indulge in one another's cuisine, as we're doing now.

My family has been my greatest teacher. They've given me tremendous perspective, an appreciation for every day, every culture, and every viewpoint. Just as my 80-year-old French grandma toils in her garden each morning, I put pen to paper, mind to textbook, and reap knowledge. Just as my grandpa in China leads his blind wife by the hand during afternoon strolls, I strive to exemplify leadership and service in my community, even if it's as seemingly trivial as offering a freshman a ride home. And just as my own parents dedicate their lives to raising a pair of rambunctious kids, I hope to commit mine to endeavors that are truly meaningful, at least to me; those are currently film and politics. The greatest lesson: No matter his or her background, any given person's struggles and dreams—and entire life, in fact—are analogous to my own.

Looking back at my plate, I begin devouring chicken with newfound gratitude, mindful of the crazy family that's so shaped me.

About the Author: My name is Frank Boudon. I'm from Troy, Michigan, and I aspire to become a lawyer or filmmaker. No matter where I end up, though, my greatest goal in life is simply to be happy.

High School Attended: Troy High School, Troy, MI

The Process: Like many other students, I struggled to answer the question, "What makes me unique?" I found, after some reflection, that the diverse people, places, and experiences I've been exposed to are central to who I am.

Acknowledgments: My family, of course.

MOMENTS THAT SHAPE A LIFE

Sydney Wagner

Ingrained in my memory is the dirty, burnt-orange couch reeking of cigarette smoke. Sitting inside the "party house," I watched as my new "posse" raged to hard-core rap and lit up cigarettes as they passed by every few minutes offering me one. "Thanks, maybe later," was my mantra. I wanted to be part of a different crowd, with people who cared, but didn't care too much.

Growing up, I had always been a "perfect" child—getting straight A's and always being polite and well behaved. But something changed within me the day my Aunt Gretchen was diagnosed with cancer. I was angry and I needed my new posse to help me escape.

Aunt Gretchen was the person who had every reason to be angry. Instead, she stayed positive through every stem cell transplant, radiation therapy session, and disappointing result. There was always at least a subtle smile on her face. I believe that she smiled because she found her strength in the love of everyone who surrounded her. She found peace, but I, who loved her, only found emptiness.

I needed to find the light again, but I didn't know how to ask for help. I will be forever grateful for my mom, who sensed that I was reaching out. I sobbed into her shoulder as every emotion I had stored up was finally released. "I love you, Aunt Gretchen loves you, and even though she isn't here, she is still watching over you," she reminded me in her soothing voice.

Those words hit home. I wanted to honor Aunt Gretchen and everything she symbolized—strength, kindness, and courage. Then and there, I decided that I would not let that one dark period of my life define who I was as a person. I am now excited for my future because I accept challenges and know that I will have a positive impact in the lives of others.

To be successful in college and in life, I will need to be true to myself, trust in my values, surround myself with people who will be encouraging and supportive, be able to weather the stormy times, and not be afraid to ask for help. I will face more challenges as I grow into the person that I am meant to be, but I will face them using my armor of strength, kindness, and courage. (Just like you, Aunt Gretchen.)

About the Author: My name is Sydney Wagner. I'm from St. Joseph, MI, and I hope to graduate from Michigan State University with an undergraduate degree in nursing.

High School Attended: St. Joseph High School, St. Joseph, MI.

The Process: Michigan State University had a couple of different essay prompts to choose from. I wrote two different essays that went along with two different prompts and chose the one that I felt like I connected with the most. After choosing which prompt and essay I wanted to use, the revision—with the help of my family and teachers—led to many new and improved drafts. It was a long process to make my essay "perfect," but I think that I accomplished it and am proud of the final product that I was able to send to MSU.

Acknowledgments: Mom; Tracy Wagner, guidance counselor; Mitzi Tomkins, teacher/coach; Lauren Hill.

LOST IN PARADISE

Darla Macel Anne Canales

Lost in thought, but found happiness. I am always preoccupied by past events and conversations taking place in my head. I once found paradise where it's usually overlooked. That paradise was a country where I noticed some of the biggest paradoxes of life and learned lessons that can only be understood through experience. My paradise, where all three lessons took place: the Philippines.

First Lesson—Finding Beauty

During class when I was in third grade, my teacher asked us to write a paragraph about something beautiful. I couldn't think of anything. "How about this country, the Philippines?" she said. I knew all about poverty and hunger, and I didn't think that was beautiful. I used her idea anyway. But noticing that I still had no reasons explaining what makes it beautiful, she told me "Sometimes what you see isn't all there is. Behind those dirty and starving faces are millions of people full of kindness and hope. The air might be polluted, but their souls are not." I've never forgotten that lesson. It was strangely beautiful.

Second Lesson—The Neighbor

When I was about ten years old, I lived next to a neighbor who was perceived as rather odd. I had short conversations with him, usually when we passed each other by. The conversations would last ten seconds, consisting of the everyday hello and how are yous, good, and good-byes. One day as I came home from school, there was no one home; the lights were off and the old rusty gates were locked. Seeing that I was alone on an unpredictable street, my neighbor walked up to me and offered to stay until someone arrived. He then said that he'd be right back and when he returned he had a tray full of food. He asked if I was hungry. We both ate and talked until my grandma arrived back from the market. I immediately introduced her to our neighbor after I saw a concerned look on her face. This, I thought, was one of those paradoxes of life. We have successfully traveled to the moon, yet we fail to travel a few feet to meet our new neighbors.

Third Lesson—The Bow and Arrow

I have always been someone who didn't like to be bound to one thing, especially when I know there is so much more out there. I disliked it when people chose one thing to master when they could have been really good in numerous things. One of the skills that I learned enough to be reasonably good at is archery. Archery, I believe, is a lot like life. To reach the target, the archer must have a reason, take action, and accept the results. The first time I picked up a bow and arrow I was horribly unsuccessful. I could barely pull the bowstring back, and when I gathered enough strength to pull back and let go, the bow string would always collide with my arm, leaving it marked with bruises. Just like life, there are challenges, and making adjustments are always a choice. Once alterations are made, the quote is quite true: "An arrow can only be shot by pulling it backward, so when life is dragging you back it means that it is going to launch you into something great."

Now these moments are lessons that are forever ingrained in my mind, captivating me so much that I tend to get lost in paradise. No matter where I am, my mind is elsewhere, far, far away, immersed in mental time travel. I usually stay there until someone gets my attention and that's when I return to reality.

About the Author: My name is Darla Macel Anne Canales. A multilingual and originally from the Philippines, I am a senior planning to become a physical therapist.

High School Attended: Peak to Peak Charter School, Lafayette, CO

The Process: Before, and while, I wrote the essay, I reflected about the things that mattered most to me, something that has shaped me and something that I carry with me wherever I go. I gathered up ideas and decided to write about three lessons I have learned in the past that continue to be true, time and time again. Finally, after I developed my first draft, I had it critiqued and made changes to what is now the final work.

Acknowledgments: Ms. Kristie Letter, teacher.

TO INFINITY AND BEYOND

Reine Defranco

On a dark road drenched from a torrential downpour, headlights gradually emerged, illuminating the arduous path. A '92 Mercedes-Benz whizzed through the night with two bickering girls in the back seat and an older one navigating the road. While united in a common destination, their minds stood worlds apart.

In the far back corner of the Benz sat a squirmy fifth-grader with bangs covering her eyes, and dirt smudged on her school uniform. At her feet lay a flourishing pile of crumpled drawings with *Toy Story* characters sprawled on the pages. "To infinity and beyond!" she squealed, kicking the back of the driver's seat. Her backpack flopped open, and her schoolwork spilled out, revealing unfinished homework and subpar test scores. She was known as Daydreamer.

The girl opposite Daydreamer glanced up from her algebra textbook and threatened to hurl her pencil at the rascal. Nicknamed Brainiac, the young seventh-grader kept her hair pulled as tight as a rope across her head, and was adorned in a baggy Wimbledon polo. Brainiac had set aside her artistic inclinations and found her drive in learning and academics. She reveled in beating all the boys at math.

"I have maps for our adventure!" exclaimed Daydreamer, retrieving a colorful map from her mountain of illustrations.

Brainiac grimaced. "Her maps offer no direction whatsoever," she claimed, turning to the driver. "Read my instructions; they describe our route in perfect detail." Brainiac proudly raised a seven-page essay, font 10 Helvetica.

"Where are the landmarks?" Daydreamer asked, reaching for the essay with her grimy hands. "Did you add *any* pictures?"

Brainiac jerked the papers away, flicking her taut ponytail. "We don't need visuals. I spent hours pinpointing the exact location with seven alternate routes."

"Sorry, but I can't use either of your directions," the driver finally answered from up front. The seventeen-year-old glanced over her seat, revealing her short, edgy haircut.

"A map with only doodles and no specific directions could lead us to the opposite end of the country," the driver continued. "But this rainstorm is too brutal to drive through without guiding visuals. Both maps fall short. However, if we use the detail and work put into the essay, as well as the artistic flair in the maps, we can then venture to our college destination."

At first, the two girls in the backseat stared stubbornly out the windows, each favoring her own means of guidance. But after a few minutes of studying her essay, Brainiac eventually acknowledged her paper's flaws. Her essay, and schoolwork in general, lost sight of the artistic spirit that used to drive her passion. Meanwhile, Daydreamer began to notice the value within her counterpart's logistical work.

The foggy windows and battering rainfall blanketed the two seemingly opposite characters with peace. The rain washed out the voices that constantly urged Brainiac to work to her limits; the thunder silenced the teachers demanding that Daydreamer pay attention.

The driver paused at a red light and finally turned to the two young girls. The graphite smudges on her hands glistened from the traffic light, and on the opposite seat lay a stack of design textbooks.

"Girls," the driver said to fifth-grader Reine and seventh-grader Reine. "You both complement each other through ambition and passion. Your collaboration is what will propel us to succeed in our journey. Never forget, a day without graphite smudged on your left hand is a day wasted."

The girls giggled as they examined their hands, finally recognizing a common bond with each other.

As the red light flicked green, the driver pressed forward, carrying with her the two pieces of her soul, fully prepared for her destination: to college and beyond.

About the Author: Reine Defranco is an avid snowboarder and fiction writer in Boulder, Colorado. She will be furthering her aspirations in graphic design at New York University Abu Dhabi in the coming fall.

High School Attended: Peak to Peak Charter School, Lafayette, CO

The Process: It took me a couple years pondering exactly what would happen when college applications rolled around, and what would be the hit story that would change lives and drive admissions officers to tears. But in the end, I decided to tap into what really created the person I am today: my past mistakes. After sitting in a car in the middle of the night watching the rain pour down, I found a certain peace with myself, and an acceptance with how all my past mistakes have most greatly created me.

Acknowledgments: Special thanks to the world's greatest English teachers: Ms. Quinlin, Ms. Letter, and Ms. Amidon.

BUST A MOVE

Calvin Riss

Here I stand, gently before you, a dancer. I have been known to put on performances of such balance, focus, and precision that they have brought tears of adulation to the eyes of my admirers. I have performed feats of strength involving great strength of feet.

Yet I have never put on a tap shoe or leotard, nor have I practiced in a studio or pliéed in front of plethoras.

My physical dancing is actually rather limited; although I do possess an internal soundtrack that cannot be contained, and have been known to "bust a move" here or there and "break it down" on occasion. Yet I often find myself in a different dance setting. It requires equal amounts of focus and balance, in combination with much physical and mental fortitude. I have practiced, for years, this intricate dance in which I am constantly frolicking through classrooms, recreation centers, my desk at home, and with my entire school as an audience. This day-to-day jig has many steps, yet none set in stone. It is largely improvised, and thus forces me to think on my feet and quickly adapt. I perform this dance daily, and the steps are often easier said than done. I am well practiced, especially with my experience as a ballroom dance instructor.

Here, allow me to teach this little number to you.

The routine begins with a turn and gentle leap, up from slumber, usually executed in the presence of the moonlight to prepare for parleys prior to school days. For each day, a different dance. Some days are a waltz, planned and controlled, with a repeated rhythm and relatively few surprises. These types of dances I find easy to lead, with minimal disruptions, synchronization with those around me, and simple steps, but each day a different dance. I enjoy all styles of dance and their unique elements, but some require more contortion than others. I am not impervious to the difficulty of certain dances. Many a day I am expected to lead the dance with prowess and poise, even when every twist and turn feels uncomfortable. When you try this, you may lack confidence and severely embarrass yourself, but the show must go on. When all eyes are on you, confidence is key, improvisation is pertinent, and crumbling under pressure is not an option. It can take its toll, but the dance always continues.

I, then, begin to perspire.

And here is where many falter. When the rhythm breaks, the familiar march of fear replaces that internal soundtrack and the perspiration poisons the eyes, revel. Let the sweat console you. Sweat is a reassurance of your ability to maintain a high intensity despite struggling to sustain the frenetic pace of the more energetic dances, including the jitterbug and bachata. It requires leading with style, precision, and a careful understanding that for it to work best, I must be conscious of making sure my partner can follow and execute these moves. Despite whatever stress may arise amidst such a hustle, I advise persistence in enjoying the exhaustive experiences. So thoroughly satisfied am I, after two-stepping and twisting from dawn to dusk, tossing in numerous other types of training, and turning in, utterly exhausted, just to do it all again.

I have stepped on some toes and had my own stepped on also, and I still have many steps to learn with this dance, but I promise I will continue to lead you to the best of my ability.

It takes two to tango, so may I have this dance?

About the Author: My name is Calvin Riss, and I was born and raised in Longmont, Colorado. I plan to go on to major in biochemistry and complete my premed requirements in order to go to medical school to become an orthopedic surgeon.

High School Attended: Peak to Peak Charter School, Lafayette, CO

The Process: I struggled through a long brainstorming process before my teacher told me to stop being so chained down by the prompts and let my metaphor about my dancing just run its course. I took her advice and, after a long editing process, stumbled upon my final product.

Acknowledgments: Kristie Letter, my teacher, Harnek Gulati, my mentor, and, last but not least, Dana Riss, my mom.

THE CRIMSON TABLECLOTH

Anna Brent

For me, every night at dinner is my rite of passage. I didn't have a bat mitzvah or a *quinceañera*. I didn't grow up in a culture that had one event to initiate adulthood. Instead, with each family dinner, I grew up a little more. No matter how challenging the discussion, I was encouraged to explain my position, and through doing so I learned what it means to be an adult in a world that is rarely black and white.

I grew up around a dinner table where the only constants are the crimson tablecloth, the three place settings, and knowing the conversation will weave, serpentine, connecting many disparate topics.

My stepdad opens the oven, "Another sourdough loaf baked by solar panels!"

He hands it to me to take to the table. "I love knowing we have a zero emissions dinner, I'm sad that everyone can't. I bet sustainable energy could be made more accessible!" I exclaim. Sitting down, my stepdad looks at me, his eyes challenging me to explain myself.

And so it begins.

Contrasting my life with the lives of those I have met through volunteering, I think about how accessibility to energy impacts lifestyles.

"When I was working on the Navajo reservation, I met a group that promotes solar energy," I tell my family. "There must be a way to make solar ovens more affordable."

"If they could bake easily, they could avoid processed, white bread that has little nutritional value. That stuff can rot teeth," my stepdad claims, cutting off a slice of warm sourdough.

"Ugh! Industrialized food makes me so mad," I say, and I am reminded of Alsup Elementary, an inner city school that I have volunteered at throughout high school. "I noticed a lot of the kids at Alsup have dental problems. Maybe it's because their families can only afford cheap, processed bread," I hypothesize.

Unfolding from the ideas of unhealthy food, we talk about world hunger, disease, war, and end up discussing the juxtaposition of past and present conflicts in Israel. I wonder, in that context, what drives people to make the choices that they do.

Speaking of tough decisions, the dialogue switches to what we would have done in Nazi Germany. Would we flee or fight?

"Nazis are pounding on your door. You have 30 seconds to decide whether to send your children to a safe house with a stranger or keep them with you and risk being killed. What do you do?"

I begin to say, "I don't know," but am quickly halted. That answer is not an option, and I must defend my decision. In the end, I choose to send my children to safety, putting the future before the present. My answer appears clear-cut, but in reality, much of life is not.

We explore tough topics like these night after night, joined around a shared meal and a crimson tablecloth. By learning to answer difficult questions and defend my position, I discovered myself. I learned to be comfortable feeling uncomfortable and to be confident debating any issue, even in the gray areas.

Family dinner is not just a time to eat and run. It's a time to learn, discuss, and explore; a feeding of the body and the mind. Eating around a table where arguments buzz through my ears, and real world issues are not forgotten, I grew to be a thoughtful adult with a distinct voice. My family not only shared the food, but the ideas that became the building blocks of who I am. When I ask my mom to pass that freshly made sourdough bread, she also passes curiosity and new perspectives. Family dinner taught me that life is about the questions asked, and the answers sought. Growing up isn't always easy, that's a given, but looking back, I can proudly say I grew up at the dinner table.

About the Author: My name is Anna Brent. Having been born and raised in Lafayette, Colorado, I strive to open my eyes to the broader world around me through both education and travel. I believe connections between cultures and between people are what will lead us to a truly globalized society. Although my life path remains mostly uncharted, my goals include finishing college, finding a career that fits my interests (probably in the field of psychology or neuroscience), and using this career to the benefit of people, perhaps by starting a nonprofit of some kind. I am not 100 percent sure what I want to do, but I look forward to the journey of finding out.

High School Attended: Peak to Peak Charter School, Lafayette, CO

The Process: My writing process was basically a continuous loop of drafting, editing, drafting, and editing again. I discussed my ideas extensively with my family and with my teachers, had friends make suggestions, and ultimately drafted and redrafted until I reached a point where every word served a purpose, and every sentence portrayed a piece of myself.

Acknowledgments: I would like to thank Kristie Letter, my beloved English teacher, my parents, and everyone else who helped me.

I Said Something

Jonathan Holmes

"GET A LIFE, LOSER!" The husky seventh-grader bellowed at me as he swaggered across the playground. His compatriots snickered. Thankfully the full impact of his insult was swallowed up by the squeals and laughter of students at recess. I sat on a cold, wooden bench, fixated on the task at hand: finishing my lunch. I looked at him. I wanted to reply, "A+ for originality, Einstein," but I lacked the energy to brace myself against the onslaught of insults he and his band of brothers would hurl at me. Better judgment kept me quiet. I returned to the comfort of food.

Even with the pitfalls of recess, lunchtime was my favorite. It was always the same: Fritos, apples, cookies, and a PB&J, expertly made by Dad. What I loved most? Every time I opened the bag, I knew what to expect. No matter what the day had in store—falling on my face in PE, having my head become the target during an impromptu spitball tournament, or being the butt of endless jokes—I could count on lunch being the same and tasting good.

As I savored the last Frito, the boy returned, followed by a short, wiry boy and another, who seemed to just be following the crowd. I avoided eye contact and remained seated, hoping they'd have a change of heart and walk away. No such luck. The first boy leaned in and whispered,

"Hey fag, NO ONE likes you."

At that moment, the bell rang and the boys laughed as they strode back into school. I froze, feeling the sting of his words and their laughs. Angry and hurt, I fantasized about getting even, but fear of humiliation stopped me from taking a stand. I just watched them leave. I said nothing.

Fast-forward a couple of years. I left that small, homogenous middle school and those bullies behind. My new, larger school brought more diversity and a new start. Things were different. Whereas before I was excluded, now I was included and regained my confidence. Here, I walked the halls at lunch, head held high, with a smile. Now my friends were my favorite part of school.

Sophomore year, something happened. The gregarious din of kids at lunch turned into a comforting white noise as overworked teenagers zoned out amidst yawns and tweets. I looked for the table that my friends had claimed as "ours." Weaving my way through the chaotic cafeteria, I spotted something that didn't seem right.

In the corner, beyond the view of bored faculty serving obligatory lunch duty, I saw a scene I'd lived countless times before. A mean-looking junior was standing over a terrified-looking freshman.

I witnessed the all-too-familiar humiliation on this freshman's face as the junior mercilessly harassed him. My first reaction was to stay out of it, turn a blind eye to the situation, and keep walking. I had played the role of victim in middle school, surviving by avoiding eye contact, trying to become invisible, and never, ever saying anything.

But that day, something changed. I no longer wanted to be a victim. I wanted to do what no one had done for me: I wanted to stand up to the jerk du jour. Speaking up is a massive risk in the world of teens, but something compelled me. How I'd wanted someone to show me that what the bullies were saying was wrong.

So I did what I should have done a long time ago.

I said something.

I walked up to that junior and said three words:

"Knock. It. Off."

And through the screaming and cursing that was his rebuttal, I couldn't help but smile. I had finally stood up to the demons that had haunted me for most of my childhood. At that moment, I stopped being a victim, and I never looked back.

About the Author: My name is Jonathan Holmes. I am a senior at the International School in Bellevue, Washington. I am applying to musical theater programs at twelve different schools. The first step was to apply academically. I am now in the process of auditioning in person for each school, and I will know later this spring where I will be spending the next four years.

High School Attended: International School, Bellevue, WA

The Process: I must have started and stopped writing this five different times. One day, I was reflecting on my experience, and the words just started to flow. It was hard to contain my essay to the prerequisite 650 words, but with diligent editing I was able to tell my story in a succinct but poignant way.

Acknowledgments: Thanks to my parents and my Aunt Terry for the support along the way.

IMMEASURABLE GROWTH

Emily Thompson

Fifteen pounds, two pant sizes, and "extraordinary" could all describe my growth during my junior year in Spain. I choose to accept the extra pounds and increased pants sizes as evidence of an unpredictable, yet immeasurable, experience.

On September 4, 2013, as a skinny fifteen-year-old ball of nerves, I kissed my parents good-bye and joined over a hundred other exchange students from around the United States, who were gathered at the JFK Marriott to participate in the American Field Service exchange program. It was going to be the best time of my life! It had to be! I had been fantasizing about it for the past year as I worked to raise my spending money and took extra classes so that I could stay on track for graduation.

The experience began on a positive note as my fellow exchange students and I bonded over jokes, stories about ourselves, and what we imagined our next year would be like. The friendly personalities and shared enthusiasm reflected all that I expected this experience would hold. This remained true with each leg of our three-day journey and was confirmed by the warm greeting that I received from my host family when we finally reached Barcelona.

However, it didn't take long for the honeymoon phase to wear off. While my host siblings were friendly, they attended a different school and were rarely around to spend time with me or introduce me to new Spanish friends. It was overwhelming to take courses such as psychology, philosophy, and economics in the regional language of Catalan. The language barrier and unfamiliar culture made it almost impossible. I began to ask myself, *What have I done?* I could be home, surrounded by my familiar friends, speaking my native language, rather than struggling to be understood by everyone around me. *Why did I do this?* Ten months away from home is an extremely long time. *What am I going to do now?* I could give up and go home to my comfort zone or stay in Barcelona and embrace the opportunity to grow. I chose the latter.

My first step toward growth was to join a local dance team. With this new group of supportive friends, I participated in my town's promotional tourism video, danced in the district's sports award ceremony, and traveled to two cities to perform in a major production of *Dracula*. I dove into every team-building event AFS had to offer, from a three-legged scavenger hunt through Barcelona, to a campout on top of a mountain, and many activities in between. With my AFS friends, I arranged a trip to Galicia, Spain, to complete El Camino de Santiago, a 100-kilometer walking pilgrimage to the famous Catedral de Santiago. I coordinated my own trip to Italy to visit distant relatives and explore the area from which my mother's family originated. I bonded with my host family during road trips to Madrid, Granada, Valencia, and a ski trip to the Pyrenees mountains. By seeking out new opportunities, and, of course, trying new and exotic dishes along the way, my experience took on a whole new form, and so did my body.

Now when I think, *What have I done?* I have grown in many ways that could never be measured in inches or in weight. I have developed money management skills, coordinated my own travel arrangements, navigated around many foreign cities, become fluent in a second language, and made many friends worldwide. *Why did I do this?* I did this so I could grow into an independent, confident problem-solver who doesn't crack under pressure but makes the most of difficult situations. *What am I going to do now?* I am going to apply the growth that I have attained from my study abroad and seek every opportunity that Appalachian State University has in store.

About the Author: My name is Emily Thompson. I am from Amenia, New York, and I have a serious case of wanderlust. In the future, I hope to have a career in the field of communications and acquire a job that allows me to work while simultaneously traveling the world.

High School Attended: Stissing Mountain High School, Pine Plains, NY

The Process: For my junior year of high school, I studied abroad in Castelldefels, Spain. I knew this memorable experience would undoubtedly be the topic of my college essay, so when I returned I chose a prompt that was applicable to my topic, and the words flew from my mind to the paper with ease. It was like the story just told itself.

Acknowledgments: Thank you, Mom!

LAS TRES SOFIAS

Sofia Mascia

My grandmother bursts out laughing amidst a cloud of flour. She has accidentally dropped the bag on the floor in the frenzy of preparing dinner. As her giggles fill the air, I think about how often I see her smile. My mother watches my Abé with admiration. The resemblance between mother and daughter is uncanny. They are both defiant and energetic and covered in flour! When I see them together, I see my future, and I know that the qualities I admire most in them, run through my blood. Together, we are "Las Tres Sofias" -- three generations of "Sofias," each adding ingredients to our collective legacy.

In this memory, my mother and my grandmother chat about our upcoming move to Hong Kong, where we now live, as they pass each other spices and spoons. "Estarás bien Sofia!" my grandmother exclaims. They are making *Bacalao, Croquetas de Jamon* and *Flan* – dishes that integrate my Mexican, Spanish and Cuban heritage. My mother occasionally scribbles in a black notebook, whose pages are stained with sauces and oils, and filled with recipes that define our family's history.

It seemed like there was never a moment in which my Abé wasn't smiling, especially when most of us would sigh and frown and feel like giving up. She had this unbelievable happiness to her that you would never expect from someone whose life had begun as hers had. Never one to hide her opinions, she was exiled from her home in Cuba at twenty-two for her involvement in anti-communist revolts. She left Cuba as a woman with a medical education and family, and arrived in her new home of Mexico with a wristwatch, the clothes on her back, and a degree that was no longer recognized. Spilled flour would not ruin her evening, as Fidel Castro would not ruin her life.

I see both of my cherished namesakes running around chopping and stirring, making a flawless Tuesday night dinner, because they are physically incapable of undertaking any task half-heartedly. This strong will transcends the kitchen: both my Abé, an oral surgeon, and my mother, an architect, break the paradigms of what is expected of women in our culture.

My mother has shown me that with blessings come responsibilities. She is single-minded, and what she fights for almost always benefits others more than herself. She never takes shortcuts because she only feels satisfied when she gives her all. This has not only been true in relation to little things, but in how she keeps our family together, in how she ran her business, and in how she has raised me.

The stride in her step, the joy in her laugh and the fire in her eyes are all qualities that she shares with her mother. Yet, after my grandmother's passing, my mother has had to face alone the task of teaching me how to be one of them, a Sofia. Through example, she has shown me how to be resilient, and take the combined strength of Las Tres Sofias and put it toward something bigger than myself.

The more I've grown, the more I have come to see the similarities between myself, my mother, and my grandmother. Like the two Sofias who have given me my name, I seem also to possess an unflagging, sometimes unexplainable, dedication to whatever I undertake. As I navigate the uncertain road ahead, and strive to make a difference, I hope to make proud the women who have preceded me.

Much like the recipes in the sauce-stained notebook, the Sofias represent the places that the women in my family have been and are going. My name stands for a refusal to accept defeat and mediocrity. And as long as it is mine, I have a responsibility to carry on the faith, strength and passion that I have been given.

About the Author: I am an American ex-patriot who has lived in Hong Kong for six years. I hope to study International Relations and eventually become a human rights attorney.

High School Attended: Kellett School, The British International School in Hong Kong S.A.R, China

The Process: I started with a very detailed and dense 'free write' of the event and its significance to me. Then I separated it into paragraphs and cut down on redundant, boring material over several drafts until I was happy with it (and it fit the word limit!)

Acknowledgments: Gabrielle Glancy and my parents!

College Attending: Harvard!

ABOUT THE EDITOR
GABRIELLE GLANCY

Former Admissions Director, Series Editor of *Best College Essays*, published in *The New Yorker,* and author of *The Art of the College Essay,* New Vision Learning's Gabrielle Glancy has been in the business of helping students realize their dreams for almost thirty years. With a knack for knowing just the right formula to help high school students succeed where they have struggled and get in where they want to go, she is one of the foremost professionals in her field. Headquartered in the Bay Area, Gabrielle Glancy is well known all around the world for her college admissions expertise.

Made in the USA
Middletown, DE
26 July 2017